Weeks to Prosperity

What your accountant, banker,
broker and financial adviser
might not tell you

By Peggy Doviak

THE ROADRUNNER PRESS
OKLAHOMA CITY, OKLAHOMA

The RoadRunner Press
Oklahoma City, Oklahoma
www.TheRoadRunnerPress.com

Printed in the United States | First Edition August 2018

For information on bulk orders: orders@theroadrunnerpress.com

Disclaimer

The information in this book is educational, not investment advice. Please talk
to your financial planner, attorney, and CPA before you implement any ideas.
Past performance is not an indication of future performance. Investing is risky,
and you can lose money. Updates can be found at www.PeggyDoviak.com.

Throughout this book the financial planner designation is reserved for a
CERTIFIED FINANCIAL PLANNER™ practitioner.

· · · · · · · · · · · · · · · · ·

Library of Congress Control Number: 2018952558

**Publisher's Cataloging-In-Publication Data
(Prepared by The Donohue Group, Inc.)**

Names: Doviak, Peggy.
Title: 52 weeks to prosperity : what your accountant, banker, broker and financial
adviser might not tell you / by Peggy Doviak.
Other Titles: Fifty-two weeks to prosperity
Description: First edition. | Oklahoma City, Oklahoma : The RoadRunner Press, 2018.
Identifiers: ISBN 9781937054755 (trade paper) | ISBN 9781937054847 (ebook)
Subjects: LCSH: Finance, Personal. | Wealth. | Taxation.
Classification: LCC HG179 .D68 2018 (print) | LCC HG179 (ebook) | DDC 332.024--dc23

10 9 8 7 6 5 4 3 2 1

To my mom, who made it all happen

Table of Contents

Welcome

Hello! I'm Peggy Doviak, and this is a book written for you—to help you. It's the book I have wanted to write ever since I became a CERTIFIED FINANCIAL PLANNER™ practitioner many years ago and realized that most people didn't know that a financial adviser doesn't legally have to put a client's interests before his or her own.

It just seems so counterintuitive. Why would anyone put money in the hands of someone who didn't need to protect it as though it were his or her own? But that's the law, at least for now. That's reality. It is also the kind of thing you need to know before you choose a financial adviser or let someone create a financial plan for you.

Personally, I believe every single person should have a CERTIFIED FINANCIAL PLANNER™ pro, someone who adheres to a set of standards and practices . . . someone who will always put their needs first. In lieu of that, every person should have a book by a CFP® professional, a book that can guide people through the financial quagmire—a book that can point out the pitfalls and pratfalls along the way.

I hope this book will be that for you.

I've designed *52 Weeks to Prosperity* to give you a sensible path to follow as you begin to take control of your financial life—52 topics, 52 chapters, 52 steps to take over the course of 52 weeks.

It sounds simple. But more important, it's doable.

And better yet, you don't have to do it alone.

I'll be right by your side. And when you have a question, I'll be there, maybe not physically, but accessible—thanks to my weekly radio program and weekly podcast "Ask Peggy Doviak about your Finances" and the "Ask Peggy" feature on my website.

There are many financial books out there. Some are excellent, and some are downright scary. I found some common flaws in them. The scary ones try to tell you how to get rich by following some complicated trading algorithm. They claim you'll never have to pay taxes again through some pretty creative accounting or promise some other secret way of acquiring or guaranteeing your wealth.

In our guts, we know these books aren't on the level. They remind me of sea anemones, or the flowers of the sea. They look pretty, but they are not what they appear to be. You've seen sea anemones on television. Little fish swim up to the pretty "flowers" only to be enveloped and eaten by them. Now, most financial books aren't quite that bad. Yet all too often, readers approach them as one might a lottery—a magical way to get rich fast. Then, the books ensnare the readers in ways that either confuse (if they're lucky) or, (worse), cost them their life savings.

Good financial advice books by respected authors don't do this. They explain financial topics in a way meant to help the reader. Their flaw is they tend to address only one topic.

One might focus on strategies for people in financial difficulty; another might provide tax techniques for the wealthy. To gain a basic understanding of all the topics that come into play when creating a financial plan, you would have to read many, many books. In a perfect world, that would be fine, but people today rarely have that kind of free time. (If this title had 52 volumes instead of chapters, I suspect you would have put it right back on the shelf.)

My least favorite financial books are also scary, but in this case, it's deliberate. These books are usually written by people in the financial industry, and they are designed to confuse and frighten the reader into taking quick action. There are entire marketing schemes in financial services designed to teach advisers how to make clients afraid. The thinking is that a client who is afraid will more likely make a fast decision and purchase whatever the adviser is selling.

I will promise you right now, my book will not scare you. People are already afraid enough of their money. When people enter my office for the first time, too often they look apprehensive at best, angry at worst. They talk quickly, and they avoid looking at me. Sometimes, they are almost belligerent as they try to convince me that they already know everything I am going to say and just need for me to confirm their current strategies.

On the other extreme is the weeping client. The first time a client began to cry during a meeting, I had been in business for about six months and had no idea what to do. Today, I keep tissues in my conference room, and I have come to learn that generally people cry when they are totally stressed out and ready to give up. They have come to me as a last resort. Many times, they don't know what to say, they don't know what to ask, and they are terrified that I am going to trick them or take advantage of them.

This book is for them, and this book is for you. Although you will learn many things in this book that you may well be able to implement on your own, there are other topics for which you will need professional advice of some kind. I want to give you the language to have that meeting not looking down, not feigning confidence, and certainly not crying because you are so overwhelmed.

I want you to become comfortable with the vocabulary and issues of your financial life. What I don't want you to do is just turn everything over to someone else, even a CFP®

professional. Instead, I want your relationship with your financial professional to be a partnership, one in which you understand what the adviser is recommending and why. I want you to see that you have options as you make and implement your plan.

I want you to be empowered, not fearful.

52 Weeks to Prosperity is divided into seven financial-planning sections: cash flow, insurance and risk management, investments, retirement, taxes, estate planning, and other planning issues.

The 52 chapters contain practical information and are designed to introduce you to some concepts about the topic and explain why that topic is important to you.

Each chapter begins with a story, and I drew these stories from experiences I have had with family, friends, and clients. All the stories are true, and in most cases, I chose the topics as a result of the stories. I tried to select the ones I thought were most important and most compelling. In fact, the story in the last chapter is about my mother, and it explains the title of the book and why I am a financial planner.

52 Weeks to Prosperity can't be completely comprehensive—the field of financial planning is just too broad and complicated. However, I did want to write the book as broadly as possible to show you what *good* financial planning should entail. Some of the chapters might not apply to you. That's okay; you might need the information sometime in the future. Each chapter ends with an activity that you can complete to help you better organize your financial life. The chapters are short, so you shouldn't have difficulty reading one a week. (That is, after all, why there are 52 of them!)

Because the chapters are short and financial planning can be complicated, you shouldn't expect the chapters to tell you everything you need to know, especially in some of the more complicated areas. However, they will serve as an introduction—a way to begin the conversation.

The book's organization is designed to improve that conversation. The CERTIFIED FINANCIAL PLANNER™ Board of Standards divides financial planning into the same sections that I use here, except for "Other Planning Issues." I had a few more things I wanted to share with you that didn't fit well anywhere else.

It's important that this book follow the Board's model because this is how the financial planning industry looks at your financial life. Remember, this is a book designed to help you speak the language of financial planning, so I wanted to organize it in a way to reinforce that.

I also want you to understand that financial planning is more comprehensive than just investments and insurance. It is much more than having a broker who recommends stocks and places your orders for them. Most of what is covered here is unlikely to be discussed by that kind of broker.

Financial planning begins by looking at your specific financial needs, goals, and dreams and then tailoring a plan that helps you achieve as many of them as possible. It takes you where you are in your financial life and helps you move forward to where you want to be by the time you're a spouse or a parent or a retiree.

Finally, this is a book to help you prosper.

I love the word *prosper* because you can be prosperous without being anywhere near as rich as the 1 percent.

True prosperity is about having confidence, happiness, friends, family and, of course, financial stability. *52 Weeks* isn't designed to help you get rich quickly but rather to help you increase your prosperity.

Let's begin—and if you have any questions, feel free to Ask Peggy!

— **Peggy Doviak**

Meet Your New Friends

Ashley: Ashley is in her twenties and lives in an apartment. She and her fiancé are trying to decide whether they should rent or buy a condo after they are married. She can't find a job in her degree, so she is working two part-time jobs. She has no benefits at work. She has a few store credit cards but no real credit history. She is living paycheck to paycheck with student loan debt.

Michael: Michael is in his thirties, and he has become eligible to participate in his retirement plan at work. He's excited, but he doesn't understand the plan, and he has no idea how to go about saving for retirement. He is married, and they have two children, ages five and eighteen months. He has a small life insurance policy from work but no will. He is a big fan of his college's teams, and he likes new cars.

Lisa: Lisa is in her fifties and single. She has no children but loves her nieces and nephews. She is a mid-level manager and is saving for retirement. She would like to lower her taxes. She worries about her elderly mother and how she will manage her own care when she is older.

James: James is in his sixties and still working. He has company health insurance, and he sees no reason to take Social Security yet. In his retirement savings, he has accumulated a large amount of his employer's stock. He has always felt comfortable investing, but he wonders about his risk tolerance now. His estate is currently worth a little less than the estate tax phaseout. He and his wife would like to be sure that their family is financially secure, and he would like to eventually be able to leave some money to charity.

7

Cash Flow

Chapter 1

Cash Flow: Financial Planning Is More than Stocks

The Woman Who Wasn't Sure What She Needed

A woman had been working with a financial adviser for several years, and at first, the relationship was great. The adviser helped her make investment decisions and even assisted her with her insurance needs.

She was happy with the choices they had made, but she had some concerns. In one of her earlier meetings, she had mentioned that she had credit card debt, but the adviser hadn't seemed concerned, nor did he respond when she asked about the wisdom of saving some money for emergencies. When she asked him about taxes, he told her to ask her accountant, and when she asked him about beneficiaries for her retirement account, he told her to ask an attorney.

Stranger still, when she asked her financial adviser about how to maximize the benefits from her job, he said she should talk to her plan administrator.

The woman began to wonder if there was someone who could work with her more holistically. The Chinese philosopher and poet Lao Tzu once observed, "The journey of a thousand miles begins with a single step." But unless you are also an ancient Chinese philosopher, you might well have had trouble taking that first step—no matter how much you would like to get your finances in order.

Improving your prosperity in a year might sound like a great idea, but what we know about human nature tells us that for most of us, it would be so much easier to *start* that journey in six months, three months, next week, or even tomorrow—any day but today. That's because tackling a long-term goal—any long-term goal—can be intimidating. You might have some apprehension: What if you can't do it? What if it doesn't work for you? Let me assure you that taking the time to begin this journey toward a more prosperous life will be worth it, and you can do it.

If you dedicate a full year—52 weeks—to understanding your money and making financial decisions based on the financial education you will gain here, you will certainly make great progress this year.

So let's take that first step, shall we . . .

When people think about the work of a financial adviser, they usually think in terms of someone managing some kind of investment account, holding stocks and bonds or funds for, say, a child's future education. That's far from a complete picture. Financial planning is much more than just handling investments. Ideally, it also includes:

- setting your financial goals
- managing cash flow
- addressing education funding
- dealing with insurance and risk management
- overseeing retirement funding
- spearheading tax strategies
- overseeing estate planning.

That's because every investment you make should be done in the context of meeting a particular goal or goals in your life, such as paying off your student loans, saving enough for a honeymoon, being insured in case of a fire or medical emergency, or having your house paid for by the time you retire.

Rarely would an investment portfolio be created with the sole goal of "beating the market" all the time. Instead, prudent financial planning helps you understand your money as it exists—and comes into play—in all areas of your life.

Because good financial planning tries to be holistic in its approach, the financial data you will need in the coming weeks is located in all kinds of documents. Therefore, the first step fro Week 1 is to have you gather all these documents. Most of them—pay stubs, insurance policies, house deeds—are provided to you. You receive a pay stub regularly, and you can find copies of your tax returns and insurance policies. It might take a little effort, but once you have located these documents, you will be able to lay your hands on them at a moment's notice going forward.

Once everything has been gathered, your documents, check registers, and receipts need to be organized. Embrace this part of the process. It is critical. Many times during a meeting, people try to tell me how much they think they have invested or how much they think they spend on groceries. Sadly, they are never right. They usually think they have more money than they have and spend less than they do.

This kind of thinking can lead to a financial disaster if you base a financial plan on faulty numbers. Don't be afraid to get organized. Simply locating all your financial documents and getting them in one spot is a great first step.

· · · · ·

 Ashley: Wow, I never tried to locate all my money documents before! I wonder where my bank statement is.

Michael: Since my 401(k) plan issues only one statement a year, I think I will use my online summary.

 Lisa: I thought financial planning was my investment return. A woman in my yoga class uses a financial planner. I wonder if she's done this.

 James: I remember the first time I tried to organize everything. Took me a week just to find even the most recent tax return!

· · · · ·

WEEK 1 ACTIVITY

This week, I want you to gather all of the documents on the following list that pertain to you. You might not have every single one—if you don't own a business for example, you won't have any of the business documents.

Put all the documents for you and your family in one place where they are easy for you to find. I don't care if it's all electronic or all paper copies. If you think of something you'd like to see on my list, please add it to your stack and drop me a note at www.PeggyDoviak.com using the message form. These documents will be used to complete the rest of this book—and it will feel great when all your important papers are in one spot and easy to access. Use the list below to check each one off as you find it.

Basic Documents
_____ adoption papers
_____ birth certificates
_____ divorce documents
_____ educational/training certificates
_____ graduation certificates
_____ passports

Financial Documents
_____ advance directive
_____ bank statements
_____ brokerage statements and other investment accounts
_____ business documents (if you own a business)
_____ business plan (whether you have or hope to start one)
_____ buy-sell agreements (if you own a business)
_____ estate documents
_____ investment documents
_____ leases (car or home/apartment)
_____ living will
_____ pension statements
_____ powers of attorney/durable powers
_____ Social Security statements
_____ succession plan (if you own a business)
_____ trusts (family, literary, etc.)
_____ wills

Insurance Documents
_____ auto
_____ disability
_____ health (including Medicare, Medicaid, supplemental)
_____ home (including flood, etc.)
_____ life
_____ long-term care

Latest Tax Return(s)

Cash Flow Document(s)
_____ appliance/electronic equipment/etc. warranties
_____ bank transactions (ATM)
_____ pay stubs
_____ receipts
_____ recurring bills (including credit card statements)

Net-worth Documents
_____ current liabilities (loans, notes), interest rates, payoff
_____ current value of major assets

. . . . .

Ask Peggy

Question: Peggy, what is the single most important takeaway from this chapter?

Peggy: Financial planning is more than your investment portfolio and a life insurance policy.

. . . . .

Notes

Use the following lines to jot down notes about what you did this week.

_____

_____

_____

_____

_____

_____

_____

_____

_____

Chapter 2

Cash Flow: Setting Financial Goals and Dreams

The Complacent College Student

A young man was nearing graduation and had no idea what to do next. He had been active in his fraternity and played college ball but not well enough to go pro. He hadn't gone to college seeking a specific career, so now that he was about to graduate, he had no idea what he wanted to do with his life. So he got an office job. Although he did fairly well in his position, he never enjoyed it.

Days turned into months, and months turned into years. He married a couple of times but not successfully, because he never knew what he wanted in a wife. He retired as soon as he could, only to discover that his plans to travel in his twilight years just didn't work financially.

Having never had a dream he pursued and because he had never planned, even the few desires he did have now in retirement were out of reach.

Are you a dreamer? Do you like to imagine how things could be better if you could just accomplish a few things— maybe get that GED or master's degree or learn a new language or skill? Do some of your dreams involve money or the things money could provide for you? Do you dream about being prosperous?

I have always been a dreamer and a believer in other people's dreams. And I am here to tell you that financial planning supports dreams, especially when the dreams are carefully created. Dreams are important. Some Native American cultures hang "dream catchers" over the bed. Made of a willow frame, sinew webbing, and dangling feathers, a dream catcher filters dreams, allowing only good dreams to reach the person sleeping beneath it.

The less romantic name for a specific dream is a goal. I like to think of goals as dreams with more detail. Dreams tend to be vague: I want to own a business. I want to make more money. Goals are specific: I will take that accounting class so that in two years, I can be a tax preparer. I will give up my daily fancy coffee and put the money into an emergency account instead as a financial safety net.

People often fail at their financial plans because they never make the transition from dream to goal, from general to specific. I see this frequently with my clients. Consider this conversation I had with one:

Me: How much money do you think you will need in your retirement?
Client: I want to be rich. Make me rich.
Me: How much money does "rich" mean to you?
Client: Lots of money.
Me: How much?
Client: Enough to make me rich.

Maybe the client has the financial resources to become rich or maybe not. The bigger issue is that the goal is just too vague. It hangs there on the horizon like a pretty rainbow. Because it can't be captured, it can't be achieved. Eventually, such a vague dream leads to frustration and defeat.

The other thing about vague goals is they don't require you to be accountable. It isn't difficult to say you want to be rich. Financial services ads capture this well, featuring healthy, silver-haired couples sailing, traveling, or relaxing in a Tuscan villa. Don't buy into such stereotypes and vague descriptions of wealth. You have to be disciplined enough to know what *rich* means to you: Being able to live near family? On the coast? To send the children to college? Being able to travel? Or in a position to give to your church or favorite charity? Once know, you can take specific steps to try to achieve the goal. In hindsight, I don't believe my client knew what *rich* meant to him.

And that's okay at the start, if you have a good financial planner. You see, it's the job of a financial planner to help you bring your dreams into enough focus that they can become a goal. That might go something like this:

Me: How much money do you think you will need in retirement?

Client: I don't know—a lot.

Me: How much do you make now?

Client: I make $5,000 a month now, and my expenses will drop a little. The house and car will be paid off, but I would like to travel more, so I'm probably not going to live any less expensively.

Me: So you think that having about the same amount coming in as you have now would work?

Client: I think so.

Me: Good, let's start with that assumption. You're still ten years from retirement, so we'll revisit the question each year to make sure you remain on track.

See the difference? This client didn't come in with a specific dream, but with a little guidance, he quickly narrowed his wants into a specific financial goal.

Good financial dreams have a purpose (in this case, travel), a length of time in which to accomplish the goal (in this case, ten years), a specific dollar amount ($5,000 a month), and a length of time for which you will need the money.

If you create your financial dreams in such a manner, starting with the general and moving to the specific, you can greatly increase your probability of success. Of course, there is some initial work to do before you can create a specific dream. Much of it involves becoming aware of how you are currently living and the cost of things. We will spend several weeks this year helping you to organize such information.

If you are still a young adult, you might not know all the answers, even at the end of the year. In fact, even if you are fifteen to twenty years from your goal, you still might not be sure of all the specific details. That's okay. Estimate the best you can. There is a reason the profession is called financial *planning*, not financial *planned*. Financial planning is a process, and over time, things that are hazy now will come into focus. Your dream-catching financial plan will help you to create clear, achievable goals that will allow you and your family to prosper in all the ways that matter.

. . . . .

Ashley: I want to save enough money to pay for our wedding and honeymoon! Mom and Dad will help, but I don't want all of it to fall on them.

Michael: Retirement seems way off, but maybe if I plan now, I can live better in retirement than I do today. I'd like more discretionary income.

Lisa: I would love to wake up every morning in the mountains. Maybe I could purchase a vacation home that becomes a retirement home!

James: We have everything we need, but I would like to leave something for the kids and grand-kids after we're gone. I know our church would appreciate a little money too. We should look at our plan and decide how much we want to leave as a legacy.

· · · · ·

WEEK 2 ACTIVITY

This week, your assignment is to dream. Where you can, turn the dreams into specific goals. When you don't know details, provide estimates. Remember that you might have many types of dreams: owning a home, buying a car, starting a business, getting out of debt, taking a trip, paying for college for a favorite niece, or leaving an inheritance to a foundation to continue your good works. Remember, these aren't my dreams or your financial adviser's. They're yours!

This week talk to the people you love about how you want your future life and financial state to look. During the year, revisit the list. Henceforth, look at the list at least annually, updating the numbers and maybe even the dreams!

· · · · ·

MY DREAMING PAGE

Dream	Years Until Dream	Cost

· · · · ·

Ask Peggy

Question: Peggy, what is the single most important takeaway from this chapter?

Peggy: Concrete goals may be difficult to achieve, but vague goals will rarely be realized.

· · · · ·

Notes

Use the following lines to jot down some notes about what you did this week.

_____

_____

_____

_____

_____

_____

_____

_____

_____

_____

Chapter 3

Cash Flow: Managing the Ins and Outs of Money

*The Professional Couple Who Had
No Idea How Much They Spent*

A husband and wife in their forties decided it was time to plan seriously for their retirement. Their cash flow was more secure than it had ever been, but they wanted to ensure that they could travel when they retired.

They went to a financial planner, and he told them he would be happy to help them, but he wanted to begin with their monthly spending. The couple looked at each other blankly. They had no idea how much they spent each month. They knew what their mortgage and car payments were. They had vague ideas about their average utility and cable bills. But they had no idea how much each other spent at coffee shops, much less as a family eating out on their way back and forth from their children's soccer games. The financial planner laughed politely and told them not to feel too bad. They weren't alone. Few people know how much they spend each month.

At the end of the month, do you ever wonder where the money went? Do you find yourself buying more than what was on your grocery list, not because it was a good deal or because you needed it but because it just looked like something fun to purchase? When you're feeling a little blue or overwhelmed, do you practice "retail therapy" at the local mall or with your favorite online retailer?

Certainly, if you do, you're not alone; there's a reason stores put seasonal and impulse purchases at the end of every aisle and by the cash register. There's a reason an ad for those shoes you admired yesterday online have popped up on your Facebook feed. Shopping becomes a problem only when you don't know how much you spend. In that case, the results can be disastrous.

The center of all financial planning is cash flow—the money you earn and the money you spend. Positive cash flow means you have more income than expenses. One of the most important numbers you need to know is how much you spend each month. It becomes the basis for not only your emergency fund, but also how much insurance you need, how much you need to save for retirement, and many other things. Unfortunately, we don't like to calculate this number. We would rather estimate it. And over the years, I've never had clients estimate a number higher than what they spend. Even when they create categories of estimates, they are too low. One client actually forgot to list the cost of the food she ate!

This week's activity will help you avoid this mistake. Spoiler alert: This will take you longer than a week to complete. That's because for one month, I want you—and everyone in your family—to write down everything you spend. No purchase is too big or too little. Withdrawing ATM money is not a purchase. You need to write down what you bought with that money. If you go to a superstore, try afterward to break your bill into categories such as household, groceries, or clothing.

Keep your records any way that works for you. If you run everything off your smart phone, keep it on a note app or a cash flow app. If you prefer paper, buy a small notebook. Keep receipts in an envelope with the month written on the front. If you tend to lose receipts, take pictures of them with your phone as soon as you receive them.

Then at least once a week, transfer the data to the table I've provided at the end of this chapter. That table will provide categories of expenses for you. I've left a couple of blank columns in case you have a different type of expense than I have listed. I've even included a *miscellaneous* category for purchases that do not fit into any other category, but please don't let that category carry more than 1 percent to 2 percent of your expenditures. A purchase is not miscellaneous; it's *something*.

The next step will involve determining what needs to be purchased, what you want to purchase, and how to create a game plan going forward. For this week, however, I just want you to begin by writing what you buy down.

Many times, when clients come in at the end of the month, they begin the discussion about their buying habits by explaining to me how the last month wasn't representative of what they normally do. Unexpected expenses threw them off course, or a business trip caused them to eat out more than they typically would.

Interestingly, this conversation has never gone the other way, with the clients having spent less than they expected with anticipated higher bills the next month. If you also believe that your spending patterns are abnormally high during the month, then extend the activity for another month.

Last but not least, I have a tip to help you prosper not only financially but within your family relationships as well. This month, don't judge the spending habits of your family members. If someone always runs through the drive-through window for a snack, don't say anything. If trips to the supercenter lead to unbelievably high bills, let it go. If Mom always racks up on-demand chick flicks on the weekend cable bill, let her be. This is not the time to censor those other people in the house who spend all that money! At the same time, if you try to "look good" yourself, suddenly giving up that weekly golf game or Tuesday lunch at the club, you will only create an unrealistic picture of your own spending habits. Don't judge anyone—even yourself. It will only build resentment and encourage the withholding of information. Trust me: To improve your prosperity in a year, you need to know what your family's monthly spending *really* looks like.

· · · · ·

 Ashley: I can't believe how much money I spend going out with friends!

 Michael: We went on vacation and came home needing to replace the air conditioner. I'm going to track our spending for a second month.

 Lisa: I really need to start making a grocery list before I go to the store.

 James: Our cash flow is fine, but I'm going to lose some monthly income after I retire. I need to compare our spending to that number too.

· · · · ·

WEEK 3 ACTIVITY

Have everyone in your household write down all spending for a month. The format doesn't matter so long as you create one consolidated list by the end of the month. You can do it on paper, the kids on their phones, and your spouse on a laptop. Just be sure to include recurring bills along with discretionary spending.

_____ Week 1 completed

_____ Week 2 completed

_____ Week 3 completed

_____ Week 4 completed

OUR MONTHLY BILLS	
EXPENSE	**MONTHLY TOTAL**
Savings / retirement contribution	
Mortgage / rent	
Home Utilities / security systems	
Insurance (health, auto, home)	
Phones	
Alimony / child support	
Groceries	
Eating Out	
Education	
Charitable Giving	
Entertainment / vacation	
Clothing	
Holidays / gifts	
Work	
Other _____	
Other _____	

. . . . .

Ask Peggy

Question: Peggy, what is the single most important takeaway from this chapter?

Peggy: The secret to creating a successful financial plan is to know down to the penny how much you spend every month.

. . . . .

Notes

Use the lines below to jot down notes about what you did this week. Later, it'll remind you of your progress.

_____

_____

_____

_____

_____

_____

_____

_____

_____

_____

Chapter 4

Cash Flow: Budget and Diet Are Four-letter Words

The Young Mother Who Loved Holidays

A young mother prided herself with being good with money. She and her husband had no credit card debt and were saving to buy a house. She shopped on a budget—that is, until the holiday season. For this mother, the holidays began with mid-September's silk fall leaves and Halloween costumes and went through Easter's pastel sweater sets and decorated eggs. She even slipped a little during the summer with American flags, red-white-and-blue bunting, and patriotic picnic supplies.

Each time she went to the store during those nine to ten months, she bought more than she intended. Napkins, socks, wreaths, holiday-themed cookie cutters—nothing was too large or too small to delight her. Afterward, she was always mad at herself. She knew the items weren't in the family budget. And often, once she bought even one extra item, she felt so guilty for the off-budget purchase that she usually ended up leaving the store with three or four more.

If you think about human behavior, this woman's made perfect sense. Think about the last time you tried to go on a diet. (If you have never been on a diet, you can read this for entertainment value.) Chances are high that you set unrealistic goals. Once you failed to keep them, you believed you had failed your diet and ate more than you would have on a typical day. If you vowed to avoid all sugar, there were donuts at the office. If you wanted to eat no fat, your colleagues went out to lunch at a burger place. If you went to the trouble to make a vegetarian entrée for dinner, the rest of the family wouldn't touch it.

We start out with such great intentions, and then we watch them fall by the wayside. One slip, and we eat two donuts, order a double cheeseburger, or take the kids for pizza. Bad behavior breeds bad behavior, and we end up in a worse place than where we started. Think about the last time you tried to control your spending and go on a budget. You went into the grocery with great intentions—and even a list. Then you were tempted by a sale on your favorite salad dressing or an offering by your favorite TV chef in the frozen-food section. You know the drill. Maybe it was gardening items in the early spring or the latest electronic cooking gadget or seasonal chocolate sandwich cookies—we all have something that seems to call out our name. Once we succumb to that first impulse purchase, we buy anything that catches our fancy. It might add up to only a little overspending, yet we arrive home with impulse purchases that cost two to three times more than the original temptation.

Do you see parallels between dieting and budgeting? I see them in my own actions and those of my friends and clients as well. Once we have broken the rules we created, we lose heart, with the result being the appearance of additional behaviors that we wanted to avoid.

I can't help you with your diet, but I can help you with your budget. The secret is not to create a budget that is a short-term, unsustainable fix to a problem. Instead, begin to alter your lifestyle bit by bit. For spending decisions to be effective, they require changes that last years, not minutes. Like *diet*, *budget* might as well be a four-letter word to most of us. However, a good budget can be a useful tool.

I have noticed that clients fare better when they realize that *their budget* is *their own creation*. In fact, not only is your budget your creation, your entire financial plan is your creation. When you feel in control of your money, you will be more successful than if you think your budget is in control of you. A budget is simply a compilation of expenses you can't avoid, expenses you don't particularly want to control, and expenses you can control. The expenses you can't control, or "nondiscretionary" expenses, include your home mortgage/rent and your basic utilities.

I know downsizing is possible, but I find that most people avoid that option. Expenses you don't want to control are payments for the car you want to drive, your cell-phone and cable plans, and other expenses that create the core of your lifestyle. These can vary between nondiscretionary and discretionary, depending on how important they are to you. The easiest expense to control is discretionary spending, that is, spending we can always control and could eliminate.

Still, almost daily we spend money without even realizing it. We pull through the drive-through burger or coffee joint, pop into the convenience store on the way to work, or go to the mall, where we buy whatever catches our attention, come home, and obliviously put it all away. Later, we might not even remember purchasing the items. Ironically, when we try to create a budget, it is usually the discretionary spending that takes us off course.

One way you can rein in discretionary spending is by giving yourself a predetermined amount of spending money each month. I am not going to try to tell you how much spending money you should have. That is based purely on your personal situation. Maybe it's $5, maybe it's $50 or $500. The principle remains the same. When you shop, give yourself a set amount of walking-around money to use for whatever you want. This gives you permission to spend money on the things you enjoy, albeit prudently. I've found that this makes following a budget a challenge most people can live with. It also provides a feeling of accomplishment that should encourage you to continue your budget.

. . . . .

Ashley: I've always been afraid to make a budget because I'm afraid I don't have enough money, but I'm going to give it a try.

Michael: Maybe we should review our cell-phone bill to see if we can find a cheaper plan.

Lisa: I'm going to start adding some spending money to my grocery list!

James: We're in good shape on our budget, but reviewing discretionary expenses is great advice.

. . . . .

WEEK 4 ACTIVITY

In Week 3 you tracked your spending, determined how much of each expense was "discretionary" or "nondiscretionary," and calculated how much money remains after you pay all the nondiscretionary bills. That's your cash flow, and armed with it you're ready to determine how much weekly spending money you can afford to set aside. When you go shopping, add two or three blank lines with a dollar amount beside each line. Don't let that number exceed the amount of spending money you have given yourself. Then if you want to splurge on something, it's built into your budget.

Expense	Monthly Total	Discretionary
Savings		
Retirement		
Mortgage/rent		
Utilities		
Insurance		
Phone(s)		
Groceries		
Cable / Internet		
Eating Out		
Clothing		
Alimony		
Other:		
Other:		
Other:		
Other:		
Monthly discretionary spending	$	

. . . . .

Ask Peggy

Question: Peggy, what is the single most important takeaway from this chapter?

Peggy: Your budget is your creation, so as a result, don't be afraid of it, and modify it if necessary.

. . . . .

Notes

Use the following lines to jot down some notes about what you did this week. When you look back on it later, it will remind you of your progress.

_____

_____

_____

_____

_____

_____

_____

_____

_____

_____

Chapter 5

Cash Flow: Creating an Emergency Fund

The Car That Enjoyed Sabotaging Plans

Okay, this isn't a Stephen King novel, but you couldn't tell it by the young man in this story.

The young fellow wanted to pay off all his credit cards, and he had some success. Then something else would happen to the car. It never failed. He called the car "Christine," and had become convinced that "she" hated him. First, Christine needed new tires. She broke down and left him stranded by the road—more than once. As the years passed, her maintenance needs became more frequent and more expensive, and always came at exactly the wrong time, usually on the heels of another unexpected expense. The young man wanted to save for an emergency fund. He wanted to keep to his budget. But it all seemed so fruitless.

How about you? Right now, do you have any money in the bank? What would you do if the dishwasher, tires on the car, and the air conditioner all went out next month? If you're like many people, your answer involves a small piece of plastic you probably carry in your wallet. Unfortunately, with no money in the bank, you likely won't have enough cash to pay off the bill at the end of the month. Suddenly you're accumulating new credit card debt.

If you follow any financial celebrities or read personal finance columns, you have heard of the oh, so important emergency fund, if only because it is usually the first thing they tell you to do to improve your financial situation.

Having an emergency fund gives you ready cash to cover unexpected expenses no matter when they pop up so that you don't break your budget. I believe having an emergency fund is a great thing. Unfortunately, most financial voices will tell you that you should have enough in reserve to cover three, six, or even nine months of nondiscretionary living expenses. (You know how much money that would be for you because we already calculated it.) However, when you don't have an emergency fund, being told that you should have nine months' worth of living expenses in savings is kind of like telling you that you should also build a rocket and fly yourself to the moon! It's an impossibly big number, so you soon give up and eventually you quit even trying.

Over the years, I have given many financial seminars, and when I ask people if they have an emergency fund, the response is universally the same: They laugh! However, it's a nervous laugh, and it is always followed by an anxious silence that makes it only too clear that they are afraid what I will say next is to get an emergency fund, which they believe they cannot do.

That is why I would like to propose a much different plan for you. Remember the nondiscretionary bills we calculated in Chapter 3?

Instead of taking those monthly nondiscretionary costs and multiplying them by six, I want you to divide them by two. That's right—the question I want to ask is, do you think you could save two weeks' worth of your expenses? Maybe doing so will take you several months, but do you think you could do it? When I ask people that question, the answer is usually yes. I'm going to bet you would give me the same answer if I asked you.

So here's our next step. Rather than trying to save six months' worth of expenses, I want you to try to save two weeks' worth of your bills. Enlist the help of everyone living in your household. Once you have accomplished this, I want you to all celebrate reaching that goal. I want you to be very, very proud of yourselves. Many Americans don't have a cent in savings—and the vast majority has less than $1,000. By achieving this one goal, you move into the above-average ranks of Americans when it comes to personal finance. I can also say without a doubt that it will give you the confidence to do more. So next, I want you to do it again. If it takes several months to do it, that's fine. The important thing is that once you get there, you will have a full month of emergency funds saved and will be truly ahead of the game.

I want you to continue this process until you have saved several months' worth of expenses. The exact amount of your emergency fund depends on many things, especially your job security. If you aren't likely to lose your job, you might not need an entire nine months' worth, although it would still be nice. Typically, I set a goal of about six months for my clients, but I would like you to try to do it two weeks at a time, celebrating each success with a splurge that stays within your budget.

· · · · ·

 Ashley: Wow, even though two weeks' worth of my bills is a lot of money, I bet I can do it! I wonder what I can do to save money?

 Michael: I've been so discouraged trying to save as much as I thought I should. This doesn't seem so overwhelming.

Lisa: I already have an emergency fund saved, but I bet I could use the same strategy to save for the down payment on my vacation home. I need to divide the amount into smaller pieces and save that much each month.

James: I have friends my age who don't have a cent in savings. This sounds like a strategy that people could try, regardless of how old they are.

· · · · ·

Ask Peggy

Question: Peggy, what is the single most important takeaway from this chapter?

Peggy: Saving an emergency fund can feel overwhelming, but the important thing is to start.

· · · · ·

WEEK 5 ACTIVITY

Look at the nondiscretionary expense total that you calculated in Chapter 4. Take this number and divide it by two. That's the first goal for your emergency fund.

· · · · ·

NOTES

_____

_____

_____

Chapter 6

Cash Flow: Creating a Savings Plan

The Executive Who Needed to Keep Up Appearances

By all appearances, the mid-level executive had it all: a good job, nice home, memberships in all the important local civic groups. He wore expensive suits, designer watches, and high-end cologne. He could usually be seen carrying a latte in one hand and his leather attaché in the other. There was only one problem. He had no money in savings. He feared losing his image as a successful businessman, but he knew he needed to cut spending somewhere. He hoped there was a way to cut corners in places that would not be obvious to his fellow members at the club.

In Chapter 5, we calculated how much money you needed to save for your first emergency-fund goal. Unfortunately, it can be challenging to try to save that much money if you look only at the big picture. A better way to make progress is to try to look at every nickel you spend, even on the smallest purchases.

I remember coffee machines that sold cardboard cups of jet-black bitter coffee overly sweetened with sugar. For a dime, I could purchase a cup of this brew that always tasted faintly of cardboard. Fancy coffee shops like those we have today didn't exist, and if you were going "upscale," you went to a restaurant or diner with ceramic mugs.

Coffee cafés have now sprouted on nearly every corner of America, in shopping malls and airport terminals. The specialty is a fancy cardboard cup filled with coffee sold in sizes with European names. Now, sugar is artificial, white, or raw and can be found beside the napkins and cinnamon. A dime won't even pay the tax on such a brew! Yes, six-dollar coffee beverages are now a common sight.

I have a friend who buys a "designer" coffee every day on her way to work. She is rarely seen without a white cardboard cup in her hand. Trendy and popular, my friend's habit is also an expensive one, especially if you are trying to save money for your emergency fund or other goals.

Many times when we think about saving money, we think in terms of big goals. We want to save enough to fund thirty years of retirement, four years of college, or a new home or vehicle. This leads to the same difficulties as trying to save a six-month emergency fund. We become overwhelmed, and we quit. Instead, I recommend trying to save smaller sums of money.

So let me pose an idea that I have heard several times but which bears repeating: Change where you buy your cappuccino. Rather than blowing $30 a week at your local coffee café, try spending just a dollar at a time for convenience-store or drive-through coffee.

If this is too horrifying a suggestion, invest in a cappuccino machine and brew your own. The pots can be had for a relatively low price—especially when compared with spending more than a $100 a month at a café —and you can brew what you like best and carry it to work in a cup that does not taste like cardboard. Before you say no way, give it some thought. What could you do if you cut your coffee expenses by $25 a week?

The savings for one year alone would be $1,300! Assuming that you invest this money and earn a 6 percent rate of return, you would have approximately $7,575 in five years! Now that's a savings plan.

Of course, inexpensive coffee is not going to turn around your financial situation, but it's a start. And the logic behind the change could be applied to many things you purchase. Maybe you never drink coffee. Do you drink bottled water? It's not as expensive, but it still adds up. Replace it with a filter pitcher and your own container.

Other nonbeverage purchases can be trimmed easily also. Consider purchasing generic items at the grocery store instead of brand names. If you can't live without your name brands, then watch for coupons. Entire websites are dedicated to the sport of "extreme couponing," and Sunday and Wednesday newspapers still feature coupon inserts.

Eating out is always expensive—whether for coffee or a meal. If you must eat out, do so at lunch rather than dinner, and you will enjoy the same food for less money. Better still, bring your lunch and then turn dinner into a revolving task at which different family members are responsible for preparing favorite dishes or trying new recipes. Maybe you want to learn a specific cooking style or help your teens learn kitchen survival skills before college. Even young children can enjoy preparing salads and desserts. Keep it simple and fun, so it doesn't become a burden. Who knows, you might even lose a few pounds!

I find entertainment is another way for dollars to slip through your fingers. Try attending matinée events on the weekend rather than evening shows, and you will see the same entertainment with change left in your pocket. Avoid opening night or the latest blockbuster movie opening and instead wait for the DVD to come out. Plan a family movie night with pizza that you make yourself. Your goal in doing this is to save a little money many times, and you will be

amazed at how quickly the dollars add up and how pain-
less it will be. Remember, you have not given up anything
you love or particularly need; you've just found a less expensive way to enjoy it. We waste a lot of money without
thinking—from habit or happenstance. Becoming aware
of our daily spending helps us to make decisions more
thoughtfully. Rather than drinking, eating, and spending
mindlessly, we can choose to be careful about what we con-
sume—saving money for the occasional treat. Triple half-
caf mocha lattes are not gone forever. They just aren't part
of your daily life. Trust me, you will be so proud of yourself
when you have that emergency fund safely in the bank.

· · · · ·

 Ashley: I think I'm going to start taking my lunch to work.

 Michael: Okay, I'll admit it. I'm a coffee snob. I think I'll invest in a good coffeemaker at work as a compromise.

 Lisa: I always save my change, and I only let myself go to the coffee shop when I've saved up enough to pay for it.

 James: I could save a ton of money if I paid twilight green fees and took advantage of Senior Wednesdays at the club.

· · · · ·

WEEK 6 ACTIVITY

1. What are your regular discretionary purchases?
2. Which three on your list have a less expensive alternative?

3. What would you save each time you purchased a cheaper option of these three purchases?

4. How many times per year do you make the purchases?

Multiply the answers to Questions 3 and 4 to determine your annual savings. Whenever you consider straying from your plan, return to the number you calculated in Question 5 and decide if it's worth it. After all, it's your choice.

· · · · ·

Ask Peggy

Question: Peggy, what is the single most important takeaway from this chapter?

Peggy: In addition to controlling your major purchases, try saving a little money many times over the month.

· · · · ·

Notes

Use the lines below to make notes about what you did this week. When you look back later on them, it'll remind you of your progress.

_____

_____

_____

_____

_____

_____

Peggy Doviak

_____

_____

_____

_____

_____

_____

_____

_____

_____

_____

_____

_____

_____

_____

Chapter 7

Cash Flow: Paying Off Debt

The Woman Who Went Shopping Too Often

A young woman was in a relationship that had become rocky. Every time she and her boyfriend had a fight, she went shopping. At first, she wrote checks, but gradually, she began to use credit cards. As the relationship deteriorated, her credit card debt grew. One day, she made the connection between her love life and her spending habits. Once she saw it, it was easier to avoid, and she began to try to pay off her debt. However, she was frustrated with the slow process she was making on her debt and wasn't sure how to improve her chances of being successful.

People are ashamed of their debt.

When new clients meet me for the first time, they often mumble a little as they describe the debt they have. Usually, carrying a mortgage doesn't impact them that way, but almost every other kind of debt makes them crazy. Although this chapter is about paying off debt, I want you to know that you are not a bad person because you have debt.

Debt happens for many reasons, and even if the reason is that you engage in too much "retail therapy," please do not feel shame about that or feel that it makes you a "bad" person somehow.

Shame and guilt about money can actually hinder our ability to make good money decisions or perform better. We do ourselves no favors when we categorize ourselves as people "who just aren't good with money." That only discourages us even more as far as changing our behavior. My advice to you is to ignore everyone who is saying or doing things to make you feel bad about your debt obligations, even if that person is a financial celebrity. This is your opportunity to forgive yourself and make a new start.

I recommend that you tackle your credit card debt by categorizing your loans into debt that is tax deductible when it comes time to file your taxes and debt that is not. Usually, the interest on home mortgages, student loans, and investment debt is deductible, as is interest on loans for rental property. To know how much you spend on debt, you will need to adjust it for your tax bracket.

Now, organize your debts from highest interest rate to lowest.

Obviously, accounts with high interest rates are the best to pay off first. Money spent on interest is wasted money. However, sometimes the number of debts a person has impacts the person psychologically. In that case, or if you have many credit cards, you might want to pay off the small ones first and then work your way up to paying off the larger balances. As you pay off a card, add that money to what you're paying on the next card—you will be surprised how quickly the balances go down, even on your largest cards.

Yes, I know paying off your cards this way is not saving you the most money. But what I have discovered is that people need to pay off loans in the way that inspires them and makes them feel the most successful. If lowering your number of debts from seven to three shows you that you can be successful, then that is what you should do.

Wherever you can, however, pay off the cards with the highest interest rates before you pay off those with lower interest rates, and pay off nondeductible debt before you pay off deductible debt. The interest on a home loan is deductible debt if you itemize on your taxes—the interest on a new boat is probably not. These strategies will lower the amount of interest you will pay. However, there are a few other important considerations.

Be careful of additional debt traps, especially those that put your assets at risk. Do not mortgage your house and use the money for an investment. Investments can go wrong, even when you have done all your research and due diligence. You don't want to lose your home in addition to your investment. More than that, some debt, including most consumer loans, can be relieved by bankruptcy if your financial situation does not improve. If you take out a mortgage to pay off your credit cards, you are paying off a debt that you can discharge in bankruptcy with an asset you probably don't want to lose. It's rarely a good idea or even prudent.

In fact, I don't like the idea of borrowing money at all to invest—too many people don't understand all the risks that come with investments.

Contrary to what some financial celebrities espouse, I don't worry about clients who have a mortgage on their home if it is one conventional, low-interest mortgage on a property they can afford, and they've made a reasonable down payment. However, don't refinance to create money for investments, using the difference between the old and new rates, even if the investment return appears to be great. Often, you might be taking on more risk than you think.

I have found that clients often oppose paying off certain kinds of debt because they want the tax break. I usually find that they rethink their position when they realize that unless the tax bracket is 100 percent, any money they borrow, even deductible debt, still costs them money.

No matter who you are, you can be debt free someday. It might take a long time, but it is possible. In the meantime, celebrate every victory you achieve—no matter how small—and every bill you pay off. Some months will be more successful than others, and you will pay more toward your balances at different stages in your life. Keep your chin up, though. You're playing a long game.

· · · · ·

Ashley: It is clear that I need to pay off my department store credit cards first. The interest rates are terrible! I just hope I can stay resolute and use cash when it comes holiday shopping season.

Michael: I think I may finally understand good debt versus bad debt. My credit card does also have a higher interest rate. Looks like I am better off paying down my Visa before I pay off my student loans.

Lisa: I need to talk to my friend Debbie about this. She was meeting with someone about using the equity in her home to invest in something that promised a higher return. I think maybe I should warn her that may not be such a good idea.

James: One of the best days in my life was paying off my mortgage before I reached retirement age. I'm so glad we never refinanced the house.

· · · · ·

WEEK 7 ACTIVITY

1. Organize your debt into categories—deductible and nondeductible.

2. Then organize it from highest interest rate to lowest.

3. Create a strategy for attacking debt. Whatever way you choose, continue to make payments toward the loan until it is paid.

4. Remember not to use your home as a revolving line of credit for anything you want.

· · · · ·

Ask Peggy

Question: Peggy, what is the single most important takeaway from this chapter?

Peggy: Pay off debt using whatever system motivates you to keep at it.

· · · · ·

Notes

Use the lines below for notes about what you did this past week.

_____

_____

_____

_____

_____

_____

_____

_____

_____

_____

_____

_____

_____

_____

_____

_____

_____

_____

_____

_____

_____

Chapter 8

Cash Flow: Improving your Credit

The Young Man Who Won Pizza, Frisbees, and Visas

Although it is illegal in most places now, not so long ago credit card companies stalked college students. Away from home for the first time, one college student was excited about the freedom college life provided him. When the credit card companies offered him T-shirts, pizza, and Frisbees and access to money with low monthly payments, he thought it was a win-win for him.

He was one of the lucky ones. He was always able to pay the minimum payments on his credit cards; however, by the time he graduated, he had a large amount of credit card debt for one so young. He later realized that if he needed to borrow money for anything else, such as a car, that the lenders would look at his credit score, he decided he needed to raise his score high enough to lower the interest rates he paid on other purchases.

Your credit score is one of the most important financial numbers you'll ever have. It determines the interest rate you pay if you need to purchase a car or a house, and could keep you from even qualifying for such a purchase.

In recent years, your credit score has also become increasingly important in ways unheard of in the past—it can now impact how much you pay for car insurance, whether you can get home insurance, and even whether you get a job. More and more employers have added your credit score as something they review before deciding whether to hire you.

As your financial condition deteriorates, predatory lenders often step in to offer "help," help that comes with sky-high interest rates and payments that can rapidly become impossible to repay. Poor credit can be financially devastating—long before a young person even realizes the importance of good credit. Thankfully, there are steps you can take to raise your credit score. It won't happen overnight, but by following some basic principles, you will be able to watch your score rise in a matter of months.

One caution: Be careful before you cancel your cards.

An important component to your credit score is the ratio of the credit you are using to the total amount you could potentially borrow. The more access to credit you have, the better your score. For example, if you have $1,000 of credit and you are using $800, it appears worse than if you have $2,000 available and are using $800.

As a result, closing cards once you've paid them off can actually lower your credit score, especially if the card had a high limit. Rather than canceling the cards—and thus canceling your ability to borrow that money, put the cards away so they aren't easy to access or use. Then, make a purchase with them once or twice a year to keep them open. And, of course, pay off the balance each time!

For those new to the business of credit, it pays to know that even applying for credit can lower your credit score. Be wary of stores that offer a small discount on a purchase in return for your applying for the store's card. First, the terms of store cards are frequently poor, and the cards usually have very high interest rates. Second, requesting credit suggests that you cannot pay your bills, and if you apply too often, your credit score will drop. For the same reason, you also want to be careful with lending services or credit card companies that make multiple applications on your behalf looking for the best rate—those bonus frequent flier miles are not worth a drop in your credit score.

Paying your bills on time is critical to keeping a good credit score. Set bills up on auto-pay systems to avoid costly mistakes. Being timely with your payments is easy to accomplish; it just takes a little organization and discipline.

If you're young, you might have an entirely different problem with credit—the problem of not having any. This can make it difficult to purchase a car or rent an apartment. There's a move to let regular payment of utility bills to be used to establish credit, but it's not yet a reality. If you're trying to build your credit rather than repair it, you might acquire a credit card to pay for an expense that you would buy anyway, such as gas. Then, pay the bill in full every month.

Your credit report is compiled by three companies: Equifax, Experian, and TransUnion. To ensure that you know what is on each report, you have the right to one free copy of your report from each company each year. Unfortunately, the free reports often do not include your actual credit score. That is available from the same sites for a fee, or you can learn your score any time you want to borrow money. Once you have the credit reports, be sure to carefully review them for discrepancies. Report any you find to the bureaus.

We'll talk about identity theft more later, but for now, just know that annually reviewing your credit report will help you to discover anything that you might need to dispute or resolve. If you request the free reports at different times during the year—rather than all three at once, you should be able to monitor activity just fine using only them.

I can't stress enough how your credit and credit score are important for your prosperity. I don't say that to scare you but rather to encourage you to tend to them as you would your health. If you have a poor credit score, don't panic. It can be improved. As you work to do that, try to remember you didn't create your debt overnight, and it will take some time before your positive actions are reflected in your score.

Although it might seem bleak when you begin, basic steps will help you to gain control of your score. As your score improves, the associated financial crisis will lessen. Interest rates will drop, employment opportunities will no longer be impacted, and the weight of the debt will fall away.

· · · · ·

 Ashley: I don't have any idea what my credit score is. I should find out before I try to buy a condo.

 Michael: I was shocked when my friend Jarrod didn't get that job he wanted because his credit score was low. I wonder what my score is?

 Lisa: I am going to transfer all my bills to auto pay. The way I travel with business, I pay late fees more often than I should.

James: If my children want to purchase something on credit, I want them to apply on their own. I don't want to cosign a loan and run the risk of their lowering my credit score.

· · · · ·

WEEK 8 ACTIVITY

1. Check your credit score and credit report.
2. Review your credit report carefully for any errors.
3. If your credit score is low, use the note section this

week to list three strategies that you will implement to raise it. Realize it can take a few months for the changes to be reflected in a better score.

. . . . .

Ask Peggy

Question: Peggy, what is the single most important takeaway from this chapter?

Peggy: Your credit score is more than the data that impacts the terms of your loan; it is also reviewed by potential employers and landlords.

. . . . .

Notes

Use the lines below for notes about what you did this week.

_____

_____

_____

_____

_____

_____

_____

_____

_____

_____

_____

_____

_____

_____

_____

_____

_____

_____

_____

_____

_____

_____

Chapter 9

Cash Flow: Saving for Special Events

The Dad Nostalgic for Christmas Past

The father did not think he was a pushover or that his children were particularly spoiled. Yet when the new toys came out before Christmas, the kids wanted them, and he and his wife bought them. They reasoned that when they were young, they received the toys they wanted, and wanted their children to have the same childhood they'd experienced. But toys had changed. Balls and homemade dolls were replaced by expensive video games and computer tablets. The dad dreaded January, because the bills from the holidays would begin to arrive. Often, the bills weren't paid off until long after the Fourth of July—sometimes not until it was time to start the holiday shopping all over again.

Even when you have your basic cash flow well under control, certain events can throw you off your plan. With a good emergency fund, you can handle an unexpected expense, but you still have all those extra annual events that must be paid for, ones that should not come out of your emergency fund. Vacations, birthdays, and holidays can quickly crater a budget.

Banks used to offer "Christmas accounts." The point of the Christmas account was that you would put aside a little money each month so that by the time it was December, you had your money saved and were ready to shop. You bought your presents and started the process again come January. Financially, you were always ahead of the game, earning a little interest and spending money you had already saved. It was fun too, because you could watch the account grow each month. The value of the presents you gave was a direct result of the amount of money you had saved. Stores also offered layaway, which let the toy of the season be reserved while you made payments to the store until the item was paid for in full. Then, the toy was redeemed. If you didn't finish paying for it, you didn't get it, but you did get your money back!

It has been said that the Ghost of Christmas Past is last year's credit card bill from the holidays. Most banks no longer offer Christmas accounts, and although they still have savings accounts, the accounts come with more strings, such as balance requirements. Many stores have also abandoned the concept of layaway, and so the modern-day holiday is put on a credit card. So instead of being ahead of the game as your mom and grandmother were in the old days, you're behind—paying interest instead of earning it, and owing money for a holiday that is already in the rear window.

Because it's "only plastic," you don't have as many spending limits either. Studies have found that people simply buy more when paying with a credit card than with cash. And while a person living on cash has to stop when the cash runs out, your credit-card spending is limited only by your card's credit limit. Presents aren't purchased because they are what you can afford—they are purchased because they are what you want at that moment. Of course, this crisis is not limited just to Christmas. Family vacations invite the same problem. Often we find ourselves paying for our honeymoon or family cruise long after we've returned to work and the tan has faded.

I recommend that you start saving money for your special events and expenses. If you take vacations or exchange gifts with family and friends, you have the choice of saving for them in advance or putting them on a card. When you're looking for those little ways to save money, remember that it will always be cheaper to save the money in advance because you never have to pay interest to save money.

I know most of us don't do that. Instead, we get ourselves behind. Suddenly, the holiday is stressful, not fun. Expectations aren't grounded in what we can afford. Before long, we come to dread the holiday season and big events such as weddings and graduations. Sometimes I'm amazed at how many people view the holidays as something to endure or survive. Although many things play a role in this, I'm pretty sure financial stress is part of it.

Why not take some easy steps to end this vicious cycle? Have a family discussion, ideally long before it's time to make a list for Santa. Let everyone know what the budget for the holiday, purchase, or event will be. Children can be brought into the conversation on a simple level. Typically, they have little concept of how expensive things are. Try to use analogies they can understand. If they get an allowance, let them know how long it would take them to save up that much money. If they still want the toy and you want to buy it for them (remember that you can say no), tell them that you will buy it for the following holiday, and it is up to them to remind you that they still want it. Odds are high that they will have forgotten all about it by then!

And don't feel as though all of this is on your shoulders. Let everyone help save money. When I was little, I saved a quarter a week in my "vacation" fund and a quarter a week in my "Christmas" fund. That meant I had my own vacation money if I wanted something on the trip that no one else wanted. I remember buying vending-machine nuts with it one time, and I felt so very grown up! I also used it to buy small gifts and souvenirs.

With dollar stores on every corner now, children can purchase a gift for a dollar. Let them do it, and it will help teach them financial responsibility. If teenagers have jobs and they want to contribute more, then let them help plan the family vacation. Help them see that having money has positive consequences. They don't have to pay their own way, but they can help. Pass on the idea of a prosperous life in all its many incarnations. And in the process, teach them financial responsibility, one of the best gifts you can give your children.

As you and your family look for clever ways to save money, remember that you can save a pretty penny by purchasing holiday wrapping paper or decorations the day after the holiday. Store them in their original containers, and they will still look fresh and new for the next season. Just remember where you stored them!

I have known wealthy people and not so wealthy people, and I can say with confidence that spending time with people is more valued by most people, especially the young and the old, more valued than any amount of money you might spend on a gift for them.

Our children might pester us for the latest toy or gadget, but chances are that long after the latest gadget has lost its thrill, they will remember time spent with you doing something together. Rather than buying a birthday cake, make one together as a family. On vacation, fix a picnic and eat it in a special spot. Time is the one commodity that none of us seems to have anymore. You might be surprised that after you have spent less money than you have done in years, your family declares it the best holiday or vacation they ever had!

· · · · ·

Ashley: I was never able to spend much time with my mother because she was always working so hard, I want to find that balance between work and home in my own life now. I would love to plan some picnics on the beach for my honeymoon.

 Michael: I get so busy at work—I know I buy expensive gifts to make up for it.

 Lisa: I remember baloney sandwiches that we ate on road trips. I just loved them. Do they even make baloney anymore?

James: The best Christmas we ever celebrated was when we didn't have any money at all, but the baby had started to crawl, and he played with all the ornaments he could reach on our tree. He liked to roll them. We didn't find the last one until the Fourth of July!

$$\cdots\cdots$$

WEEK 9 ACTIVITY

It is so easy to overspend on the holidays that many people resist even looking back—much less adding up the total spent. But if you want to move closer to your financial goals, I suggest that you take a moment to review a couple of years of old holiday spending.

1. Dig out your old spending records. If you no longer have your old statements, you can find them online or order them from your bank and credit card companies. You might cringe when you see how much you ended up spending on holiday gifts last year. Which begs the question: How much did you spend on birthday gifts? Other gifts? Vacations?

2. How much money would you need to save monthly to have a healthy holiday fund saved by next year?

3. Brainstorm as a family about ways you could save money when it comes to gifts and vacations.

· · · · ·

Ask Peggy

Question: Peggy, what is the single most important takeaway from this chapter?

Peggy: Start shopping early for holiday gifts, so you can avoid costly last minute, panicked buying.

· · · · ·

Notes

Use the following lines to jot down some notes about what you did this week. When you look back on it later, it will remind you of your progress.

_____

_____

_____

_____

_____

_____

_____

_____

Chapter 10

Cash Flow: Keeping Up with the Joneses

The Woman Who Understood Prosperity

A woman in her fifties remembered well the years when she had worried about looking successful. She recalled the wasted hours worrying about how she dressed. Now, don't misunderstand. She still liked to look nice, but she had abandoned the designer purses and expensive watches of years gone by. She and her husband had decided it was more important for them to have a peaceful life than it was to have all the latest gadgets and fashions. Their house wasn't huge, but they owned it free and clear, and they had taken to paying cash for their cars.

The change was rooted in a dire phone call from her doctor a few years ago, and her realization in that moment what mattered most—all the things money can't buy.

Her children and grandchildren had always known without a doubt that they could count on her. She never missed a recital or birthday, and she remembered every holiday with a homemade gift. With the money she and her husband were saving from their new habits, she knew they should never be a financial burden to their children, and she thought that might well be the best gift she would ever give her children and grandchildren.

Congratulations! You've made it through all ten of the chapters on cash flow. If you're on track, you've established some concrete goals, you know how much you spend each month, and you know how to create a budget. You also have strategies for creating an emergency fund and saving money, whether it is for holiday gifts, vacation, or something more. You're also paying off debt and improving your credit.

There's just one last cash flow tip I want to share, and it is this: Don't let other people derail your financial plan.

No one likes to admit it, but sometimes we look at a colleague's new car and then at our old one and wish we could have the new one. Or maybe friends take us out for a day at the lake on their boat, and we start doing the math to see if we can afford one. It can be even harder when it is our children raving over what one of their friends received as a birthday present. We would love to give them such a gift if we could, but sometimes children don't realize that it just isn't financially possible.

Most everyone, at one time or another, has wanted to keep up with the Joneses. Unfortunately, if that becomes a consuming desire, it can lead to one spouse wishing the other would get a better job or a lifestyle financed with debt. Sometimes, the stress of financial difficulties can lead to tragic outcomes. Trying to keep up with the Joneses rarely has a happy ending.

I wish everyone could understand that prosperity is about so much more than your money. Many financial services companies, books, and celebrities talk about easy ways of becoming *rich*. Early on, I decided I didn't want to use that word, and instead, I would use the word *prosperous*. To me, the word *prosperous* is deeper and more meaningful than the word *rich*. For one, I don't know how you could be prosperous *and* be unhappy. I know plenty of people who are rich and also miserable. That's because our family, friends, and children (including any fur babies) make us prosperous. You can be prosperous and eat beans and rice every night.

Yes, your prosperity is so much more than your money.

Of course, you are more prosperous if your financial world is under control. And that's why you and I are spending a year together to help you gain control of that part of your life. You see those two goals—prosperity and financial security—are tightly interlaced.

It also bears saying that just as you watch the Joneses, someone else is watching you. Give them something positive to watch. Inspire them to create a financial plan and live within their means. Even if you never know who they are, you just might save a marriage, a family, or a life.

· · · · ·

 Ashley: I never expected a financial planner to encourage me to eat beans and rice as a way to a happy, financially secure life! I thought this book would be about how to invest my portfolio or how to take on more risk—or how to get rich fast.

 Michael: I guess I need to quit resenting seeing my neighbors' new truck and boat in their driveway.

Lisa: Prosperity is more than money. I do love my life, and I'm grateful for all I have. I'm not rich, but I'm happy.

James: I found the advice in this section to be good—both prudent and smart, but I think I am ready to tackle some of the more advanced financial-planning topics now.

. . . . .

WEEK 10 ACTIVITY

Gather your family and friends around you and have a "prosperity party." Serve potluck so no one has to work too hard or spend too much, and then let everyone know they should be prepared to share one thing that makes them happy about their life. You will laugh all evening, create new memories, and leave in a wonderful mood.

. . . . .

Ask Peggy

Question: Peggy, what is the single most important takeaway from this chapter?

Peggy: Prosperity includes financial security, but it is also about friends, family, pets, spirituality, and self worth.

. . . . .

Notes

_____

_____

_____

_____

_____

_____

_____

· · · · ·

Ask Peggy!

 Ashley: Peggy, I've never given any thought to my finances other than hoping I had enough money to make it through the month. What is the very first thing I should do?

Peggy: Ashley, don't feel bad. Most people only rarely and vaguely think about their money. It's too intimidating. The first thing I want you to do is see how much money you spend every month, of course for bills you have to pay but also for your eating out habits, shopping, and all your other expenses. Once you know your monthly bills, use this information to help you create a budget, save an emergency fund, and begin to get a sense of your retirement savings needs—even though I realize that this is so far in the future, it doesn't seem real!

Michael: Peggy, I would like to save money, but I'm so busy I take a lot of shortcuts. I know I eat out too much and purchase a lot of cups of coffee. Worse than that, I have a little more money now, and I still find it difficult to budget. How do I break these old habits?

Peggy: Michael, you know that recognizing all this is a huge accomplishment. Try to create meals in advance that you can just pull out of the freezer or from a crock pot. Buy a coffeepot with a timer you can set the night before, so the coffee is waiting for you in the morning. I do not want you to think you can't purchase things. I just want you to refrain from mindless spending. Why don't you make yourself take two trips to a store before you make the purchase? It will slow down your impulse buying, and you aren't likely to go back to the store to buy it unless you need it!

67

Lisa: **Peggy, I know my nieces and nephews love the great gifts I give them for holidays. What can I do to help them see the importance of giving more than just receiving?**

Peggy: Lisa, as I said in the book, prosperity is more than money. It's fine to give your nieces and nephews gifts, but why not go down to the homeless shelter and help serve meals some time over the holidays too. Or better yet, why not go other times of the year when the shelters actually need more help. Everyone seems to get charitable during November and December.

 James: **Peggy, I'm always worried when my friends tell me that they are spending more in retirement than they anticipated. How can we stay on track?**

Peggy: James, you will always have fluctuations in what you spend, and in the early days of retirement, you have to realize that you will have to form new spending habits to reflect your new circumstances. Sometimes it can take a few months to realize you're over spending. The problem is when the overspending continues month after month. If you spend too much money on something, then cut back for a few months. Hopefully, you've calculated your spending needs accurately in advance. If you haven't, admit it early; don't be afraid of it. Maybe you could go back to work part time for a while. That would help your cash flow significantly.

Insurance

Chapter 11

Insurance: Life's a Risky Business

The Woman Who Didn't Want to Work

A lot of things will go both right and wrong in your life—and surprisingly, most of them, risky or not, will require insurance of some kind. Whether it's the joy of a first home or a new baby or the challenge of a major weather event or unexpected fender bender, things will certainly go better if you have the right insurance already in place. You might not like to think about life's risks, but they happen, often unexpectedly, and they have the potential to derail your life, including your financial life.

Cash flow is the core of good financial planning, but risk management is a close second. Often, we manage risk through insurance, and that is our focus here. However, other ways of managing risk also exist, and in the spirit of full disclosure, I believe we should review them as well.

One way to manage the risks of life is to be willing to retain them. That means you don't pay for insurance. What happens happens, and you roll with the punches. The downside is that you also have no protection or financial fallback if an unfortunate event occurs. If you do not have any life insurance and you die, your heirs receive no death benefit. If you need nursing home care and you don't have long-term-care insurance, you pay for the care out of your own pocket or you go without.

Certain kinds of insurance, such as auto insurance, are required by law or lenders. Those aren't optional for you.

Some types of insurance are your choice.

However, no matter how golden your life has been to this moment, I would urge you to read all the chapters on insurance before you decide that you don't need coverage. And I suggest you talk with your family or friends to see if they agree with your decision. Remember, they might be the ones left holding the bag in the end.

Insurance can seem expensive when you're paying the premiums, but believe me, it feels priceless when you need it. It is a significant monthly or annual expense, but one that you can sometimes lower by how you go about your daily life. And to keep the cost of insurance from escalating, you can exercise due diligence. For example, if you wear a bicycle helmet when you ride your bike around the neighborhood, you can lower the possibility of severe injury to your head and all the life-threatening and costly consequences of such an injury, including an increase in your premiums.

True, you could eliminate the risk of any bike-riding incident or subsequent rise in insurance premium if you simply never ride a bike. But this book isn't about turning you into Scrooge—it's about creating a prudent personal financial plan that will let you prosper in life. Riding a bike is one of the simplest joys of life—and if you plan ahead, you should be able to cycle to the park with nary a worry in the world.

I realize most people don't want to change their lives. That's why a good financial planner will suggest that you look at ways you might lower your risk and then insure any activities that might lead to expenses that would cause a financial crisis for you and your family.

My goal here is to also remind you of some common risks we all face. Chances are that you already know what these are. We just typically don't like to think about them. But you might also face additional risks that I have not mentioned, especially if you own a business, are active duty military, or have a high net worth.

In this chapter's story, a couple decided that they needed life insurance, so they asked their financial planner to review the life insurance policy that their insurance agent was recommending. It was a whole life policy with a multimillion-dollar death benefit, and the clients wanted to be sure they were making the right decision in purchasing it.

The planner interviewed the couple and learned that the wife had a degree in education. When asked if she thought she would want to teach again if anything happened to her husband, the wife looked aghast. She said she never wanted to work again and expected to live in exactly the same manner as she did now, whether her wealthy husband was alive or not. Because of the permanent and expensive expectations of the wife, the planner agreed that whole life insurance was a good decision in their situation.

Whole life insurance usually carries a higher price tag, and it has fallen out of favor with many people. Term life insurance is widely loved by financial celebrities, and the phrase "Buy term and invest the difference" is so common that I am asked about this advice at least once a month.

My advice? Be cautious of anyone who gives you an answer that is too easy! There is no one "correct" type of life insurance to buy. The kind of insurance that you need depends on the goal of the insurance and your particular situation. Realize that many kinds of policies exist, with different characteristics. You should familiarize yourself with all these choices before you make any decisions.

Life insurance manages the risk of your death. It is at its most basic one risk-management tool available to you.

Everything in this chapter will underscore that belief, so this chapter takes a specific perspective on insurance and risk that you might or might not agree with. That's fine. One of my major goals is to help you think through every one of the financial decisions you are making. If you insist on using insurance as a savings vehicle or investment tool, I want you to know the risks and expenses associated with that decision.

So let's get started.

Insurance can be divided into two major categories: *temporary* and *permanent*.

Temporary life insurance, or term life, provides insurance for a set period of time, whereas permanent life insurance, whole life or universal life, can provide coverage until you die. Term life is in place for a set period of time. It provides a benefit if you die within the period of time the policy is in force (literally, the *term* of the policy). Because it is a *temporary* benefit, it is typically priced less expensively than permanent insurance. That is partly because if you're young, the insurer has good reason to believe you won't die before the policy ends. If you're an older customer, the product has been priced to take your age into consideration.

Term life can be appealing for someone who is young without as much income to spend on benefits. Term is also effective when it insures a specific event or liability. A term policy might match the length of an overseas assignment or a mortgage to insure that the family home is paid for in case someone dies. Unfortunately, when the term ends, so does the insurance, and all the insured person has to show for it is past peace of mind and receipts—but no insurance.

By the time the term policy has expired, the insured might no longer qualify to buy additional insurance because of poor health, so any future insurance needs cannot be met. Although the difference in the premiums can be invested, if a large future insurance need is expected, the investment might not have grown enough to cover the expenses.

Term insurance can't be counted on to pay estate tax because the insured could easily die after the policy expires. Finally, term might not be effective in business continuity planning, depending on the age of the business owners and how long they plan to work.

Whole life insurance is permanent life insurance that can stay in force until you die, as long as you keep the premiums paid. Whole life is more expensive than term when you are younger, but it becomes more financially beneficial as you age because a private term policy purchased when you are older can be very expensive. Whole life policies build up a cash value and are sometimes sold as a savings tool. However, the purpose of insurance is risk management, not cash savings. If the creation of a savings vehicle is the only reason you're considering whole life, consider other savings options before you purchase it.

To lower the cost of the insurance later, the cash value can eventually be used to pay premiums as long as the death benefit does not drop below the amount of your insurance need. You can also borrow against the cash value, but again, that will impact the amount of insurance you have. And remember, your life insurance shouldn't replace your emergency fund.

A variation of whole life insurance is *variable whole life insurance*. This is a life insurance policy that can be invested in the stock market. Again, before purchasing this kind of policy, I caution you to remember the reason you are purchasing your insurance policy in the first place—also be sure the death benefit is not tied to market performance. If it is, and if you purchased the correct amount of insurance at the outset, you could be underinsured if you die during a market decline.

If performance does not impact the death benefit, look at the fees being charged to be sure you're not paying more than you'd pay if you had an investment account separate from your life insurance policy. Your financial planner can help you to make this comparison.

A third type of life insurance, *universal life insurance*, provides great flexibility in payments and benefits. It can be modified throughout your life, allowing you to adjust the premium and death benefit while you own the policy. However, universal policies can be confusing. Be sure you understand what options you have and what you pay for that flexibility.

Variable universal, like variable whole life, adds the investing component into the policy. It has the same risks and advantages as variable whole life.

In general, you need to examine whether you want to mix your investments with the need to control the risk of your death. Some would say the twain should never meet.

Finally, remember that term, whole, variable, and universal insurance policies all come with many differing characteristics and items specific to the policy. Before you decide exactly which plan works best for you, look at your available options and the costs associated with them.

· · · · ·

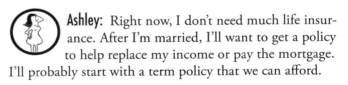

Ashley: Right now, I don't need much life insurance. After I'm married, I'll want to get a policy to help replace my income or pay the mortgage. I'll probably start with a term policy that we can afford.

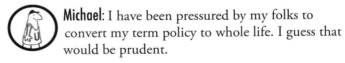

Michael: I have been pressured by my folks to convert my term policy to whole life. I guess that would be prudent.

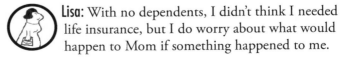

Lisa: With no dependents, I didn't think I needed life insurance, but I do worry about what would happen to Mom if something happened to me.

James: We have a whole life policy that we bought when I was about fifty. I just didn't want my wife to have financial issues if something happened to me. Maybe I should see if it still provides the security she might someday need.

$\cdots\cdots$

WEEK 11 ACTIVITY

In this week's activity, I would like you to review each of your current insurance policies for the following:

1. *What type of policy is it?*
2. *What is the death benefit?*
3. *If it's a term policy, how long is left on the term?*
4. *Why did you buy the policy in the first place?*
5. *Are those situations still the same or has anything changed?*

$\cdots\cdots$

Ask Peggy

Question: Peggy, what is the single most important takeaway from this chapter?

Peggy: If you want to buy term insurance and invest the difference, be sure you have no need of permanent coverage, and then be sure to invest the difference as planned.

$\cdots\cdots$

Notes

_____

_____

_____

Peggy Doviak

_____

_____

_____

_____

_____

_____

_____

_____

_____

_____

_____

_____

_____

_____

Chapter 12

Insurance: How Much Life Insurance Do You Need?

The Hammer That Saw Everything Like a Nail

Sometimes, I talk with people in financial services who don't seem to understand holistic financial planning. During one such lunch with a colleague, we began to talk about how much life insurance clients ideally need. The adviser told me that he sold large life insurance policies to meet estate needs. When I asked him if he ever recommended trust techniques to lower estate tax liabilities, he told me no. In such situations, he just recommended that his clients buy more life insurance. He bragged that he had never seen an estate issue that couldn't be solved by purchasing more insurance. I nearly choked on my breadstick.

One of the most random decisions that I see clients make concerns how much life insurance to purchase. Some clients decide they simply don't need any insurance and settle for whatever is provided by their employer's benefit package. Others decide they need a large personal insurance policy, and purchase a million-dollar policy in the hopes that their loved ones can be wealthy should they die. Others pull a random number out of a hat, a number that sounds like it would be enough if something should happen to them. The one thing all three clients often share is that once they decide how much insurance they need, they rarely think to revisit their decision on their own.

Calculating life insurance needs is a formula that will change through your life. In the last chapter about types of life insurance, I talked about the purpose of life insurance. It is designed to manage the financial risks associated with your death or the death of your spouse, if you have one.

If your income is no longer available to meet the needs of your family, what is the shortfall?

Another risk associated with your untimely death might be estate taxes. Did you know that life insurance can be purchased to pay any estate tax liability that remains after good estate planning? Calculating how much life insurance you need and reviewing it annually along with your other investments is a way to ascertain your insurance needs at different times of your life, and you might well find that such an annual review will reveal that you have different insurance needs today than you did yesterday.

If your projections show that you have a perennial insurance need to either pay expenses or estate tax, you probably would want to consider some type of permanent insurance. However, if your calculation reveals that you no longer have an additional life insurance need in the future, then that is an indication that term insurance might be a good decision from that point on. Each part of your life needs to be analyzed. Although this chapter doesn't offer a calculator, I would like to give you some major categories of expenses that might need to be covered by life insurance.

The first category of expenses is your funeral expenses and any debt that needs to be paid at the time of your death. Remember that if you want to pay off your home or other long-financed debt, you must select an insurance policy that lasts as long as the liability.

Next, what income will your surviving spouse have while the children still live at home? After your death, your children will receive a monthly Social Security payment until they are grown—but you might be surprised to learn that in this situation, "grown" means sixteen years of age (unless the child is disabled). With usually two more years of high school remaining at that age and college looming, you might not find that Social Security payment to be sufficient.

What other expenses or obligations might your family face? What's the difference between the income and the expenses? That is the gap you need to fill with insurance. Do you want to pay for your children's college? How much will that cost, and how much do you have saved? The difference between the two is the amount that needs to be filled with insurance.

The third category is often the hardest gap to estimate—after your surviving spouse's children are grown and no longer receiving Social Security assistance but before your spouse qualifies for Social Security and any pension you might have earned.

Sometimes, retirement accounts can be accessed during this time, but using those funds before your spouse turns sixty-five might leave him or her with a shortfall during retirement. You need to calculate the difference between your spouse's income and the family's need and purchase insurance to fill that need.

Finally, after you have completed your estate plan (we will discuss this later), do you still have an estate tax liability? That need can also be covered by insurance; however, you should not add it to your total insurance need.

An Irrevocable Life Insurance Trust can purchase life insurance to pay estate tax liability after all other planning strategies have been exhausted.

In the meantime, talk to your estate planning team about creating a trust that can hold life insurance. This is a very specific use of insurance, and you will want to plan for this separately.

Randomly choosing an amount of insurance can be dangerous or expensive—tying up funds that could be better used or even saved. If you calculate the need too low, financial disaster can occur when someone dies. If you calculate the need too high, you can waste money on insurance premiums rather than meeting other underfunded parts of your financial plan.

Giving some thoughtful attention to your policy now will help the people you love for years to come.

· · · · ·

Ashley: Right now, I do not have anyone I love or feel responsible for who would have a financial need if I died. All I need to pay for is my funeral, which is sort of depressing.

Michael: I just know I want to be able to pay for my children's college no matter what might happen to me or my wife. I think we need more insurance than we have now.

Lisa: Although I love my nieces and nephews, they don't need a large inheritance when I die. Right now, I can't imagine needing a lot of insurance after I'm seventy.

James: My accountant, financial planner, and estate attorney are helping me track whether or not we should fund insurance to pay for a possible estate tax. So far, we're still under the net worth phaseouts. Of course, the risk is that when I need it, I might not be able to purchase the insurance anymore.

· · · · ·

WEEK 12 ACTIVITY

Research shows that the only thing people like to talk about less than death is money. Combine the two, and it is no surprise why so many couples have no idea what each other thinks when it comes to end-of-life issues. Yet if there is one thing we do know, it is that every single one of us will die—maybe young, maybe old—but for sure and someday. That is a certainty. People who face that reality often find that their lives become sweeter and more purposeful as do their relationships with family. When people stop resisting end-of-life planning, they often feel the relief that comes from knowing you've taken care of your family no matter what the future might bring.

This week's activity will help you organize into a table the possible financial risks that would be associated with your death. Once you total them, you can calculate how much life insurance you need, and it'll be possible for you to have more confidence that you are neither dramatically overinsured nor underinsured. It will also provide excellent data for an insurance agent to use to help you choose a policy.

Period of Time	Deficit in Resources
Expenses to be paid at death	
Expenses until children are 18	
College expenses	
Expenses for children after age 18	
Expenses during retirement	
Estate tax liability	
Additional expenses to be paid	
Total Deficit	

. . . . .

Ask Peggy

Question: Peggy, what is the single most important takeaway from this chapter?

Peggy: Use a cash flow analysis rather than a rule of thumb to decide how much life insurance to buy.

. . . . .

Notes

Use the following lines to jot down some notes about what you did this week. When you look at the book later, it will remind you of your progress.

_____

_____

_____

_____

_____

_____

_____

_____

_____

_____

Chapter 13

Insurance: Disability Coverage

*The Entrepreneur Who Didn't Believe
It Could Happen to Her*

It is difficult to start a business, and maybe even more difficult to run one, even if you are highly successful. In some cases, it may be even harder because you are successful.

An entrepreneur ran her own small business for thirty years. Well respected in her profession, she had the reputation of providing honest, quality service at a fair price. Her business carried little debt, and she had a company retirement plan. What she did not have was disability insurance. It was an expense that had just never seemed necessary—until her cancer diagnosis.

The seemingly endless treatments left her unable to work. She assumed she could apply to Social Security because she had paid into the system, but Social Security denied her claim. Friends and family raised money online and through fund-raisers, but the proceeds couldn't come close to replacing her income. Fortunately, the cancer treatment worked, and she was eventually able to return to work.

But what would have happened if she had not been able to return to her business?

With medical advances and the changing job landscape, you are much more likely to become disabled than you are to die during your working career. Yet disability insurance is often overlooked as an important element in your financial planning strategy. True, if you have sufficient resources saved, disability insurance might be irrelevant. However, for most of us, that just isn't the case. If we couldn't work, financial catastrophe would be just around the bend.

Traditionally, employers have often provided disability insurance as a fringe benefit. However, with the rise in the use of contract labor and the trend of even big companies cutting back on benefit packages, that can no longer be assumed.

It's also important to understand that disability insurance comes in two forms: short-term disability and long-term disability. The names are self-explanatory. Short-term insurance covers an inability to work for a period of months to approximately two years. Long-term insurance provides coverage for longer periods of time, generally beginning when short-term coverage expires and ending at full retirement age.

Employer benefit packages typically offer short-term policies if they include disability insurance at all, whereas long-term disability is generally a privately purchased insurance. Anyone who has been diagnosed with cancer or has had a serious medical emergency can tell you that it is important that you understand the dollar value and length of time for which your policy provides benefits.

No disability policy is likely to completely replace your salary. Disability insurance is usually designed to offer a benefit worth about 60 percent of your salary. This is important to know from a cash flow perspective, and it should also reinforce the need for an emergency fund.

It is important to know the taxability of your benefit. Generally, if you pay your own disability premium, benefits are income tax free when you use them. But if an employer pays the premium for you, the benefits are taxable to you when you use them. As a result, many people choose to pay for the premiums. I suggest that you talk with your human resources department to be sure you enroll in benefits in the way most beneficial to you. And, of course, be sure to make what you learn a part of your discussions with your financial planner.

Typically, the price of private disability insurance is a function of how likely you are to be injured on the job (the more risk, the more you will pay for coverage), how long you want to wait before you begin to receive benefits (the elimination period), and the disability you want your insurance to cover.

Sometimes, you can have the option to receive benefits at different levels of disability. The inability to do your own occupation (also called "own occ") provides benefits more quickly than a policy that only provides benefits only if you cannot work at all (called "any occ"). A policy for modified occupation ("modified occ") provides benefits when you cannot perform work that is similar to what you do now. These options are not available in all professions, so it is worth asking your agent if you have such choices.

It is difficult to qualify for Social Security disability benefits. Yet many people assume that Social Security disability will be there to help them should injury or illness make it impossible for them to work. Thus they also mistakenly think that Social Security disability replaces any need to purchase disability insurance on their own. Certainly, when it is granted, Social Security disability is helpful in a bad situation. However, Social Security takes an "any occupation" definition of disability, which is the most restrictive kind. If you can hold any position, you cannot receive benefits.

Certain exceptions exist, including serious illness that can result in death and some other medical conditions.

However, assuming that you have easy access to disability compensation through Social Security isn't prudent.

Instead of counting on this benefit, you should review what, if any, policies you have either privately or through your employer. You might be surprised at what you find, but pat yourself on the back for taking the time to learn what your options are before something unexpected leaves you unable to work and your family in a financial crisis.

· · · · ·

 Ashley: I do wish my employer offered benefits. Once I can find a job in my field of training, I'll be sure to remember to look at the benefit package before I take a job.

 Michael: I thought my work disability covered me until I turned sixty-five. I had better review my policy to see how long the benefits last.

 Lisa: I opted to pay the premiums for my disability at work. With a 40 percent reduction in salary, I don't need taxes taken out too!

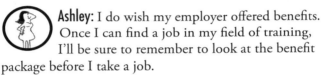 **James:** Because I could retire at any time with a good nest egg, I don't see my needing disability insurance.

· · · · ·

WEEK 13 ACTIVITY

Your task this week is to review your work benefits package to understand the terms of any disability or other insurance policy you already own. Next, I want you to review your cash flow exercises.

1. Could you and your family survive financially if you couldn't work?

2. For a week?

3. A month?

4. A year?

If the answer to any of those questions is no, you need to consider disability insurance.

· · · · ·

Ask Peggy

Question: Peggy, what is the single most important takeaway from this chapter?

Peggy: If your employer pays your disability premiums, the benefit is taxable, but if you pay the premium for the insurance, the benefit is tax free.

· · · · ·

Notes

Use the following lines to jot down some notes about what you did this week.

_____

_____

_____

_____

_____

_____

_____

_____

_____

_____

_____

_____

_____

_____

_____

_____

_____

_____

_____

_____

Chapter 14

Insurance: Health Care

The Boater Who Took Care of Everyone Else

The Fourth of July is supposed to be a day of patriotic fun in the sun. However, for one father, it became a nightmare. While on his boat making plans with friends for watching fireworks later that night, he noticed that the gas gauge registered low on fuel. He did everything correctly while refueling, but when he restarted the boat, it exploded. No one was killed, but everyone, including the boat's owner, was badly burned. They all had to be taken by helicopter to a local burn center. And the holiday tragedy wasn't over.

The man, you see, had no health insurance. After the Affordable Care Act became the law of the land in 2010, he was among the first to purchase policies for all his family—everyone that is except himself.

Few things in life are scarier than receiving bad news from your doctor. Yet when you don't have health insurance, almost any health problem can quickly become overwhelming and financially incapacitating.

Medical tests and even routine surgeries can easily run to thousands if not tens of thousands of dollars. More serious or chronic health problems such as cancer can rack up bills in the hundreds of thousands if not millions of dollars. Yet a Kaiser Health Tracking Poll in 2017 found that 45 percent of Americans said they would have difficulty paying an unexpected $500 medical bill. That is why one of the most important factors in your financial security is having adequate health insurance that covers the essentials—and that includes the large, unexpected major medical emergency.

The best way to ensure that you purchase the correct policy is to be familiar with its components—and to understand that not all health insurance is created equal.

First, you should know how much of a premium you will be paying, with the understanding that the lowest premium is likely not the best choice, because the benefits are likely to be quite limited. The Affordable Care Act attempted to address the proliferation of health insurance policies that offered super low premiums without making it clear should you ever have a medical emergency, your actual coverage would be minimal or limited or even nonexistent.

The ACA made it the law that all health care policies must provide essential coverage. But where there is a will, there's often a way. Efforts have been made to allow policies that don't cover the essentials. Once again, consumers need to be on the lookout for policies that parade as full health coverage but only cover catastrophic medical emergencies or exclude doctor's appointments.

You might tell yourself that neither you nor your family will ever need to go to the hospital or visit a doctor, but that reality can change in an instance. Your child might wake one morning with one of the new drug-resistant infections, or you might be in a car accident. Suddenly you are at the emergency room needing tests and specialists and medication—the bills that result could be extremely expensive.

And then there's the deductible. You need to know the size of your insurance deductible. The deductible is the amount of money you have to pay out of pocket before the insurance policy takes over.

Larger deductibles are likely to make a policy less expensive. Just be sure that you have the resources, such as your emergency fund, to pay them.

Deductibles can also come in different forms. If you are purchasing a policy to cover all your family members, be sure you know whether the deductible needs to be met for every member of the family before bills are paid or whether bills are paid for each person once that individual has met the deductible.

Although the second structure is more common, I have seen policies in which a certain percentage of the family members had to meet a deductible before any benefits would be covered by the insurance company. And, yes, that information is often in the small print of your plan.

You will probably have a co-payment each time you use the policy. Although typically not expensive, co-pays also vary depending on the policy. Be sure you know how much the co-pay is for different kinds of expenses, such as a hospital stay or visiting a specialist.

If being able to see a doctor you've used for a long time is important to you, be sure that doctor is inside your network. Your policy will probably involve a network of physicians, hospitals, and laboratories. That doctor may or may not be in that network. Find out what happens if you choose an out-of-network provider or need to use one while on vacation or a business trip. Sometimes, even when you think you have anticipated every scenario and asked every question, a piece of your treatment will slip out of network.

I know someone who carefully planned a minor surgery. However, she had never thought to ask where a biopsy would be taken for testing—a development that arose while she was still under anesthetic. The analysis went to a lab that was considered out of network—not one approved by her health insurance company. All I can say is, it was a very expensive little exception.

And that is why it pays to try to anticipate any medical procedures you are having and confirm with your doctor and health insurance company that all parts of any procedure will be covered by your insurance. Asking the right questions could save you a bundle in the end.

One new question when it comes to health insurance these days involves what wellness procedures are covered in a policy. In an effort to rein in health care costs and improve Americans' health, the ACA requires health insurance to cover preventive wellness care. Such procedures—say an annual physical or a mammogram—are designed to catch problems early to avoid more serious and costly illnesses that could arise later; they can add years to your life. But don't assume your insurance policy covers them—check and confirm that for yourself, ideally in writing.

Another area to ask about is whether your policy covers prescription drugs. Drug costs are staggeringly high in the United States compared to other countries, especially if no generic alternative is available. With many pills costing more than a $100 apiece, good prescription drug coverage can save you a lot of money.

With everything you need your health insurance to cover, it probably comes as no surprise that if you can get insurance through your workplace, it is likely your best choice. Still some people remain uninsured. If you fall into that category, look at the coverage available through the Affordable Care Act in addition to reviewing private policies.

Your options will depend on the state where you live and how much you earn. And if you are eligible for health insurance through, say, a university or a Native American tribe or the U.S. military or the U.S. Department of Veterans Affairs or some other outside entity, take the time to investigate—and then choose what is best for you and yours.

· · · · ·

 Ashley: I need to start learning about my health insurance options. My coverage has been through my mom's policy, thanks to the ACA extending the age older children could be insured.

 Michael: My employer offers good insurance for both me and my family. I know I'm one of the lucky ones.

Lisa: It amazes me that some people still think they can function without health insurance. It takes just one big medical emergency to bankrupt you.

James: I'm going to need to be careful to ensure that I keep continuous coverage for the period of time between when I retire and when I begin to receive Medicare benefits. I don't want any nasty surprises!

· · · · ·

WEEK 14 ACTIVITY

If you don't have health insurance, you should purchase a policy. It's one of the pillars when it comes to protecting your family's financial prosperity. If you have insurance available through work, that is probably your best and most affordable choice, although you may want to compare the cost of including your spouse and children on the policy.

In some cases, independent policies are less expensive for them. Don't overlook policies available through the Affordable Care Act. You can look at online options or contact an insurance agent. In either case, be sure you understand the coverage—what it does and doesn't cover— and the expenses. Don't forget to review prescription-drug coverage and other types of health coverage, including the benefits of dental and vision insurance.

· · · · ·

Ask Peggy

Question: Peggy, what is the single most important takeaway from this chapter?

Peggy: In our fluid regulatory environment, be sure you understand all the components of your health insurance plan, including what is covered and at what level.

· · · · ·

Notes

Use the following lines to jot down some notes about what you did this week. It will help you track your progress.

_____

_____

_____

_____

_____

_____

_____

Chapter 15

Insurance: Long-term Care

The Man Who Lived Longer than He Expected

When you make financial decisions because you are sure you know the future, you're likely to make a mistake. A man had been devastated as a teen when his grandfather died at a young age. Then his father died in his sixties, and the man became convinced that he would not live to see retirement. Although he saved for his retirement, he didn't worry about how he would pay for his eldercare, because he never intended to get old.

He was blessed with a loving wife, two sons, and a long life, which was wonderful for many years. Then he began to forget where he put the car keys, what he had eaten for lunch, and finally, the name of his older son. The family had enough money to live on but not enough money to care for him. Both sons had families and financial responsibilities of their own.

Eventually, the man's resources dipped so low that he qualified for Medicaid and was moved into a facility—unfortunately one more than thirty-five miles away from his beloved wife; it was the closest Medicaid space to be had.

She drove there to see him until she couldn't, and then her sons took her as often as they could. The family's pain over the separation from the father would never be forgotten.

The crisis of eldercare has directly impacted my life, my friends' lives, and many of my clients' lives. I believe it might be the greatest unseen and certainly undiscussed crisis of the next twenty years. It's the elephant in the living room that no one wants to address.

I hope I'm wrong, but I don't think I am.

The issue of paying for eldercare is going to overwhelm American families. We are living longer, and for much of our extended longevity, we are sailing, traveling, hiking, holding hands, and doing all those other things we see the retired couples do in television ads. However, when it comes to the very last part of our lives, no one is shooting video, because it is ugly.

You need a plan for how you'll pay for care when you become too old or ill for you to live alone or with family. Typically, if someone enters a nursing facility, the average length of stay is three years. Care at home extends life at least that long. Unfortunately, those three years can bankrupt you. Long-term care, whether at home or in a facility, is easily $6,000 a month in Oklahoma, by far not the most expensive state in the union, but let's just keep that number as a frame of reference. Many people don't have $72,000 a year to pay for care for themselves or their parents. At that rate, a three-year stay costs $216,000! But before you panic and close the book—stop. Turning away won't help anything, instead let's talk about a few strategies that might.

First, some tough love: Medicaid is not the immediately all-encompassing solution you might think it is.

Medicaid provides long-term care for the indigent, which means that nearly all the financial resources of the person must be exhausted. You should check with Medicaid for exactly how many assets can remain with the recipient. The person must qualify for the program, which can take a little time, although there isn't a specific elimination period. The greater crisis comes in finding a facility that accepts Medicaid patients in your area. Although many facilities take a few, the space is very limited—and they are dealing with a wave of aging Baby Boomers.

If this is the long-term care plan for you or a family member, realize that you might well end up with Grandpa or Grandma in a different town.

I am not going to be critical of Medicaid care, because I believe the caregivers do the best they can with limited resources, but most people who are ill need an advocate who is readily available 24/7. I do recommend that people visit the facilities to check on their loved ones at unexpected times, even if the facilities are private and expensive. When the patient is an hour or more away, the ability to be a regular advocate for a loved one becomes difficult.

Second, Medicaid now has a five-year look back period. This means if you had planned to give away resources in order to qualify for Medicaid, you need to do it five years before you apply for Medicaid. For many people, this time horizon is just too long.

A third issue is Medicaid fraud. Because Medicaid was not designed for wealthy people who gave away their assets to become "paper poor," the government takes a dim view of the behavior. If you are even considering doing this, talk with your financial planner, accountant, and attorney to be sure that you are not breaking the law. Certainly, if the finances are gone, Medicaid is an available resource. I just worry about people who believe they know how they will pay for their care when they have no idea it is so difficult—or how falsely moving assets around can be illegal.

Long-term care policies are not perfect, but then what is? Yet to compound the problem, many people focus on the negative characteristics because they don't want to pay the premiums in case they die quickly or in a way that does not leave them in need of a long-term care facility.

I have another caution as well.

Research is suggesting that with advances in other forms of medical issues, most of us will die with dementia. Dementia can remove the ability for families to offer care, and if it is too severe, it can limit home-care options as well. Certainly, it requires a caregiver. That caregiver can be a family member, but that person will likely need to quit his or her job. If a caregiver is hired, the bill quickly becomes thousands of dollars a month again.

Long-term care insurance creates a benefit that far exceeds its expense if and when care is needed. Although expensive, it isn't anywhere close to $72,000 a year. You don't have to purchase the best policy. Even a smaller benefit without an inflation adjustment will go a long way toward helping to meet a need. Personal resources might be able to make up the difference.

Finally, insurance might not be the appropriate solution for everyone. If you and your spouse have roughly half a million dollars set aside that you can dedicate to your care, then you probably can self-fund your care. If you don't have that much money—and many people don't—then have a family conversation about how you will pay for your care. You might discover your children would happily pay the policy premium now to avoid the anguish of trying to work two jobs later to pay for your care. You could self-fund it as a family unit, so everyone would pay less.

One way or another, you need to create a plan for your care when you are elderly. If Medicaid is your choice, you need to begin planning early and carefully. Otherwise, you need to allocate a portion of retirement and investment resources for the care at the end of your life. Ignoring this elephant won't make it go away, but it will cause it to squash you when it sits down.

· · · · ·

Ashley: I need to focus on accumulating an emergency fund before I worry about how I will pay for a nursing home.

Michael: I'm still too young to purchase a policy for myself, but I wonder about my parents.

Lisa: I don't know how we will pay for Mom's care. I don't want her in a facility—and I don't think she'd ever want to go into one, but if it came to that what would we do?

James: We bought a long-term care policy for my wife because women usually outlive men. I hope it was the right decision.

· · · · ·

WEEK 15 ACTIVITY

This week's activity involves a combination of cash flow analysis and family conference. I suspect someone you care about does not have long-term care insurance. Obviously, if that person is you or your spouse, your analysis needs to begin there. However, you might also have parents without coverage, and if so, the family needs to make a plan. Talking about it before you need it is the prudent thing to do, and then you can make some sort of plan.

If long-term care is available as a fringe benefit from your work, look carefully at the plan. It might offer benefits at a lower rate than a private plan does. Even if the benefit amount doesn't cover all the costs, it might be worth the price of the premium to create the income stream.

Finally, be sure you understand all the components of whatever you purchase. How much is the daily benefit?

How long is the elimination period (the period of time before the policy begins to pay)? Is there inflation protection? Are there benefits if you and your spouse purchase a policy at the same time? You will need to weigh these questions and possibly others as you make a decision.

Remember that you aren't doing this for yourself; you're doing it to reduce the stress you will cause your loved ones if you don't.

· · · · ·

Ask Peggy

Question: Peggy, what is the single most important takeaway from this chapter?

Peggy: Medicare provides *very* limited long-term care benefits—take the time to consider additional options.

· · · · ·

Notes

Use the following lines to jot down some notes.

_____

_____

_____

_____

_____

_____

Chapter 16

Insurance: Automobile

The College Graduate with Too Much on his Mind

Teenage boys have notoriously poor driving records—something that I can assure you is not lost on the insurance industry. As a result, insurance policies for teen males are extremely expensive and often used. A responsible but busy young man set up all his bills to auto debit from his bank account. His twenty-fifth birthday came and went, yet he never thought to notify his insurance company. Instead, his premium continued faithfully to go to the insurer each month. If his company tried to notify him, he didn't see it. He read his e-mails but wasn't so diligent with letters. It never occurred to him that anything might have changed.

In fact, he had moved to a different rate pool.

He paid several months of higher insurance premiums before he finally realized that maybe he needed to update his policy information.

Assumptions are made every day in the business world. We assume young men know the age at which their insurance premium will drop. We assume everyone knows you have to have car insurance, even though often the only way young people figure this out is if they have to get insurance to apply for a car loan or if their parents tell them.

Buying a car can be fun, but then you have to insure it. All those features that made it so appealing on the showroom floor can cause it to be a more expensive endeavor once you have driven it home.

Choosing the right insurance policy can be challenging—even for an adult. Unfamiliar terminology can make you uncertain about what you need and what to choose. That's why before you buy a car, you should run the purchase by your insurance agent so you know exactly how much car insurance is going to cost for that vehicle.

You might well find that what you set aside in your budget for a car is not enough once you include car insurance and tag. The best way to avoid such a nasty surprise is to choose the insurance company first. As you look at your options, review the financial health of the insurance company and reviews about its customer service.

One of the worst mistakes you can make is selecting an insurance company that sounded good on TV but can't pay a claim if you have a problem—be wary of insurance companies hawking low premium prices that seem too good to be true. They probably are.

That's why the service record of an insurance company also matters. It is a relatively easy thing to learn, since most companies provide such information and reviews through Web analysis tools and social media. Don't forget to ask your friends about their experiences too. You don't want to purchase a policy from a company that delays payments or doesn't provide good service.

The type of car you purchase will also impact how much your insurance will cost. Typically, the newer and sportier the vehicle, the more it costs to insure. However, it is a myth that red cars are more expensive to insure. Most people don't know it, but the insurance industry is color-blind.

As you look at your car purchasing budget, remember that you have to include that monthly insurance policy. The older car might not be as exciting, but its lower operating costs might be just enough to keep you on track to meet other goals, such as taking a vacation or retiring someday.

Automobile insurance has different classifications. Although state regulations differ, liability insurance is the minimum level of insurance usually required by state law.

Liability insurance covers your liability in case you cause an accident. The policy is written to cover bodily injury per person hurt, total bodily injury coverage for all people hurt, and property damage coverage. With the high cost of medical bills, it is important that your coverage levels are high enough to protect you from being sued for medical bills that your insurance doesn't cover. Of course, if you hit an expensive car, the amount of property-damage coverage also needs to be high.

Collision insurance, the second classification, covers damage caused to your vehicle by an accident that is your fault.

The third classification, commonly called *comprehensive insurance*, covers damage to your vehicle from another cause. Collision pays if your car hits a tree; comprehensive pays if a tree branch falls on your car.

Other features of an automobile policy might or might not make sense for you to purchase. Always look at the benefit, its cost, and whether it would be cheaper to retain the risk. A rental-car provision might be nice, but if it is an expensive feature in your policy, it might be worth finding your own replacement vehicle in the case of an accident. The same can be said for roadside assistance. And remember: You must have the financial means to replace or repair your car if you carry only liability coverage—or you could find yourself walking to work or taking the bus.

Periodically, review the coverage of your policy. Although some people drop everything except liability when a car is old and is owned free and clear, be sure you could afford to purchase a car without any insurance benefit before you drop the other coverage.

If you have any life changes (say a move to a new state), be sure to notify your insurance agent. You might also want to review the policy if you or a family member cross an age milestone, or if you've gone a while without a ticket. You might find a discount that you would otherwise have over-looked without the review.

The price of the car in question will have an impact on your rate, but your driving record is more important. If you have too many violations or accidents, you might end up in a state pool, paying an exorbitant rate just to maintain man-datory basic coverage (this is something to start stressing to your children before they are old enough to drive). And as we mentioned earlier, your credit score may impact your ability to get insurance as well as its cost.

No matter what kind of car insurance you purchase, you will likely want to consider adding uninsured motorist cov-erage. This provides you coverage in the case that you're hit by an uninsured, negligent driver.

And remember: Don't be so desperate to save a little in premiums that you cause yourself a financial crisis should something happen to your car.

· · · · ·

Ashley: I love my car, but I wish it didn't cost so much to insure. Maybe next time, I'll choose an economy car or a more basic sedan—I had no idea that could make a difference.

Michael: Finally, I'm out of the high-risk group, and my premiums have gone down. I don't know how my folks ever afforded it when I was a teen.

Lisa: Recently, I looked at my policy and realized I needed to increase coverage in case I should ever cause an accident and someone else was hurt.

 James: We have comprehensive insurance on our good car, but I just carry liability on my old truck. It isn't worth insuring for more than that.

· · · · ·

WEEK 16 ACTIVITY

This week, I want you to find your auto policy and read it. Look at the details, highlight any terms or parts you don't understand, and then make a call to your insurance agent and go over them with him or her one by one. That's an agent's job, and it's included in the price of your insurance.

While you're at it, make sure all the levels of coverage you're carrying on your vehicles are high enough. You don't want to be financially destroyed should you cause an accident that results in other people being injured.

If you have a car loan, your lender probably also has insurance requirements.

If your car or truck is paid for, you need to carry enough insurance to allow you to replace that car or truck. If you have the financial means to buy a replacement vehicle, you might need only liability and uninsured motorist coverage.

· · · · ·

Ask Peggy

Question: Peggy, what is the single most important takeaway from this chapter?

Peggy: Be sure to carefully review your auto policy to ensure the coverage levels are adequate, especially to cover medical bills that might result from an accident.

. . . . .

Notes

Use the lines below to jot down any notes about what
you did this week.

_____

_____

_____

_____

_____

_____

_____

_____

_____

_____

_____

_____

Chapter 17

Insurance: Protecting the Home Front

The Woman Who Owned a Beach House

Owning a beach house is a popular dream, and one lucky woman had made that dream come true. She was careful to immediately insure her property against floods, windstorms, and the typical home issues of fire and theft. In fact, she had three insurance policies on her new beach house. Back inland at her old home, it was a different story. One day it began to rain there, and it just kept raining. Her home had floor vents for the heating and air-conditioning. After a couple more days of rain, she noticed that the living-room carpet was wet. Much to her horror, water was bubbling up through the ductwork.

Because flood insurance was not required where she lived, she did not have coverage. As she began to move furniture and pull back carpet, she realized her policy wouldn't cover the damage. Flood insurance isn't part of standard homeowner's insurance.

Owning your home is the American dream, and home ownership provides you with a little piece of this planet that is all yours. However, home ownership is not for the faint of heart. As you are looking to purchase your home, remember that you will need to care for it, maintain it, and insure it, especially if it has a mortgage. Yet even if you decide to rent, you will need insurance to cover your possessions.

Here are some tips to help you select an appropriate home or rental policy: First, choose a reputable carrier. Insurance does you no good if you can't make a claim or if a claim won't be honored. Review the customer service of the company and choose a firm that is easy for you to reach and known to be responsive to clients in their time of need. Many consumer-driven publications and websites offer reviews and ratings, and you can also use social media or conversations with friends and family to help you make a decision.

Always be careful to purchase the correct type of policy. Usually beginning with the letters "HO," a homeowner's policy covers different types of property associated with having a home. Typically, policies cover your dwelling, other structures on the lot, personal property, liability claims, medical claims for injuries on the property, and loss of use but always verify this.

Other types of insurance policies include rental policies that cover contents or policies that cover only older homes. Review your property and any unique things about it that need to be insured, and study your options to decide what is best for you.

Make sure you understand how your insurance company decides the amount of benefit it will pay, as set out in your policy. Although opting to insure the current value of your contents might make the policy less expensive, you might not be able to afford to replace your belongings if something happens. Your home appreciates in value, but most of the contents usually do not. To be able to afford replacing all the possessions you lose, you need to have paid the extra sum for a "replacement" policy.

Ask your agent about the percentage of coverage you choose. Although the law might not require that you carry 100 percent coverage, if you choose less than that, it can drastically impact your benefits. Because laws vary from state to state, you need to examine them before you decide to skimp on coverage.

Know the details of your policy—and, more important, understand them. It's critical that you know what your policy does and does not cover. Different states provide different kinds of home coverage, but there are two things that a traditional homeowner's policy does not cover.

For one, your traditional home policy will not cover flood damage. Flood damage is caused from external water, not a broken pipe in your home—a good homeowner's policy won't cover the broken pipe, but it very likely will cover any water damage it caused. If you live in a flood zone, you're usually required to carry FEMA flood insurance. Look at the zoning of any property before you purchase it as well as any potential nearby water sources such as creeks or ponds. Storms are becoming more extreme and frequent as a result of climate change, and so what was a fifty- or hundred-year storm might now happen every few years.

Your traditional home policy will also not cover earth movement. Earth movement is usually defined as landslides and earthquakes. Although you might be able to purchase a rider to cover such events, they will not be part of your traditional coverage. Again, read your policy carefully and know what is and is not included.

Look at coverage limits in the policy as well. If you have expensive art, jewelry, antiques, or other luxury items, you might need to purchase a rider to cover them. And one friendly tip: If you stash cash under the mattress or gold in the walls, know that most policies will only cover a small amount of the loss. You could be out a lot of money if you are ever robbed.

Higher deductibles typically result in policies that cost less. Look at the amount of your current deductible and ask what a higher deductible would cost. Then, decide if you could afford to absorb the deductible in the case of a claim.

Be careful before you make a claim too. One component of whether a company will carry your policy and how much premium you'll pay can be the number of claims you have made in the past. If you make a claim for a small dollar amount higher than your deductible, you might lose more money than that in increased premiums or, worse, have your coverage canceled.

If you need to make a claim because of damage, be sure you have secured the damaged area as well as you can. If you have a broken window and you don't fix it, additional damage resulting from rain might not be covered. This sometimes causes difficulties for people during natural disasters. When multiple insurance companies are providing benefits, finger-pointing can make it difficult for a policyholder to collect the full insurance value on their losses.

If you run a business from home, be sure that your homeowner's policy covers business losses, because many times, such policies don't. You might need an additional policy or a rider to cover anything related to your business.

Finally, it is also prudent to review your policy from time to time to make sure everything is up to date. If you have made any major improvements to your home, you want to be sure that they are insured. You also will want to review the value the policy puts on your home to make sure it is appropriate, especially if you live in an area where property values are rising or in an old neighborhood that is becoming gentrified. Don't let your American dream turn into a nightmare. My grandmother used to say, "If you can't afford to insure it, you can't afford to have it."

Store your policy and contact information for the carrier in a fire-proof box of important documents. Keep it where you could find it in an emergency. If you need to make a claim, you want it to be as easy to find as possible.

. . . . .

 Ashley: I think I need to get a renter's policy—and the sooner, the better!

 Michael: I have good coverage, but I haven't read my policy in a while. I've never read any of my insurance policies much less reviewed them on a regular basis. But that's changing. I'm going to do that this week. It is one way to protect my family.

Lisa: I never knew I might need more than one policy to cover a piece of property—learn something new every day!

James: I'm always careful to keep up with the value of the property on my policy. I wouldn't want to own a home or personal belongings worth more than the policy covered.

. . . . .

WEEK 17 ACTIVITY

This week, I want you to find your homeowner's policy and read it. Now, I'm not suggesting you never read it before, but this time, slow down and study the details.

1. Does the policy cover your possessions?

2. Do you have flood coverage?

3. Do you have earth-movement coverage?

4. Do you need any extra riders for valuable collectibles?

5. Do you know if you are keeping more cash at home than your home policy covers?

. . . . .

Ask Peggy

Question: Peggy, what is the single most important takeaway from this chapter?

Peggy: Common homeowner's policies do not cover weather-related flooding or earth movement.

. . . . .

Notes

Use the following lines to jot down some notes about what you did this week. When you look at the book later, it will remind you of your progress.

_____

_____

_____

_____

_____

_____

_____

_____

_____

_____

· · · · ·

Ask Peggy!

 Ashley: Peggy, I don't need much insurance right now. I'm thinking about waiting until after we're married to figure out our insurance needs. Would that be okay?

Peggy: Ashley, the point of life insurance is creating the funds to cover the financial risks associated with your death. You can wait until you are married to figure this out, or you can try to decide now what your expenses will be. This would be more important if you and your fiancé purchase a home together now or created another major expense either before you were married or immediately afterward. As soon as you have major shared expenses where you are helping to pay the bills, you will want to decide how much insurance to purchase.

 Michael: Peggy, remind me again. If I pay the premiums on my disability policy, the benefits are income tax free, right?

Peggy: That's right Michael. If you pay the premiums, you don't pay taxes on the disability benefits if you ever needed them. If your employer pays the premiums, then the benefits are taxable. Remember that your benefit is likely only 60 percent of your salary anyway, so that tax savings can be extremely important.

 Lisa: Peggy, I'm worried about how I will pay for my end-of-life care. So many of my friends say that long-term care insurance is a waste of money, but I want to know, will I be okay without it?

Peggy: Lisa, I know that long-term care insurance is expensive, but that is because the claim rates are so high. Many carriers are no longer even offering policies. What I know for sure, though, is that conservatively, you could pay a quarter of a million dollars for three years of care. When monthly bills for nursing homes or memory care centers are at least $6,000, and home care can go even higher if you use an agency, you need a plan to pay for it. If you have enough personal resources, you can opt to pay these bills yourself. Most people, though, can't do it. Insurance is sometimes the best option, especially since Medicaid can be problematic for some people for a number of reasons.

 James: Peggy, you mentioned that standard homeowner's policies have limits on coverage for items such as jewelry. Does that mean our policy might not cover a theft?

Peggy: James, you should check your coverage levels. Call your agent and review your policy; you may need to supplement it. Remember that you will need receipts or appraisals to support the value you place on items.

Investments

Chapter 18

Investments: Stocks, Bonds, and IRAs, Oh My!

The Investor Who Didn't Know her Portfolio

A woman was in her first meeting with her new financial planner. When asked if she had any investments, she told the planner that yes, she had an individual retirement account. The planner said an IRA was great, and then asked how it was invested.

The woman looked at him blankly and said, "What do you mean? I just told you it's invested in an IRA."

Many people do not understand what constitutes an investment account, much less what constitutes the investments themselves. Raise the topic, and their eyes glaze over, and they tune out. Most are convinced they could never get familiar with such money matters, so why even try? But if kindergartners can master the names of all the kinds of dinosaurs that once roamed this planet—from Brontosaurus to Tyrannosaurus rex—you can do this!

Investment accounts are comprised of two parts:
1. the type of the account and
2. the investments within that account.

Basicallly, the types of accounts can run the gamut, from

company retirement pensions, IRAs, education funds, and annuities to plain old taxable accounts (the latter being the one type you are least likely to have). Inside, say, your retirement account, you choose the types of investments you want. Even then, there are two layers. You can invest directly in securities (stocks, for example), or you can purchase a fund for which someone else invests the securities for you.

Funds are so popular that they have their own chapter in this book. However, to understand them, you need first to understand the investments inside them. Once you understand the underlying investments, you can choose the funds that will help you meet your investment goals.

When people think about investing, they usually think about the stock market. They believe investing means buying and selling stocks. They're also usually thinking of the American stock market as measured by the Dow Jones Industrial Average, the NASDAQ, or Standard & Poor's 500 indices, although many other exchanges exist.

So, let's dig into the big three index funds. Each one is comprised of companies—the Dow has thirty companies, and the S&P 500 has five hundred companies. Each company issues its own stock and sells small pieces of ownership through the sale of a share of stock. Your purchase of a share or more of stock provides capital for the company to use when conducting business. Basically, if you own stock you own a small piece of the company!

The price of the stock is determined on the stock exchange, and it is always a function of a balance between the buyer and the seller.

The better the company is doing, the more money the seller requires for selling the share to the buyer. As a result, the price of the stock goes up, and the buyer pays more money. Conversely, if the company is not doing as well, the buyer isn't willing to pay as much for it, and the seller has to accept a lower price to get rid of the stock.

A second way a buyer of a stock can make money is through the issuing of a dividend by the company. In its simplest form, a dividend is growth or profit that the company decides not to put back into the company. You can think of it as "excess growth," and this growth is given back to the company's investors as a cash dividend, usually issued quarterly.

Some companies focus more on growth and others on dividends. When you purchase a stock, you purchase a slice of the company, and you usually make money when the company performs at least as well as people expect.

Another type of investment is the bond market. It is much less understood, and investors and advisers tend to pay less attention to it. Bonds are often those holdings in your portfolio that aren't stocks, and they are supposed to help keep you safer should the stock market fall.

Basically, a bond is a loan, or an IOU—and you're the bank. You loan money to a company, city, or the government, and it promises to pay you back in full, with regular interest payments. When you purchase a U.S. government bond, you have loaned money to the U.S. government so it can pay its bills—just like the bank loans money to you to purchase a house or car. The interest the bank charges you for that loan is how it makes its money.

The bond works like every other loan. It is made for a period of time, and it earns a specific rate of interest. When you own a bond, you have made a loan. But what makes a bond slightly different than a traditional loan is that it is also traded during its life. This means a bond might be issued for ten years and pay 3 percent annual interest. However, four years into the bond, the person who owns it might want to sell it.

Nearly every new bond sells for $1,000 a bond (called "par"). If, on the day of the sale, interest rates have risen to 4 percent, the owner of the 3 percent bond won't be able to sell it for $1,000. He or she will need to sell it for less. On the other hand, if the current rate is 2 percent, the owner can sell it for more than $1,000.

Many things impact how sensitive the bond is to changes in interest rates. The most common impacts are the length of the bond term and the coupon (interest) it pays. Typically, longer-term bonds that pay less interest are more susceptible to changes in price than shorter-term bonds that pay more.

That is why I usually advise clients to buy the bond, receive the rate of return, and hold it until it matures. Once it matures, you can cash it in for $1,000. The change in face value exists only until it matures. However, there may be times when holding the bond until maturity might not be the best advice for you. Talk to your financial adviser about this. Bonds are often the type of investment that people want to turn to when the stock market becomes volatile; they see the bond market as a safe haven in such times. That is not always wise.

There is a wrinkle in bond funds that makes them different than the individual bonds they hold: Those individual bonds are constantly being traded. That means the value of a fund is fluid—it becomes a function of the bonds within it.

As a result, bond funds can and do lose money, especially in an environment of rising interests. Granted, bond volatility is not as great as stock volatility, but under the wrong conditions, it can still lead to significant losses. The impact of this is only made worse when people believe that bond funds are *safe*. Many clients have indicated to me that they don't think they will lose money if they hold bonds. I believe this comes from a fundamental misunderstanding of the bond market.

Bonds and bond funds offer interesting diversification options that are often overlooked, and funds that track many types of bonds are available, including U.S. Treasury, U.S. agency, high-grade corporates, high-yield corporates, inflation protection, international corporates, and international treasuries. Those are only a few of the types of bonds that you can choose from, and they each have slightly different risk and reward characteristics. Generally, the more yield a bond or bond fund pays, the riskier it is. That's because we are paid to take risk when we invest. Low-yielding funds are safer. This is why international bond funds pay more—they are considered to carry more risk than U.S. government bond funds.

You might be surprised to learn that real estate is a separate asset class. If you're a homeowner, your home is one of your assets. In fact, for most Americans, their home will be the single biggest investment of their life.

Other asset classes include commodities, such as gold or oil or ethanol or ostriches. Other less common investments are also available, but I don't want to spend a lot of time discussing them. What I do want to do is offer a word of caution: Nothing is without risk, and if you don't understand how an investment works, even after asking questions, never invest in it blindly.

Your risk tolerance will determine how your portfolio should be constructed. Typically, stocks are higher-risk investments, and bonds are lower-risk investments. Real estate and commodities are often added in small percentages because they tend to rise and fall in value more independently.

However, putting together a portfolio takes a lot of thoughtful discussion. Work with a financial planner to be sure your portfolio is comprised of the right investments, within your risk tolerance, that will help you meet your goals. Remember, you're invested in more than just the IRA!

Please don't ever invest in something you don't understand. If, after you study this chapter this week, your eyes are crossing, my advice would be to sit down with a financial planner and review it all again in person until you do get it. It is important that you understand every investment in your portfolio—why you have chosen it, what it costs, and any restrictions it might come with.

Taking the time to talk with your financial professional is the sign of someone who takes their finances seriously. One caveat: Don't agree to an investment purchase—be it stocks, a beach property, or a high-tech start-up—until it makes sense to you.

· · · · ·

 Ashley: I think I'm just taking a broad bite of the market with my one mutual fund.

 Michael: I'd like to invest in some sectors within the stock market, but most of my funds are basic, core holdings.

 Lisa: I remember how badly people got hurt from focusing on one or two sectors during the last market crash—and all those people who lost their big houses worth hundreds of thousands of dollars!

 James: I prefer buying bonds to bond funds, but it can be expensive. It's hard to get good diversification when each bond costs $1,000.

· · · · ·

WEEK 18 ACTIVITY

This week, I want you to take the time to review your portfolio—from any stocks you might have inherited to your retirement fund. Now that you know the difference between stocks and bonds, look at your investment holdings. If you own funds, you will have to do some research about them.

You can find a bundle of information about them at www.MorningStar.com. A financial planner should also be able to help with the research. Before you can understand investing, you need to begin by simply knowing what you already own.

. . . . .

Ask Peggy

Question: Peggy, what is the single most important takeaway from this chapter?

Peggy: When you buy a stock, you are buying a small piece of ownership in the company, and when you buy a bond, you are loaning an entity money.

. . . . .

Notes

Use the following lines to jot down some notes about what you did this week. When you look back on it later, it will remind you of your progress.

_____

_____

_____

_____

_____

_____

Chapter 19

Investments: The Menu of Funds

The Doctor Who Thought He Understood his Portfolio

A doctor retired from private practice and moved to Florida. He began to interview new financial professionals to help him with his investments. One of the planners asked him to bring a copy of his current investment portfolio, and he proudly showed it to her. He was pleased to point out to her that he had a dozen mutual funds, and he even made a comment about being glad he was so diversified.

The planner looked at the portfolio and realized the diversification was mostly an illusion. In fact, most of the doctor's mutual funds tracked the same group of stocks—large American companies. Only two or three of the dozen offered any real diversification. As she explained this to the doctor, he couldn't hide his surprise. He had thought he understood what he owned.

Funds—whether full of stocks or bonds or real estate—are popular investment tools for many people. However, when pressed, most individuals do not understand what they are purchasing when they buy a fund. They might grasp that it is a collection of investment instruments, such as stocks, so it is less risky than putting all their money into just one stock. They also might think they have heard that they should purchase funds, so they believe they are making a good investment. But if you were to ask them to explain what a fund is or why they picked it, most couldn't tell you.

Fortunately, those common beliefs about funds are usually true, and funds can be a prudent investment option. However, before you decide what is best for you, be sure you understand what funds are, what they do, and what their advantages and disadvantages are.

What do I mean by that? It's not that understanding what is in, say, a stock mutual fund is so difficult. It's actually quite simple: Such a fund holds a collection of stocks.

What many people don't know is what comprises the holdings in their mutual fund. That's right, most people could not name one stock in their fund. They just trust their financial adviser to get it right.

That's not okay. Being an informed investor means knowing what you own—if only so your children don't learn at your death that you were invested in a corrupt company just because you didn't care enough to learn where your money was going. Being aware of what is in the funds you own is also another way to be an active partner in the investment relationship you have with your financial adviser. It is a way to learn slowly but surely as you become a more sophisticated investor.

That said, the most common types of funds are mutual funds. They are created by mutual-fund companies, and the funds are comprised of many different individual investments that share common characteristics. A mutual fund might track the U.S. stock market or an index, such as the S&P 500, or a sector, such as precious metals or technology.

Funds can also track bonds or other fixed-income items, so selling all your mutual funds because you are afraid of the stock market might well be the wrong decision. I commonly hear people say they want to liquidate their portfolios to cash because they are afraid the market will go down.

When I ask them if they own any bond funds, too often they tell me that they have no idea, but they want to sell everything anyway.

This underscores that earlier important first lesson: You have to know what type of funds you own. You have to know the characteristics of each fund and how market and economic conditions will impact it.

Funds typically come in two broad categories—actively managed or tracked by index.

An index is a collection of investments that have shared characteristics, such as size, region, or industry. Most indices are created from a set of rules, and as a result, managers do not make arbitrary decisions on the holdings. Because of this, the price of a fund that tracks an index is usually less expensive than an actively managed fund.

An actively managed fund has a fund manager who is choosing the individual holdings of the fund and watching how each one performs.

If you are considering purchasing a fund that has a manager, be sure that you are gaining enough additional return to offset the higher expenses.

By this, I mean be sure that the return you are shown uses an appropriate benchmark for comparison. Your actively managed fund should outperform the closest available index on a risk-adjusted basis consistently, in good and bad market conditions. If the fund manager can't do this, you might be better off with an index fund.

Active management is an expertise and is very difficult even for the best managers. Selecting individual securities requires extensive training, constant tracking, and a good bit of luck. Although such fund managers do exist, they aren't common. Most actively managed funds underperform the appropriate index on a risk-adjusted basis.

Bottom line: Be sure you understand the cost of your fund. Speaking of fees, you should also understand what owning a fund costs you. Among the possible fees you might incur are a transaction cost, a load if the fund is sold in a commission model, and an annual expense ratio. Sometimes it is difficult to figure out the costs associated with a fund, but don't be afraid to ask your financial professional to explain the fees to you. That's the professional's job.

Funds are products, and products are never free. You need to be sure you understand exactly what it costs you to own one. Be sure you have the fund ticker symbol so you can do your own research—usually the fund symbol is five letters ending in X, like ABCDX. It is the symbol that will help you find the expenses associated with your investment.

Mutual funds typically have several share classes for each fund. Some classes have loads, meaning they come with a sales charge or commission; some don't. Some have higher annual expenses; some do not. Some have trading expenses, such as a transaction charge; some do not. Put simply, the fund name will not give you enough information. You need to know the ticker symbol. Fund information is found in many places, but the binding document is the fund prospectus.

A fund prospectus is a long, extensive document with tiny type. If you look at one online, it will typically be a .pdf document that you can download—so you can either read it online or print it out. You can also then search for terms you are trying to research. Once again, be sure you understand the fine print before you make the purchase.

Even purchasing an index fund, which by design is created to match or track an index such as the S&P 500, requires some research. As investors have begun to request index funds, fund creators have begun to create more indices. Some of them are interesting, but most center around the latest investment craze, gimmick, or sympathetic cause.

Purchasing a fund that tracks an index of breast-cancer drugs might make you feel better if you or a loved one has had breast cancer; however, that index is likely comprised of a very small number of companies focused on a very specific area. Indices usually fare better when they provide a good level of diversification. You would be better served to send donate to your loved one's cause and then purchase a broader index that has a better opportunity to provide you with an investment return.

Your investments are not designed to promote all of your causes (although you certainly can set restrictions on what you do or don't want to own), and investing should avoid becoming highly emotional. We need to remind ourselves that we are investing to earn a rate of return on our money that enables us to meet our goals in life. We do that by managing the investment risk through diversification, time, and other risk-management techniques. Before you select an index fund, be sure you understand the index it tracks.

The age of the fund can also help you track management performance or index appropriateness. In general, try to avoid new funds that have an unproved track record unless you have a very compelling reason to want to invest in them. Generally, funds with a longer track record will be easier to evaluate.

Mutual funds are not the only kind of fund you can choose for investing. Exchange-traded funds (ETFs) are popular investment tools because of their low expense ratios and index orientation. However, you still need to be certain that the index the ETF is tracking is an appropriate investment. Many ETFs have transaction fees because they trade like stocks.

Even if you like ETFs, you will want to be careful that you do not create a situation in which you never make a profit. Recently, actively managed ETFs have become more popular; they have the same risks and potential benefits of actively managed mutual funds. Properly used, funds provide you with a way to gain exposure to more stocks than you could afford to buy individually. You are also less likely to have a company-related investment crisis that results in great loss.

However, popularity can breed unscrupulous behavior on the part of some people and sometimes lazy behavior from others. Do your research to be certain the funds you have selected will help you prosper. If funds will comprise the largest type of the investment you own, take the time to understand them.

· · · · ·

Ashley: My fund is a blend of stocks with a few bonds. Right now, it's easier for me to invest in just one fund. Every month on the first, I invest $100. I don't even look at the market before I do it.

Michael: The government started to require a quarterly 401(k) plan report that shows the rate of return on my investments and the related fees and expenses in 2012—it has been such a help!

Lisa: I hate funds that have names I don't understand. What's a "New Horizon Voyager Frontier" fund anyway? I realize now I should never invest in a fund for its name until I know what is in that fund.

James: I like having a portfolio with funds that serve specific purposes. I have different asset classes and different fixed-income items, all in separate funds. It makes changes easier. I don't think people should need a secret decoder ring to understand their investments.

· · · · ·

WEEK 19 ACTIVITY

First, find your most recent investment statement.

That statement should show your holdings, and it should provide you with a ticker symbol associated with each holding. For example, Apple stock has the ticker symbol AAPL. If you can't find the symbols, call your financial planner, online brokerage firm, 401(k) adviser, or whoever else helped you set up the account. They can surely provide the symbols for you.

Once you have the symbols, go to Morningstar's free website, www.MorningStar.com. I like Morningstar because the site provides unbiased information about nearly any fund. You can look up the symbols at the search box on the top of the page. You will bring up an overview of each fund that will help you to understand how much the fund costs (called the expense ratio), how much dividend it pays, and how it is invested. The page will give you additional information as well.

I realize it may look overwhelming at first, and you might or might not find the other data interesting, but believe me, the more you become familiar with the terms and concepts the better off you'll be. Of course, if this is more than you want to deal with, you can hire a reputable financial planner to help you sort through the details. However, having a way to check out a fund yourself can be a useful exercise.

· · · · ·

Ask Peggy

Question: Peggy, what is the single most important takeaway from this chapter?

Peggy: Mutual funds are often comprised of stocks, bonds, or a blend of both, so always look at the asset allocation of a fund to see if it is appropriate.

Notes

Use the lines below to jot down notes or questions about what you did this week. When you look back at them later, it will remind you of the progress you are making.

_____

_____

_____

_____

_____

_____

_____

_____

_____

_____

_____

_____

_____

Chapter 20

Investments: Annuities

The Teacher Who Didn't Read the Fine Print

A teacher retired from her job. She planned to structure part of her retirement as a series of annuity payments from her 403(b) plan. She liked the idea of a steady stream of income.

Before she completed the paperwork, however, she received a call from a local financial adviser offering her a different annuity package that included guarantees that the annuity from her retirement plan did not have. She signed the new papers without studying the fees and the terms.

Later, when talking about the plan with a friend who had retired with her, she was upset to learn that her fees were nearly twice the fees of the annuity offered by her original 403(b) plan.

Annuities are popular investment vehicles that are also sometimes controversial. They are designed to create an income stream so the owner does not outlive the investment. Creating this stream of income is called "annuitizing," and once it is set up, changes can be expensive or even forbidden by the policy. Therefore, it's important that you understand the basic rules of annuities before you decide whether one is appropriate for you.

Annuities can have a fixed rate of return or can be tied to market returns. Fixed annuities have a guaranteed annual rate of return, but because it is a guarantee and it is not invested in the stock market, the rate is low. However, for someone who does not have a pension plan, a fixed annuity can provide a return that doesn't involve worrying about the stock market.

One concern with fixed annuities is the expenses they come with. Although fixed annuities typically are much less expensive than variable annuities, it's important to compare all the costs as a percentage of return because the rate of return is low. If the net return is too low, more flexible investments might be a better choice.

The other risk to a fixed annuity involves the rate of return—the question of whether the annuity can keep up with inflation. With historic inflation rates averaging 3 percent, it's important to make sure the annuity earns a real, inflation-adjusted return. This becomes more important than a bank account's interest rate because the fixed annuity typically commits the money to the investment for a longer period of time.

Variable annuities are invested in subaccounts that track the stock and/or bond market in ways that resemble other funds. Variable annuities have the potential for rates of return similar to the market but also carry the same risk. Be sure you understand the investment strategy and the fees.

A new feature for annuities is market-based annuities with guarantees of no loss and positive returns typically capped at a percentage of the stock market's performance. These annuities can be amazingly appealing at first glance, but they bear a closer look. First, all annuities have costs associated with them. Variable annuities tend to be more expensive than fixed annuities, and variable annuities with guaranteed-return components are more expensive than just traditional variable annuities.

Once you enter the annuity structure, if you need to withdraw the money as a lump sum for an unexpected emergency, you might find that the fees have eaten into your account more than you expected. The guarantee assumes you are keeping the annuity in place and taking periodic distributions. If you need the money at a faster rate, the terms might change. Still, the guarantee can be a positive feature when very few of us have actual pension plans.

Annuities are funded in two ways—immediate annuities and deferred annuities. Immediate annuities are funded with a lump sum, and the owner begins to take distributions from them immediately. Deferred annuities are funded over time and are often used as retirement vehicles.

Even an immediately funded annuity can be used for future benefits, however. Sometimes these annuities are used to shelter money from lawsuits, making them more popular with those in professions that bring fears of litigation. In this strategy, the professional might fund an annuity with a lump sum with the intention of taking distributions years later. The money inside the annuity is more difficult to access as part of a lawsuit.

Annuities typically have a life insurance component to them, often providing a death benefit to a beneficiary. However, distributions from the annuity might lower the death benefit. Other annuities maintain the death benefit, but only if the account keeps a minimum balance.

Be sure you understand any life insurance benefits that are part of the annuity. Realize that typically, annuities are seen as investments that happen to provide life insurance as an additional benefit. Most of the time, with the declining value of the insurance, an annuity is not purchased primarily as an insurance policy. From a tax perspective, annuities do not result in capital gains when subaccounts are bought and sold. However, annuity distributions are taxed as income (if it was funded in pretax dollars through a retirement account) or the basis is returned tax free (if it was funded in after-tax dollars).

Basis is defined as the cost of an investment when you purchased it.

Remember that basis is most important in investments subject to capital gains. Although you should track basis in retirement accounts, the basis has no tax impact on them because every dollar is taxed on distribution. The growth of the annuity is taxed as ordinary income on distribution. Annuities can result in early-distribution penalties if distributed before age fifty-nine-and-a-half, and they can have required minimum distributions at seventy-and-a-half years.

Typically, transferring between annuities does not result in a taxable distribution, but other fees and restrictions of the new annuity might make the transfer less beneficial. Because many retirement plans—especially 403(b) plans—can offer the same benefits, be cautious about transferring the annuity offered through your plan to a product sold by a private adviser. Although either product might be good or bad, some annuities sold by private advisers can be more expensive.

This brings us to the biggest drawbacks of annuities—fees, surrender periods, penalties, and complexity. The concept of the annuity is appealing, and some annuities are fine products; however, annuities can also be expensive. The subaccounts have fees, the annuity itself has fees, and any special features might bring additional fees. Finding the fees, even in the prospectus, can be difficult, but insist on knowing them before you buy.

As you decide whether or not to purchase an annuity, remember to work with an adviser who will put your needs first rather than being more concerned with the commission earned if you purchase the product.

Most annuities pay a commission to the sales person who sells them. This can be somewhat tricky because technically, the commission is paid by the annuity company.

The annuity company protects its interest by charging the purchaser a surrender fee that is levied over a period of years. The compensation for the selling of annuities can be substantial and has caused annuities to come under scrutiny by consumer protection groups. The fear is that the complex nature of annuities causes many purchasers to not understand what they are buying.

If you're considering an annuity, the best advice is to work with someone you truly trust and then be sure you understand the structure. Find out the length of the surrender period, any other restrictions on how much money you can withdraw per year, any fees associated with the annuity, and the portfolio makeup of each of the subaccounts. The portfolio allocation and risk tolerance of the annuity should match the goal for which it was purchased, and it should help you prosper.

· · · · ·

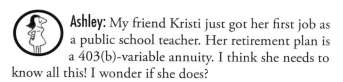

Ashley: My friend Kristi just got her first job as a public school teacher. Her retirement plan is a 403(b)-variable annuity. I think she needs to know all this! I wonder if she does?

Michael: I have a good friend who works in a high-risk industry. He told me he purchased an annuity because his assets would be more sheltered from lawsuits.

Lisa: I want to wait as long as possible before I actually annuitize my account so I have more flexibility in distributions.

James: I'm no fan of annuities, but the guaranteed rate of return helps me sleep at night. It's hard to find one that makes money after the fees.

· · · · ·

WEEK 20 ACTIVITY

If you're thinking about purchasing an annuity, take your time before you sign on the dotted line. Be sure you understand the terms and conditions of the annuity. What is your maximum annual withdrawal rate? How is the product annuitized? If the annuity has a guaranteed return, does that include the time it is annuitized? Be sure you know the length of the surrender period and your total annual fees. Armed with this information, you can begin to decide whether the investment is appropriate for you.

· · · · ·

Ask Peggy

Question: Peggy, what is the single most important takeaway from this chapter?

Peggy: An annuity is, simply, an income stream created from a lump sum of money, but too often firms complicate them in ways both expensive and difficult to understand.

· · · · ·

Notes

_____

_____

_____

Chapter 21

Investments: It's All About the Risk

*The Fiscally Conservative Military Officer
Who Earned Less Than He Expected*

A military officer was quite fiscally conservative, mainly because he never wanted to experience a major decline in his portfolio. He had explained his concerns to his financial planner. The planner understood and created a conservative asset allocation just for him.

Shortly afterward, good economic data caused the stock market to go on an extended climb. When the officer eagerly opened his statement the next month expecting great news, he was unhappy to see that the market had increased much more in value than had his portfolio. Upset with the performance, he called his adviser. The adviser reminded him that they had talked about this very thing in their earlier meeting when they discussed his risk tolerance.

An investment portfolio's returns will typically be a reflection of the amount of risk taken. If an investor takes less risk than the norm, that usually results in lower returns.

Knowing this, before you can decide how to invest a portfolio, whether it is a taxable account or a tax-deferred retirement account, you need to complete a risk-tolerance analysis. These assessments may vary in length and differ in quality, but they are designed to help you ascertain how you truly feel about risk.

Do not make an investment decision or agree to an adviser's suggestions before you have completed a risk-tolerance document that you understand and that feels right.

Personally, I believe determining your risk tolerance is much more complex and personal than many people realize, so let's review some issues you might face:

Risk tolerance is usually specific to an investment goal, so if you have multiple goals, your risk tolerance could be conservative and aggressive at the same time. How is that possible? Say you have a child going to college in the fall and you are retiring in twenty-five years, you will likely be more conservative with the college portfolio and more aggressive with the retirement allocation. This happens because you have more time before your second goal than the first.

One of the most powerful drivers of your risk tolerance should be the length of time before you need to take the money out of the market. The longer the money can be invested, the more risk you might be able to take in your portfolio—so long as a rising and falling stock won't send you into a tizzy.

It's worth noting that many of us will be spending thirty years or longer in retirement. Thirty years is a long time by any standard. As a result, if you choose a very conservative allocation and very little risk shortly after you retire, you could lower the likelihood that you will have enough money in your retirement account to last the rest of your life.

Few people seem to understand the relationship between risk and return in their portfolio. Remember that when the market is working as it should, you receive a return in keeping with the risk you are taking. When you take less risk, your return should by definition be lower. This can cut two ways. First, if you choose a very low-risk portfolio, you have to expect a lower rate of return. Second, if something is paying a high rate of return through growth, dividend, or yield, there might be more risk in the investment than you thought there was.

Although both of these observations seem easy to understand as you read them, it's important to remember them as you review your portfolio. Regularly, I have clients tell me that they want a good rate of return without taking risk. Or they insist that something is offering a high rate of interest because it is such a great investment, not because it is risky.

It falls to me to explain to them that both assumptions are basically incorrect. Risk and return are highly correlated. When you see an annuity with a guaranteed rate of return, the structure is complex and the returns are typically much lower than a long-term expected stock performance. That is because one principle of investing is the need to take risk to earn return. There are always costs associated with these guarantees. Some of the products are fine, but it's critical that you understand them well before you invest in them.

Of course, the return you need to make from your portfolio to achieve your goals can also impact how much risk you need or are willing to take. Again, you cannot expect to make a return unless you are willing to take risk.

When you calculate how you will achieve your retirement needs, you have to assume a portfolio rate of return. This portfolio rate needs to be consistent with your risk tolerance for the retirement projection to be as accurate as possible, given that it is making assumptions about future market conditions.

If the rate of return you need to earn to achieve your retirement goals is higher than your risk tolerance suggests, you need to make some adjustments. However, if the rate of return suggested by your risk tolerance is higher than the return you need to meet your goals, that's a great problem to have. That means you are more likely to achieve investing success—and to have the money you need throughout your retirement days. In such a case, you might actually choose to take less risk.

If the rate of return suggested by your risk tolerance is too low to fund your life in retirement, you have some choices to make—you need to save more, delay retirement, lower retirement expectations, or increase your portfolio assumed rate of return. The last choice will cause you to take more risk than you might originally have wanted to, so you need to think about it long and hard before proceeding.

There are many ways to create a successful financial plan, but you have to put together a scenario that allows you to be successful but also allows you to be you.

In the end, raising your level of risk to raise your return might be the wrong decision for you. Your personality and anxiety level is a factor in this equation. If you are highly anxious about your portfolio allocation or your investment strategy feels too aggressive to you, then choose one of the other strategies for achieving your goals. Working five more years is certainly preferable to creating a scenario that is so stressful that it leaves you in poor health or worse. What good is retirement if you hated every day getting there? Prospering involves creating a life of joy that is financially stable.

That said, sometimes stress comes because we just don't understand a situation. Your financial professional should describe the investment process and your investing strategy in a way that you understand. If you are confused, don't be embarrassed; ask your adviser to explain it again. There is no such thing as a "dumb" question. If your professional makes you feel like there is, you have the wrong financial adviser.

I find many of my clients to be uneasy with the stock market. Taking the time to study and understand the stock market, along with working with a financial planner, can be a good way to control your anxiety and increase your confidence in what you're doing.

By the end of the risk-assessment process, you should have a good idea of what your portfolio needs to return to allow you to meet your goal. Then you are ready to look at the actual portfolio construction.

. . . . .

Ashley: I know I'm supposed to be high-risk tolerant because I'm young, but I've been so confused by everything when it comes to investments, I haven't wanted to invest at all. I'm glad to get some explanations that make sense.

Michael: I never thought about having multiple goals with different risk tolerances. It makes sense, but I need to think about the different time horizons between my children's college funds and my retirement.

Lisa: I've never looked at my investment portfolio as a direct outcome of my cash flow needs. I should go back and make sure all my assumptions are working. When they talked to me about my 401(k) at work, they didn't make the relationship clear.

James: I know people my age who think they're conservative, assuming they'll live twenty years after sixty-five. My parents lived into their nineties. I could easily live for another thirty years or more.

. . . . .

WEEK 21 ACTIVITY

It's time to find out your penchant for financial risk. There are online tools that can help with this, and your financial planner should also have a risk calculator. The questions asked should be detailed enough that you have to think about your answers.

Remember your portfolio construction will also be limited by the growth rates required to meet your financial goals. Does your risk tolerance match your portfolio required return? If it doesn't, take time now to solve this problem. Risk tolerance can change over time but an early start helps!

You should complete a new risk-tolerance assessment every few years or after any major life changes (give yourself a chance to get back on your feet first). Your risk tolerance is a living, breathing document. Treat it as one.

· · · · ·

Ask Peggy

Question: Peggy, what is the single most important takeaway from this chapter?

Peggy: You earn an investment return because you take risk; it is virtually impossible to take little risk and earn a high rate of return.

· · · · ·

Notes

_____

_____

_____

_____

_____

Chapter 22

Investments: The Portfolio

The Executive Who Didn't Know What To Do Next

It went down just like last year. An executive dutifully attended the 401(k) annual presentation provided by her plan's adviser. Like last year, the adviser arrived with sandwiches from the local deli and a PowerPoint presentation with too many slides. He might not have intended to, but as the adviser explained the components of the retirement plan, he talked too quickly, even mumbling at times. By the time the adviser tried to explain how plan participants could calculate their risk tolerance, their eyes had glazed over.

Our executive had heard her share of presentations and believed she had accurately calculated her risk tolerance as "moderately aggressive." It was the next step that always baffled her: How did she translate that risk-tolerance level into how to invest her 401(k)?

In earlier chapters, we talked about types of investing tools available to you, and we also talked about risk tolerance. However, I often find that even with information about both topics, clients remain unsure how to proceed in creating their own appropriate investment portfolio.

Our goal this week is for you to start to put together your investments in a way that allows you to sleep at night while still meeting your goals. Let's review a few things that will form the basis of your decisions.

First, investing is never free.

That's right. Often you may have trading costs associated with your purchases. Because of this, you will want to be careful in the kinds of investment tools you choose. If you have a small amount of money or are investing a few hundred dollars each month into your portfolio, you might want to consider a blended fund of stocks and bonds. Target date funds are funds that become more conservative as you approach the date of the fund—so in 2015, a 2020 fund would be operated more conservatively than a 2055 fund.

The risk with target date funds is that the asset allocation might be different between funds assigned to the same year but created by different mutual fund companies. As a result, you should always check the asset allocation before you just choose the fund associated with your retirement date.

Blended funds are sometimes named based on their riskiness, with names such as "balanced," "moderate," "aggressive," or "conservative." Although you lose some investing flexibility when the same mutual fund holds both your stocks and bonds, from the perspective of expense and ease of implementation, it's a reasonable, although not perfect, way to get a diversified portfolio. You can look at their asset allocation on a site such as www.MorningStar.com to learn what percentage of the fund is in stocks/equities and what percentage is in cash/fixed income/other. This will help you to begin to determine the true riskiness of the fund.

Asset allocation is critically important when putting your portfolio together. That's the reason I want you to review the asset allocation of the fund. Research shows that asset allocation is the single most important tool you have when putting your portfolio together.

At a basic level, assets can be divided into four major categories: cash or cash equivalents, fixed income, equities, and alternatives, such as commodities and real estate. Remember that fixed-income investments are usually bonds, and equities are usually stocks. The categories then rapidly become more complex. Bonds can be government, corporate, domestic, or international. Corporate bonds are categorized by riskiness, with high-yield bonds, often called "junk" bonds, paying a higher dividend and carrying more risk.

Stocks are also divided by size: large capitalization (also called large cap), mid-cap, and small cap. Don't let the term cap throw you off. Think of them as large, midsized, and (relatively speaking) small companies. A large-cap mutual fund is comprised of large-cap stocks, and other funds follow a similar format. And remember, stocks can be domestic or international, and international stocks are divided between those from developed nations and ones from emerging markets. You can see how the stability of the former and the instability of the second could impact risk.

Sometimes stocks take a different classification and are organized instead by a sector such as technology, health care, or financials.

Typically, large-cap stocks carry less risk than small cap, and developed nations pose less risk than emerging markets. Sectors are risky if something goes wrong within that sector, or is likely to go wrong. Remembering the technology bubble of 2000 is an easy way to see how investing only in one sector, such as the high-tech sector, can be disastrous for your account.

Alternatives can be broad ranging—from farmland to oil and gas to wind leases. Commodities and real estate are the most common alternative investments, although this asset class is fast becoming more complicated. In the end, just remember the basic rule of investing: If you don't understand an investment after some reasonable study, don't purchase it!

In an effort to make this easier, I have created three risk pyramids:

1. One pyramid for general investing,

2. One pyramid for fixed-income items,

3. And one pyramid for equities.

Many economic and financial issues can impact these pyramids, and so they are not static. There will be times when these pyramids will not reflect the current risk and return of each investment item in them.

Nevertheless, I think you might find them useful.

The higher you go on each of the pyramids, the more risk you might be taking.

Review them with your financial planner to get perspective and to make any adjustments.

General investing, least to most risky

Fixed-income pyramid, least to most risky

Equity pyramid, least to most risky

. . . . .

 Ashley: I like the idea of a blended fund that doesn't require a lot of thought.

 Michael: My retirement plan at work has a target date fund choice, but I selected it without looking at its allocation.

 Lisa: I still don't understand some of these alternative investments. I'm going to avoid them and invest in products I understand.

 James: I would have thought people would know not to invest all their money in the latest thing. However, they never seem to learn.

. . . . .

WEEK 22 ACTIVITY

Look at your investment portfolios and be sure you understand the asset allocations. Do some research or talk to your financial planner to determine what the risk and return are of your overall portfolio—even if the only things in it are your house and retirement account. Many online tools can help you do this.

1. Does the historic rate of return of your portfolio allow you to meet your retirement needs?

2. Does the portfolio match your risk tolerance?

. . . . .

Ask Peggy

Question: Peggy, what is the single most important takeaway from this chapter?

Peggy: Creating a portfolio that is appropriate for your level of risk involves understanding how different asset classes have different risk characteristics and how to put them together in your portfolio.

· · · · ·

Notes

Use the following lines to jot down some notes about what you did this week.

_____

_____

_____

_____

_____

_____

_____

_____

_____

_____

_____

Chapter 23

Investments: Get Real about Returns

*The Professor Who Should Have Been
Satisfied with Hitting Singles*

A university professor had little interest in the stock market until a friend of his, another professor, started bragging about his trading returns. He knew the friend claimed to outperform the market year after year. Eventually, his friend offered to invest some of the professor's money, promising to hit it out of the park. The professor gave his friend some money and then more and then some more as the monthly statements reflected a consistent annual 10 percent return. Then one day, two men in black suits arrived at the office of the professor and began to ask him questions about his stock-trading friend. The agents told the horrified professor that his money was gone—his friend had been running a Ponzi scheme.

Do you want to make a killing in the stock market? Do you want to purchase that low-priced stock that shoots through the roof on the back of a big new invention or discovery? Sadly, then, this isn't the chapter for you. We're going to be talking about reasonable, prudent investing because most of the time, such advice will work far better than trying to hit it out of the park. Trying to beat the market is a fool's game at best. The moral of the professor's story is to be wary of anyone who claims to regularly beat the market or the major indices. Several things can be at work in such a situation. The worst outcome is that it's a scam, likely a Ponzi scheme. Please know most financial professionals—even ones who don't make the cut in my chapter of "Whom To Work With"—are not con artists. True cons are rare, and yet I personally know several people who have been badly hurt in Ponzi schemes. That is why you are doing the right thing by learning more about your money and investing.

I'm afraid what you're much more likely to encounter is someone trying to make things look better than they are—someone trying to put a little shine on his or her performance.

One such scam involves a return that is shown with beginning and ending dates that portray the portfolio in the best possible light. Always, always look at the dates of the return and ask questions if the reported return stretches far into the past. There can easily be a few lost days or even a month in reported returns, but the dates should make sense. They should also reflect recent market movement.

Your returns should be compared to an appropriate index, such as the S&P 500. It is comprised of the five hundred largest U.S. companies, so that comparison can be misleading if your investments aren't in large American companies. If your investments are in an international fund, it might show better returns than the S&P 500 fund, but you might also be open to more risk. Even an American fund of small U.S. companies takes more risk than the S&P 500.

You've probably heard that most portfolio managers can't beat "the index" return on a risk-adjusted level?

It's true!

Basically, if you had just put your money in an index fund, you would have done as well or better!

Appropriate index and risk measurement often take the tide out and leave managers standing there with lower returns. You don't have to understand the details here to know that if you are being asked to purchase a fund and it is being compared to something it is quite different from, there might be a problem with the comparison.

Take the time to ask your financial professional to explain your annual report. Truthfully, your greatest concern should be whether, for some reason, the adviser can't explain the results. Be also cautious of advisers who trade often, especially if they are compensated from commissions or income from the company that created the investment.

"Churning" is a popular culture term; it refers to financial advisers who "churn" your account, constantly changing investments and making money every time they do it. Trading is fine, and thoughtful trading is what you want, but a pattern of constant trading should always get a second look.

I suggest that you keep an eye on the total value of your account, not the positions. Is the account value going up or down? How does it compare to market conditions?

If the constant trading isn't outperforming the appropriate measure with the right risk tolerance, correct index, and net of fees, ask the adviser why he or she is trading so much.

Frequent trading can generate fees and capital gains tax. If your account is taxable, each trade creates a taxable transaction. If you want to pursue an active trading strategy, consider doing it in tax-deferred money so you don't trigger persistent capital gains. The second tax problem with constant trading can occur when your adviser creates a "wash sale."

A wash sale happens when:

1. you sell a security (stocks, bond, options) at a *loss*

2. and repurchase it or a substantially identical security within thirty days *before* or *after* that original sale.

When that occurs, the IRS will not allow you to claim the loss on your taxes. Instead, there is an adjustment to the basis (also known as purchase price) of the repurchased security, and the gain or loss is deferred to the second sale.

Typically, unless you were selling to generate a tax loss, a wash sale is more of an inconvenience than a crisis. It requires careful accounting to create the correct basis for the position. If the account is tax deferred, a wash sale creates no reportable event, because the account does not have a basis (the exception would be if it is a nondeductible IRA or some other unusual account).

Because the majority of us have most of our money in retirement accounts, wash sales rarely impact us. However, if you have a taxable account, you need to be on alert.

Solid, thoughtful investing that is designed to help you meet your financial goals will typically provide you with better long-term returns than frantic trading will.

Yes, Joe DiMaggio exists.

However, it isn't likely that you or your financial professional will be hitting for the record book. Try to be happy with hitting consistent singles and doubles instead.

· · · · ·

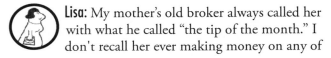

Ashley: Right now, I don't need to worry about all this. I just have one fund, and my financial adviser has never recommended that I do anything other than invest a small amount into it each month.

Michael: I'm glad to have some stability in my investment account rather than trading constantly—and it sounds like that approach has probably saved me a lot in fees as well.

Lisa: My mother's old broker always called her with what he called "the tip of the month." I don't recall her ever making money on any of those investments once she had paid the associated fees and charges.

James: This reminds me of the old fable about the tortoise and the hare. In my experience, as in the story, the tortoise wins every time. I have always tried to remember that when it came to my investments—there is no such thing as "easy money."

· · · · ·

WEEK 23 ACTIVITY

This week, you will need to look at your investment statements from the last year if you are working with a financial professional.

Each statement should show you when and where you bought or sold a security. If there is a lot of activity, go back into Morningstar and look at the composition of each "buy" or "sell." If the securities seem very similar—in other words, if you sold a fund and bought a very similar fund to replace it, that might or might not be a red flag.

Certainly, legitimate reasons exist to trade stock. However, it's worth talking to the adviser about it. If there's a lot of activity, you might want to ask why. Even if you are approving each trade, you might want to ask some additional questions to understand what the adviser is trying to accomplish by trading so frequently. Remember that you aren't seeking to hit the home run!

· · · · ·

Ask Peggy

Question: Peggy, what is the single most important takeaway from this chapter?

Peggy: Investment returns vary over time; consistently similar and high rates of return suggest fraud more than they indicate a hotshot portfolio manager.

· · · · ·

Notes

Use the lines below to record your progress this week. When you look back on it later, it will serve to remind you just how far you've come.

_____

_____

_____

_____

_____

_____

_____

_____

_____

_____

_____

_____

_____

Chapter 24

Investments: Compound Interest

The Business Owner Who
Didn't Understand a Profound Force

A small business owner had been saving money for his retirement for many years. He never saved with a plan. He just tried to make sure he invested in his retirement account each month. By the time he was in his mid-fifties, the man decided he should try to determine whether he was on track for what he thought he would need after he retired.

He took the amount of money he had saved and divided it by the number of years he thought he would need retirement distributions.

He was horrified to realize that he didn't have nearly enough money saved to see him through his golden years.

He hurriedly called a financial planner, who met with him, reviewed his numbers, and gave him a surprisingly different outcome. Come to find out, the business owner was right on track to having saved enough money, given his goal. The planner reminded him that his account would grow during retirement by however much the market provided. The growth would also *compound* over time, providing him with significantly larger distributions than he had thought.

Albert Einstein is reported to have said that compound interest was the most powerful force in the universe. That's high praise from a man who turned Newtonian physics on its head with his theory of relativity. I don't know that I believe compound interest is more powerful than, say, gravity, but certainly, keeping that profound force working for you can help you grow your money more quickly.

Interest on your savings or investments is calculated in two different ways: simple interest and compound interest.

Simple interest works this way: Assume you have a $100 investment that pays 10 percent interest per year. That means at the end of year one, your investment is worth $100 plus 10 percent of $100, or $10, for a total of $110. The $10 is not kept in the investment, so the investment regains its worth of $100, and the investor takes the $10 and does what he or she wants with it. At the end of year two, a second $10 is earned, and the process continues for the length of the investment period.

Compound interest is calculated differently.

Given an investment worth $100 and a 10 percent interest rate, at the end of year one, the investment would be worth $110.

The magic begins here.

The $10 interest is kept in the investment, and 10 percent is earned on $110 in year two. At the end of year two, assuming annual compounding, the investment is now worth $110 plus $11, totaling $121.

Compare the total investment return in the two systems. Take our $100 investment earning a 10 percent rate of return and assume that the investment has a ten-year time period. At the end of the ten years, a simple-interest investment would return the $100 principal with $10 for ten years' interest. The total return would equal $200.00, doubling your money. No doubt you would be happy with your investment decision.

However, assume you had compounding interest working on behalf of that investment. How much money would you have then? It would be $259.37. Certainly, an additional $59.37, the equivalent of a 59.37 percent of your original investment, would be preferable.

How is this possible?

Compound interest is calculated on both the principal of the investment and the growth of the investment.

Compounding allows an investment to grow more quickly, and it makes it a little easier to save for retirement, especially if dividends are reinvested. It's not always the right decision, but it should always be at least considered. You might find it interesting to know that the place where we most commonly keep our money—our local bank—uses compound interest.

Bank accounts pay interest on not only the money we originally put in the bank but also on the interest our money has earned. Literally, we make money for nothing, and this is the profound force that impressed Einstein so much.

Other kinds of investments also pay interest in either a simple or compound manner.

The kind of investment you select depends on many considerations, and certainly, many great types of investments—bonds come to mind—pay simple interest. However, understanding how your interest is calculated will help you determine how much growth you can anticipate from each of your investments.

It should be noted that paying interest is different from reinvesting dividends into additional shares of what you own, but the concept is the same. Sometimes this is a good strategy for you to follow; you just want to be careful that you don't create an out-of-balance portfolio.

That said, harnessing this powerful force known as compound interest allows your money to work for you in a way that can deliver impressive results.

Ashley: I would like to put my emergency fund into a bank savings account that pays even a tiny amount of interest—it would be better than earning nothing!

 Michael: I am not sure that my 401(k) plan is set up to reinvest the dividends of my mutual funds. I am going to check on that.

 Lisa: It's scary to imagine the impact inflation could have on my retirement savings.

James: As I start to take retirement income, I'm going to stop reinvesting dividends in my taxable accounts. If I have to pay taxes anyway, I might as well take the money to help me pay my monthly bills.

· · · · ·

WEEK 24 ACTIVITY

Compound interest is effective only when you have time to let it accumulate. Even smaller savings rates can grow nicely given time, through the magic of compounding. This week's activity is to encourage you to start saving now rather than later. If you can find a savings account at your bank that pays interest, that would be a good vehicle for your emergency fund. Most of the time, savings accounts offer better interest than checking accounts, though that might vary from bank to bank.

Consider reinvesting the dividends on at least some of your mutual funds. Be careful that the funds you reinvest into are funds in which you don't mind taking a larger position. Your portfolio can easily skew, especially if you reinvest into single stocks. Still, reinvestment is a prudent way to create a system in which dividends are reinvested into the security and continue to grow. If you don't reinvest the dividends, most brokerage accounts will sweep the dividend into a money market fund, where it will also grow at a compound rate, although the interest rate may be much lower.

It's always important for you to keep up with what interest rates are being paid by banks and money market funds along with the growth rate of your security. You want to maximize the benefit of compounding while keeping your risk in check.

· · · · ·

Ask Peggy

Question: Peggy, what is the single most important takeaway from this chapter?

Peggy: Compound interest is magic, because it is interest earned on your interest.

· · · · ·

Notes

Use the lines below to record your week's progress—or thoughts and questions you might have on this chapter.

_____

_____

_____

_____

_____

_____

_____

_____

_____

_____

_____

_____

_____

_____

_____

_____

_____

_____

_____

Chapter 25

Investments: Risk-adjusted Returns and the Rule of 72

The Grandmother Who Helped her
Granddaughter Pay More Attention

A beloved grandmother had been investing for years and wanted to help her granddaughter begin to make good financial decisions. The granddaughter's job provided a retirement plan, but the money did not seem *real* to the young woman. Because she couldn't access it, she didn't pay a lot of attention to it.

Her grandmother reminded her that the whole point of the account was to grow the funds necessary to provide her with money for her old age. The grandmother wanted her granddaughter to understand the power of beginning to invest early. She went so far as to explain the Rule of 72 to her granddaughter, who was amazed to learn how her money could grow if handled right.

Portfolio returns can be confusing. Many people choose to compare their portfolio to a stock benchmark to gauge whether it has earned as much as a recognized index such as the Dow Jones Industrial Average or the S&P 500. When they earn more than the market, they are pleased. If they earn less than the market, they are disappointed. What they forget is that looking at the stock market only gives you half the story.

How much risk do you want to take in your portfolio?

How much time do you have before the money is needed?

How much do you panic when the market declines?

All these questions and more control how your portfolio should be invested.

We've discussed risk management and its impact on your portfolio; remember that it will impact your portfolio return. If you are taking only half the risk of the stock market, you can't expect to earn a return as high as the market. That stands to reason, but it still confuses and distresses clients.

Most of us stress about having enough money to meet our goals. Generally, the reason people stress about market returns is not about the amount of money earned, assuming that the investments are appropriate and the fees charged are reasonable. No, their fear is that they will not have enough money to achieve their goals.

Simply put, they don't know what their portfolio rate of return tells them as far as how on track they are—they don't know how to use a financial calculator and they hate to keep asking the financial planner to explain things.

Fortunately, there is a shortcut that will give you a rough idea of what your market return means. It's called the Rule of 72. When your rate of return (as a whole number) times the number of years you have to earn that rate equals 72, your money has doubled.

If you earn a 9 percent rate of return on average, your money doubles every eight years because 9 × 8 = 72. If you earn a 6 percent rate of return on average, your money doubles every twelve years because 6 × 12 = 72.

So if you start with $1,000 and it earns an average 8 percent rate of return, it should be worth $2,000 in nine years.

Of course, the Rule of 72 can work against you too. If inflation averages 3 percent a year, it means that something that costs $100 now will cost $200 in twenty-four years because 3 percent × 24 = 72.

Unfortunately, that also means if you are forty years old now, things will likely cost twice as much when you turn sixty-four and are nearing retirement as they cost today.

Talk about an incentive to save more now!

Understanding how your rate of return can impact your long-term planning often makes it easier to stay on track. It can also take money longer to double than most people are aware. Knowing all that can help you control your expectations and keep you from becoming frustrated if your portfolio doesn't double in a year.

As a note of caution, I encourage clients never to assume an average rate of return higher than 8 percent or 9 percent because market fluctuation and their own risk-tolerance constraints can lower the expected rate of return over the maximum average market return. Although this might sound more conservative than you have heard before, just remember the poor professor who failed to be happy with hitting singles.

Your inflation-adjusted return is calculated by subtracting the inflation rate from the rate of return. This would cause an 8 percent growth rate to be closer to 5 percent once you accounted for inflation.

The stock market's long-term average raw return is 11 percent, but most people have tempered their stocks with bonds, money-market funds, and other items with lower returns, making their average return lower. A market disruption can also severely lower an average return significantly if the timing is poor.

I believe that expecting lower, more consistent returns makes it easier for you to achieve your financial goals. Once you understand how your returns are calculated, some of your frustration lowers, and you can apply the Rule of 72 to gauge how close you are to your financial goals.

Ashley: I have a little money invested. My financial planner suggested that it might be okay to be aggressive for a spell because I have a long time before retirement. Now I know what she meant.

 Michael: I have friends who are convinced they can double their money in a year. I think I'll let them read this chapter.

Lisa: It's a little unsettling to realize that things could very likely cost twice as much when I am ninety as they do when I am sixty-five—and that's if the world chugs along like it is now. What if there is an unexpected economic hiccup?

James: I've been through several market declines. Now that I'm almost retired, I need to keep an allocation that won't destroy me if something should go wrong.

· · · · ·

WEEK 25 ACTIVITY

This week, I want you to go back to your monthly cash flow calculations. Use the cost of your monthly bills, and then figure out how many years you are from retirement.

Take the number of years and divide it by twenty-four. If you're twenty years from retirement, calculate 20 divided by 24. You should get 0.833. That lets you know if inflation averages 3 percent, items will cost 83 percent more when you retire than they do today.

Assuming you retire at sixty-five, you can pretty much assume the cost of items will double over the course of your retirement, again assuming a 3 percent inflation rate.

It works for everyone because 65 + 24 = 89, a reasonable if slightly low life expectancy. Because 24 × 3 = 72, you know things will cost twice as much at age eighty-nine.

Finally, the good news: You can also use your average portfolio rate of return to see how long it will take the money to double. It might double several times. Remember that each additional time it doubles, it uses your last product as the base. If you have $100,000 and you earn an 8 percent rate of return, your money will double to $200,000 in nine years. Then over the next nine years, it will grow to $400,000. Of course, this assumes an 8 percent return year over year.

· · · · ·

Ask Peggy

Question: Peggy, what is the single most important takeaway from this chapter?

Peggy: Mathematically, if you divide your rate of return (as a whole number) into 72, the answer is the number of years it will take your money to double. For example, 72 ÷ 8% = 9 years.

· · · · ·

Notes

_____

_____

_____

_____

Ask Peggy

Ashley: **Can I keep all my money in a blended mutual fund?**

Peggy: You're just starting to invest so a blended mutual fund gives the advantage of good diversification in a single fund. It's an easy choice for you for now, especially if the fees are reasonable.

Michael: **When I hear my investment has increased in value by 8 percent over a year, it sounds good, but it's vague. How can I figure out what that means?**

Peggy: The Rule of 72 gives you a quick shortcut to determine how long it will take your money to double. The Rule of 72 says that when you take your rate of return, such as the 8 percent you just gave me, and divide it into 72, the answer is the number of years it will take your money to double. So for you, your portfolio would double in nine years if you average an 8 percent return because $8 \times 9 = 72$.

Lisa: **Some advisers say my portfolio should be especially conservative since I'm now in my sixties. I don't want to overact because I'm nearing retirement age. How should I respond?**

Peggy: Once retired, you often can't add a lot of money to your portfolio. They may be thinking you could spend more than thirty years in retirement. That could be tricky if you are too conservative. Consider holding several years of cash flow need in very conservative investments. That way, if the markets collapse, you can pay your expenses without selling positions while they are low—and, as always, talk to your financial planner about this.

James: **Peggy, I have a lot of my company's stock in my retirement plan at work. Is that okay?**

Peggy: James, it's likely your plan allows you to diversify out of company stock and into other investments. It can be a little risky holding a lot of company stock, because if something goes wrong, both your livelihood and your retirement portfolio could suffer. If you keep the stock, you may be eligible for net unrealized appreciation, or the difference in value between the average cost basis of your shares and the current market value of them if they're held in a tax-deferred account. Again, talk to your CPA.

Peggy Doviak

Retirement

Chapter 26

Retirement: Saving the Right Amount

The Woman Who Didn't Want To Eat Cat Food

A savvy, smart woman in her sixties went to a free dinner and seminar she had been invited to by mail. After a plate of cold spaghetti, the adviser told everyone in the room that if they didn't have $1 million in savings, they would be eating cat food in their retirement years.

Miraculously, the adviser had just the investment product they needed to buy to lower their risk of that happening. Panic-stricken, the woman called me the next day and asked if it was true: Was the presenter right? Would she be eating cat food in her old age? She had no idea how much she needed to have saved to see her through the rest of her life.

By far the single most commonly asked financial planning question I hear from people is, "How much money do I need for retirement?"

I think it's even a more common question than people asking if an investment portfolio makes sense. The roots of the question are understandable. Although most of my friends do not hold jobs with traditional pension plans, many of our parents did. By pension plan, I mean money put into an account by your employer on your behalf, in which the plan makes the investment decisions, and then, during retirement, you receive a check every month for the rest of your life.

Technically, this is referred to as a "defined-benefit plan," and it used to be the norm when it came to pension plans in the United States.

That is no longer the case, I'm afraid.

The important point of such a pension was that your retirement check was considered secure, leaving no reason for most Americans to follow the stock market at all. That pension check, especially when added to Social Security, might not create a luxurious retirement, but the pensioners had no fear of having to resort to eating cat food in their golden years—they knew what size of check would be coming in every month once they retired.

Sadly, retirement plans with guaranteed monthly benefits are disappearing, not because they aren't a wonderful benefit for workers, but because they are expensive for the company or governmental entity that offers them. Over time, companies realized they didn't want to take the investment risk—coming up with the difference between what the investment earned and the promised benefit to the worker—if they could pass that risk on to the employee. From an employer's perspective, it's much more appealing to provide a contribution or a match and leave the investment risk up to the participant.

Despite this trend, most people have no idea how to go about determining how much to save to ensure a particular monthly pension amount in their old age. I believe it is this question that overwhelms people so completely they don't even try to figure out how much money to set aside monthly.

More surprising, however, is the number of people who simply choose not to participate in their company's retirement plan at all, even if the plan contains an employer match to their contribution. That's like turning your nose up at free money.

No one is going to prosper that way.

What I abhor is people in the financial services industry who have chosen to address the issue by trying to scare people rather than by giving them solid information early enough in their lives to make funding retirement easier. Financial advisers who just try to scare you are offering a sales pitch, not financial planning.

So how do you begin to calculate what you'll need down the road? You need to choose a retirement income formula. This is an important decision and not one to make casually. People often ask me if I like the 80 Percent Rule. That guideline assumes you will spend 80 percent of what you spend now in retirement.

My answer is that I don't like it much.

If you are young and have no idea how much you will need in retirement, then it's a reasonable place to start. As you age and continue to refine your financial life, however, you will likely deviate from it—and rightly so. My fear of the 80 Percent Rule is that it often ends up painting a false picture of what you will need, especially if it's used without thought. I would prefer that you work from your cash flow analysis.

To do this, you need to go back to your earlier exercise in Chapter 3 when you calculated your monthly spending. Look at that number again. Do you see expenses that will disappear during retirement? Will you still have a house payment? Maybe a mortgage for a second vacation home? Will the house be paid for but because you plan to be an older parent, you'll still have college obligations for your children? Do you see some expenses you anticipate having in retirement that you don't have now?

You might want a larger travel budget or may anticipate more medical expenses. The closer you are to retirement, the better your estimate can be. For now, just try to decide how much you will want on an annual basis without worrying about inflation. The next steps are much easier to accomplish if you employ a financial planner or find the right financial calculator. That's because all the monetary adjustments involve compounding, so you won't be able to use a traditional pocket calculator for them.

As you read the steps, understand that we are dividing your financial future into two categories—*after* retirement and *before* retirement.

We begin by calculating how much money you will need to pay your expenses during retirement. Then we can calculate how much you need to save during your working years to make that happen.

1. *How much are you spending now? What budget adjustments should you make to figure out how much you will need in the future?*

You will need to decide how much money you think you will need each month during retirement.

2. *What will inflation do to your monthly need?*

You should inflate your monthly requirement by your inflation assumption to see what it will be when you hit retirement age. I usually use 3 percent because that is the long-term inflation average in the United States. You can use any number you choose, but you should do some research before settling on one. Remember that this calculation must be compounded each year. If you want to do it yourself, you will need to get a compounding financial calculator.

3. *What resources do you have available?*

Once you've determined your monthly need at retirement, look at sources of monthly income. Typically, these would be Social Security payments and pensions. Subtract your monthly cash flow need from your monthly benefits.

4. *Do you have a surplus or a deficit after Step 3?*

Any deficit will involve increasing your savings rate now, before you retire.

5. *How much do you think your money can grow through investing?*

The amount that you need to save for each month's deficit can be reduced by a reasonable stock-market growth rate, but it also must be increased by inflation. If you think the money will earn 6 percent, and you believe inflation will be 3 percent, the real growth rate for the money needed for your retirement years is roughly 3 percent.

6. *How much do you need to have saved by the first day of your retirement?*

Using the inflation-adjusted growth rate in Step 5, you will need to use a compounding calculator to determine the total value of the money you want to have saved by the first day of your retirement.

7. *How much do you need to save annually to meet your retirement goal?*

That number becomes the basis for how much you need to save each year until you are ready to retire. Remember that you can assume a reasonable growth rate of this amount to lower the total amount you want to save. Again, this step involves a compounding calculator. And if you're thinking that this might be a good calculation to leave to your financial planner to do, you're probably right—so don't rush out to buy that new compounding calculator just yet.

The only reason I'm giving you all the moving pieces in this situation is because you need to know the pieces exist. Way too many people do not appreciate the complexity of the calculation, and not every financial adviser is equipped to help you with the math. Even some online retirement calculators can skip steps. Yet it's important to get this calculation correct. I might suggest that a financial adviser who can't handle such a calculation is one to avoid. And as you look for a new adviser, give yourself a pat on the back for knowing what questions to ask him or her.

The idea of not having enough money in retirement is a scary proposition to most people. Planning now can help you avoid that. Having a trusted financial planner to help with that planning increases your odds for success. You can forgo planning now for your retirement, but you will pay later: Without planning today, you might well have to delay your retirement or fight Fluffy for that bowl of kibble.

· · · · ·

Ashley: Yikes! That's too many steps and too much math for me. For now, I'm going to assume I need 100 percent of my current income, but I understand why I'll need to refine that later. Because I need to save my emergency fund first, I'm regularly putting a little back at a time right now for retirement.

Michael: I ran my retirement projections, including and excluding Social Security, just to see what the difference in my savings level would need to be. Looking at the totals, I do hope Social Security is there when I am sixty-five.

Lisa: I went to a seminar dinner similar to the one Peggy attended. No matter how much anyone in the audience said they had saved, the speaker convinced them it wasn't enough. He told them they couldn't count on Social Security and even suggested that pensions weren't secure. I would have felt better about his honesty if he hadn't just happened to have the "perfect" product for us to buy to fix it all. I wonder how much money he earns for selling that product.

 James: I remember how inexpensive things were thirty or forty years ago. Inflation is a powerful force. I need to remember that.

• • • • •

WEEK 26 ACTIVITY

This week, I want you to talk to a financial planner about how to calculate your retirement need or find an online calculator. There are many good calculators available online, but they should have the characteristics that I outlined. And remember that you must take the following components into account as you calculate your retirement need:

How much do you want to spend monthly in retirement?
How many years do you have until you retire?
What are your assumptions about the inflation rate?
What is a reasonable assumption about investment growth?
What is your life expectancy?
Will you have any monthly retirement benefits?
Do you want to include Social Security?

• • • • •

Ask Peggy

Question: Peggy, what is the single most important takeaway from this chapter?

Peggy: The easiest way to determine how much money you will need in retirement is to begin by looking at your spending today and then adjusting the amount up and down for higher and lower expenses.

· · · · ·

Notes

Use the lines below to record your progress this week.

_____

_____

_____

_____

_____

_____

_____

_____

_____

_____

_____

_____

_____

Chapter 27

Retirement: What is an IRA?

*The Woman Who Thought
She Understood More Than She Did*

A woman wanted to supplement her savings by investing in an Individual Retirement Account, so she opened an on-line account at a discount broker and funded a traditional IRA. Believing it was deductible, she took the deduction on her taxes. Later that year, she received a letter from the IRS telling her that she had taken the deduction in error. She already had a retirement plan at work, and she and her husband earned too much money to take the deduction.

If you don't have a retirement plan at work or if you want to fund your retirement with asset classes not available in your plan's fund choices, you might want to consider an individual retirement account or IRA. Although the amount you can contribute is lower than a qualified pension plan, the IRA is the only choice many people have available.

Before you can decide if an IRA makes sense for you, it's important that you understand the characteristics of an IRA. You should know that IRAs come in four types: traditional/deductible IRAs, Roth IRAs, traditional/nondeductible IRAs, and spousal IRAs. Several types of small business retirement plans also have an IRA structure, but we'll address those later.

When it come to an IRA, you need to know you are limited in how much money you can put into any IRA each year. IRAs are funded by earned income. That includes your income and your spouse's income. For divorces occurring after 2018, however, alimony is no longer considered earned income for the recipient.

The amount by which you can fund an IRA is limited by the annual contribution limit or your earned income, whichever is smaller. However, if you are fifty or older, you are allowed to contribute additional money as a catch-up. In 2018, the amount of the annual contribution remains at $5,500, and the catch-up is $1,000.

You cannot exceed your annual contribution limit, even if you are simultaneously funding more than one type of IRA. You might choose to fund both a deductible IRA and a Roth IRA, but you would have to distribute the annual contribution amount of $5,500 between the two types of accounts. You can put money into your IRA as late as April 15 of the year following the contribution year. For example, if you forgot or didn't have the money to fund your IRA during the calendar year of 2018, you could fund that year as late as April 15 of 2019. And that would not prevent you from funding your IRA for 2019 as well in such a situation.

IRAs are basically savings vehicles.

You select investments to fill your IRA.

The IRA is not the investment itself.

Think of it as the bucket holding your investments. Common investments that can go into an IRA include mutual funds and exchange-traded funds, stocks and bonds, and, less commonly, options.

IRAs can't be invested in everything. In fact, they are forbidden from investing in three things: insurance, collectibles, and loans. This is mostly because of the tax treatment of those items or the difficulty in arriving at an exact value of such holding. Elaborate, complicated IRA investment strategies in fine art or baseball cards might not be in your best interest anyway. Sometimes simpler is better, and you would not want to break the IRS investment rules.

The restrictions make sense if you think about it. Life insurance death benefits usually pass income tax free to the recipient, so it would make no sense to put an insurance policy in an IRA because an IRA creates a tax liability when distributions are taken from it. As for collectibles, while your Joe DiMaggio baseball card may be priceless to you, the IRS has no way of determining its exact value as of December 31, a process that must occur when you take required minimum distributions, or RMDs.

You might read articles extolling elaborate, self-directed IRA methods of investing in real property and other less common investments. I'm not going to speak to the wisdom of such strategies, but I do know they are difficult to structure properly, and a mistake could create an enormous tax liability.

An IRA has a beneficiary, which means it passes outside the probate process on your death. However, you need to be careful when you choose your distribution beneficiary.

When you designate multiple beneficiaries for the same IRA, the annual required minimum distribution is based on the age of the oldest beneficiary of the inherited IRA. If there is a large age difference among your heirs, you might want more than one IRA. And if your beneficiary is not a person and you're leaving your IRA to a charity or a family trust, the distribution period can change from the beneficiary's lifetime to only five years. This can create a nightmare with trusts. Again, please talk to your attorney and your certified public accountant before moving forward.

The most common type of IRA remains the traditional deductible IRA. It is funded in pretax dollars, and the growth and income from any investments is tax deferred until the money is actually withdrawn from the IRA. As a result, contributions to a deductible IRA will lower your current tax liability.

Only when the funds are taken out of the IRA as a distribution are the taxes due. In most cases, you will be in a lower tax bracket by then because the assumption is that you will be retired. In fact, the Internal Revenue Service typically will penalize the filer 10 percent and require you to pay the taxes if you take a distribution before you are fifty-nine-and-a-half years of age.

Exceptions to this penalty exist, so if you're having a financial emergency, check with your financial planner to see what options you might have. The existence of a company retirement plan might eliminate your ability to deduct a traditional IRA contribution, depending on your adjusted gross income. On the other hand, if you choose not to participate in a company-defined contribution retirement plan through your own contributions or contributions by your employer, you might be eligible to deduct your contribution to the traditional IRA.

Still, as a word of caution, I'm not sure I would often recommend that a client take the latter option, especially if the employer offers a match to what you put into the account. It's difficult to beat free money, even if the company plan's options are limited and the expense ratios of the funds are higher than you might like.

If you're married and working and have a company plan, you might like to know that a traditional deductible IRA might also be available to your spouse. Remember that a single person who does not have a company plan or a married couple, neither of whom has a plan, can always deduct their traditional IRA contributions. However, if your spouse has a company retirement plan, you will have an income phase-out for deducting your contributions. The spousal IRA has a higher income phaseout than exists for people who have their own company plans, so it might still be a viable option.

Roth IRAs tend to draw a lot of praise, and rightly so. Given that it is funded in after-tax dollars, the Roth IRA is interesting. And Roth distributions can be income tax free if you meet the criteria. And you can participate in your company's retirement plan and still have IRA options available.

Distributions for a Roth IRA are not mandatory until they are inherited. Because the account is funded in after-tax dollars, you can withdraw the money you put into the account at any time with no tax and no penalty.

If the Roth has been open for five years and you are older than fifty-nine-and-a-half, the distributions of investment growth are also income tax free. The income phaseouts, or the amount you can earn and still contribute to an IRA, are much higher for Roth IRAs than they are for deductible, traditional IRAs. Participating in your company's retirement plan is not a consideration when funding a Roth; your ability to fund it is based solely on your earned income. Finally, if neither a Roth nor a deductible IRA is available because you make too much money, you have a third option. You can fund a nondeductible IRA. A nondeductible IRA is funded in after-tax dollars, and the growth is not taxable until you withdraw it from the account. Basically, it allows you to avoid capital gains if you want to trade inside the account, and that can be a valuable ability. However, a nondeductible IRA has a second, even better feature. It can be rolled into a Roth IRA, regardless of your adjusted gross income.

If you already have a deductible IRA, you must prorate all of your conversions to make them partially taxable. However, if you don't have a traditional IRA and you earn too much money to deduct an IRA or fund a Roth, you might consider another option. Because rollover rules can change, work with a certified public accountant and a financial planner to implement this strategy.

The IRS supports Americans funding of our retirement accounts through favorable tax treatment. Traditional deductible IRAs, Roth IRAs, and nondeductible IRAs can each serve potentially useful roles in your retirement strategy.

Review the options open to you and choose a strategy that helps you meet your goals.

· · · · ·

 Ashley: I've started to put money into a Roth IRA each month. I like that I can take my contributions out in the future without a penalty.

 Michael: My wife and I are watching our adjusted gross income closely. Last year, we were close to the IRA phaseout for deductible contributions because we both have retirement plans at work.

 Lisa: The idea of funding a Roth in addition to my retirement plan at work appeals to me. I like the tax-diversification feature just in case I'm not in a lower tax bracket come retirement time.

James: We aren't planning on taking distributions from our Roth. We're trying to let our children inherit it to postpone the tax as long as possible and maximize the growth. Our financial planner called it "stretching" the IRA distributions over two lifetimes. We've worked hard to be in the position so we can do this.

· · · · ·

WEEK 27 ACTIVITY

This week, I want you to look at your income and the IRA phaseout levels.

What type of IRA are you eligible to fund?

If you have already taken advantage of any match offered by an employer, does an IRA help you meet your retirement goals or lower your taxes?

Which type of IRA would be best for meeting your goals?

Talk to a financial planner for assistance in making all of these decisions.

. . . . .

Ask Peggy

Question: Peggy, what is the single most important takeaway from this chapter?

Peggy: IRAs can be opened by anyone with earned income, but there are deductibility phaseouts if you or your spouse participate in a company retirement plan.

. . . . .

Notes

Use the following lines to jot down notes.

_____

_____

_____

_____

_____

_____

Chapter 28

Retirement: The Company Plan

The Teacher Who Was in Better Shape Than He Thought

A teacher came in with his wife for a meeting with their financial planner—the couple both taught high school. The planner asked whether they participated in the state's teacher pension plan, and they said they did. The husband, however, was still anxious because he didn't understand what their pensions would and wouldn't do.

The planner explained to him that between their school pensions and Social Security, they had four sources of income for which they wouldn't have to make investment decisions. In addition, the husband and wife had deferred more income into 403(b) plans than they could have done in IRAs.

In the "good old days," many companies funded a pension for their employees. The employees knew the value of the benefit, and they didn't have to worry about anything else. They had no investment decisions to make, and when they retired, they received a check—in the amount they expected—each month. Those kind of retirement plans still exist; as we said earlier, they are called "defined-benefit plans." However, they are becoming increasingly rare. It is much more likely that if you have a company-sponsored retirement plan, you are being given some money in the form of a match to what you're putting in and a list of investment choices. I won't kid you: The process can be daunting, and so I would like to begin this topic by making sure you understand some of the basics of company retirement plans.

First, you need to determine what type of retirement plan or plans your employer offers. This might sound like an easy task, but I am frequently dismayed at the number of my clients who don't know what type of plan they have.

Larger employers might offer a variety of plans, including 401(a), 401(k), 403(b), and 457 plans. These plans are all named for a section of the federal tax code.

If you work for a small employer, you might be offered a simplified employee pension, or SEP, or a savings incentive match plan for employees, or SIMPLE. These plans are usually a form of an IRA, but allow for larger contribution amounts than the deductible, nondeductible, or Roth IRAs.

Plans come in two major categories:

1. *Defined-benefit plans*, in which, as we have said before, you receive a monthly benefit during retirement without having to make any investment decisions, and

2. *Defined-contribution plans*, in which you invest money provided by your employer or deferred by you, and you take all the risk if the market rises or falls.

Some plans guarantee employer contributions, and some leave that up to the employer's discretion. Be sure you understand what type of plan your company offers.

Once you know the type of company plan you have, you need to know the company's rules about plan participation.

Different types of retirement plans require different levels of employment, but typically, plan participation is limited to full-time employees. Generally, one thousand hours per year are required for you to be qualified to participate in a company's retirement plan. Some exceptions to this exist, but rather than turning this chapter into pages and pages of tax code, I would recommend talking to your company's human resources department about your eligibility for a company plan. You can also ask a financial planner or go to www.irs.gov to learn more about each type of retirement plan offered by your company.

Once you know what your company offers, it is also important to understand how your employer participates in the plan. Does the company make a nondiscretionary (mandatory) contribution into your account? In this type of retirement funding, you would receive a benefit even if you chose not to make your own contribution.

More frequently, employers match the amount of the salary you defer to the plan, up to a certain percent. They might match as much as 3 percent of your compensation if you also defer the same amount. If your employer matches contributions, it is important to take and maximize that benefit. Do everything you can to contribute money to your plan to the highest level your employer matches. Why? Because that will become an instant risk-free, 100 percent rate of return on the money you put into the plan. Of course, any additional gain or loss comes from how you choose to invest that money once it has been contributed.

Different plans allow for different deferral levels, and some plans allow you to invest more if you are older than fifty. To complicate things even more, a few types of plans offer additional deferral if you are close to retirement age.

One of the things you'll want to ask HR about is whether the company's retirement plan has a Roth component. That would allow you to contribute after-tax dollars and then receive the retirement distribution of principal (money you put in) and growth income tax free.

The advantage is the tax savings, but the disadvantage is the loss of the tax deduction today. And, unlike a Roth IRA,

Roth retirement-plan distributions must be taken beginning at the age of seventy-and-a-half.

Every plan that offers the Roth deferral option must also offer a pretax deferral. The employer match is always to the pretax side. You will probably want to talk to a financial planner to decide which is better for you.

I find that what confuses people the most when they choose the Roth 401(k) is that it leaves them with two retirement accounts in their company's plan—one for employer money and one for the after-tax money that they defer.

Some people forget that they have two plans and thus two accounts to make decisions about. I have had new clients come to me who have made investment decisions in only one of their two accounts. The other account remains in the plan's default choice because the clients either weren't aware the account even existed or had forgotten about it.

That leads us to the next question you need to answer: What is your retirement plan's default investment choice?

Some plans still choose a money market, although they are supposed to offer a fund that offers market growth. Usually, the choice is a target date fund or a balanced fund such as we talked about in the chapters on Investments.

Bottom line: You need to understand what happens to your money if you make no decisions.

Some companies give you the opportunity to choose to participate in their plan by filling out an application. Other employers opt to give you a "negative election," by which you are enrolled in the company plan unless you specifically opt out.

There is nothing wrong with either approach, but you need to know which one your company follows—or you well might miss out altogether.

Finally, you need to know what professionals are available at your company to help when you have questions. You should have an HR contact, and there should also be an investment professional provided by the company that is holding the investments. Usually that professional comes to your office once a year to offer a seminar and answer questions. Get the person's card, and don't hesitate to call him or her if you are confused.

The details of company retirement plans could fill an entire book on their own. This chapter is designed to show you other areas you should explore, because a company retirement plan is a critical component to the success of your own retirement plan.

Be sure that you are using it to your best advantage.

· · · · ·

Ashley: I'm hoping that once I have a full-time position in my field, I can become eligible for a company retirement plan. If that would provide some money, it would be so much easier for me to build enough of a nest egg to retire in comfort.

Michael: I chose the Roth option in my 401(k) plan almost on reflex. Now I have two retirement accounts, and I am being careful to keep them both invested the way I want.

Lisa: I've been fortunate to earn enough money to maximize my retirement deferral. Once I reached the age of fifty, I began to defer even more. It is building me a nice retirement account.

James: My plan is to keep investing in my retirement account at work and to take no distributions until I retire.

· · · · ·

WEEK 28 ACTIVITY

For this week's activity, I want you to answer the questions I asked in this chapter. Take some time to get a real understanding of your company's retirement account, how much money you can invest in it, whether or not the company matches some of your investment, and how the money is invested.

· · · · ·

Ask Peggy

Question: Peggy, what is the single most important takeaway from this chapter?

Peggy: If your company retirement plan offers to match your contributions, try to take advantage of it at the highest level possible because if you don't, you're leaving free money on the table.

· · · · ·

Notes

_____

_____

_____

_____

_____

_____

Chapter 29

Retirement: Company Benefits

The New Employee Who Was Confused

A young man finished college and obtained an extremely good job with a large corporation. He went to all the company orientation meetings and eventually was asked by human resources to choose from a long list of fringe benefits. He was given a lump sum to spend and told to select which benefits he wanted to receive.

HR also informed him that anything he selected now, such as life insurance, would not require any form of physical exam or other qualification. However, if he wanted to add a benefit later, he would have to qualify for it. Thrilled as he was with the generous opportunity, he was nonetheless confused. He simply didn't know where to begin to choose from the company's menu of benefits.

If your employer offers a benefit package, often called "fringe benefits," you need to spend some time thinking about what they are and aren't—and how they might change as your time with the company lengthens.

First, you need to know when you can enroll. Typically, if you want to avoid any potential insurance issues, you should enroll as soon as you are eligible for the benefits. If you don't, you might have to qualify for them when you do want them. In the case of insurance, an insurance company will access your qualifications through the underwriting process and decide what the cost will be to insure you.

The good news is that being a member of the group should make you eligible for at least the basic levels of benefits offered by the employer. However, some companies do make new employees wait three to six months before some benefits, such as health insurance, kick in.

Once you're eligible, realize that most benefit packages have an annual enrollment period, along with the time you can enroll as a new employee. Be sure you know when this is, mark it on your calendar, and deal with additions or changes within those time parameters.

Procrastination has caused many people to miss the deadline. And you will want to be particularly careful in years in which you have had—or expect— a life event, such as marriage, a new baby, or divorce. These can often change your benefit needs.

Typically, an employer will provide you a sum that you are free to divide between different company benefits. This is often called a "cafeteria plan." Sometimes you might be able to take cash in lieu of, say, medical coverage or child-care expenses. I would note that the money is often worth more if invested in the products or benefits that are offered. Although those benefits can vary between employers, a few of them are more common than others.

Health insurance is probably the most common benefit. And most of the time, it is in your best financial interest to insure yourself through your employer.

You should, however, take the time to compare the cost of insuring your spouse and children with other options you might have available to you. If your spouse works, that company's health insurance might be a better choice for your spouse. That leaves you with the choice of who insures the children. Because national health care is also available, it's worth your time to compare the cost of a policy through the Affordable Care Act.

Disability insurance is another common benefit offered by employers. It is usually, although not always, offered as a short-term policy rather than a long-term policy. Again, the policy available through your employer is probably less expensive than a privately purchased plan. Disability insurance is often overlooked, but as we talked about earlier, it is critically important. Remember that if your employer pays the premium for the insurance policy, the benefit is taxable to you if you receive it.

Life insurance is another common company fringe benefit. You should see how much, if any, is provided automatically by your employer. If you would like to purchase more for whatever reason, remember to do your research first.

Be sure also that you understand the type of insurance being offered by your employer and how the premiums might change in the future.

Other company benefits can be highly individualized, depending on the company or corporation. You might have a health savings account to cover medical expenses in tax-free dollars or your employer might pay some of your child-care costs or provide a long-term policy.

Other choices might help you implement your personal goals, such as a reimbursement of tuition costs for night school or an automatic contribution from your salary to your savings account. Just be sure you don't leave benefit money unused, and be sure to choose the benefits that will help you to best leverage and improve your financial situation—and your family's life.

And remember, if you are not sure which benefits those are, please ask.

That's why you have a financial planner.

Ashley: Right now, I feel like I just work for cash. I know I will have more options in the future.

 Michael: Because we were planning for children, I purchased extra insurance when I got my job, even though I didn't need all of it then. I didn't want to deal with trying to qualify for it later.

 Lisa: When I calculated the real value of my benefit package if I needed to use it, it was worth much more money than if I had just taken cash.

 James: When I retire, my company will let me keep some of my benefits, such as health insurance, but I will have to pay for them out of my own pocket. They will be more expensive than now, but the price is still reasonable, although I know that isn't true for every company.

• • • • •

WEEK 29 ACTIVITY

This week, I want you to look at the benefits package available to you from your employer. It's probably a large book that you received when you were first hired. If it has been a while, go to HR and get the latest edition.

Does your current benefit selection best meet your financial need, or would you want to make any changes? Before you decide to make any changes, be sure you will still qualify for the benefit that you want. Remember that if you reject a benefit when you are hired, you might have to go through an "underwriting," or qualification, process when you decide you want the benefit. Be careful that you choose your benefits through the lens of your overall financial plan.

· · · · ·

Ask Peggy

Question: Peggy, what is the single most important takeaway from this chapter?

Peggy: Sign up for any company benefits, like health insurance or life insurance, as soon as you are eligible to avoid underwriting issues if you sign up later.

· · · · ·

Notes

Use the following lines to jot down some notes about what you did this week. It will remind you of your progress.

_____

_____

_____

_____

_____

_____

_____

_____

_____

Peggy Doviak

_____

_____

_____

_____

_____

_____

_____

_____

_____

_____

_____

_____

_____

_____

Chapter 30

Retirement: When To Take Social Security

The College Professor Who Wanted To Work Forever

A professor at the local university loved her job. In fact, retiring early was almost unheard of in her department. The professor knew without a doubt that the earliest she would retire would be full retirement age, but she also knew that age was creeping up on her. Born in 1958, she was sixty years old. Full retirement age for her would not be sixty-five but almost sixty-seven years.

Not to worry—she thought she might well work into her seventies. Her parents had both died in their nineties, and she was going strong at sixty. However, she did worry about what to do with her Social Security benefit. She wanted to put off taking it as long as she could to continue to increase what her final monthly benefit would be.

A common question people ask me is when they should begin to take Social Security benefits. The answer is as individual as you are, because what is best for you depends on many factors in your life. That said, Social Security benefits grow at an 8 percent rate each year you delay benefits. But let's look at your choices as though they are limited to just three: taking Social Security at sixty-two, taking it at your full retirement age, or taking it at age seventy.

In fact, you can choose to take Social Security any time after you turn sixty-two. If you choose to start taking Social Security at sixty-two, you will receive about 75 percent of the benefit you would have received if you had waited until full retirement age.

If you delay taking Social Security to age seventy, you would receive approximately 132 percent of the benefit.

The *break-even* life expectancy between taking your Social Security at sixty-two versus your full retirement age is about seventy-seven.

This means that if you die before you are seventy-seven years old, you would have received more money by taking retirement at sixty-two; however, if you live longer than age seventy-seven, you would make more money by having delayed your benefit to full retirement age.

And remember: If you receive benefits before full retirement age, you are limited in the money you can earn.

However, the numbers aren't all you need to consider. There are also some questions you need to ask yourself:

Do you plan to continue to work?

If you are between the ages of sixty-two and the year that is considered your full retirement age, unless you limit your income to $15,720 per year ($1,310 per month), you will lose $1 in benefits for every $2 earned above the limit. In addition, you lose $1 in three during the year in which you reach full retirement age.

Because the amount you can earn changes each year, be prudent. Run the numbers for the year for which you are considering taking the early benefit. *Once you reach full retirement age, you can earn as much as you want without any reduction in benefits.* Remember that the money you go without for now will increase the benefit that you will receive once you reach full retirement age.

In 1999, the U.S. Social Security Administration began mailing annual benefit statements to workers age twenty-five and older, which provided critical information about your future retirement income based on what you were earning at the time.

In mid-2011, for the first time, the agency stopped the annual mailing as a cost-saving measure. However, in 2014 it resumed mailing paper statements to workers as they reached the ages of twenty-five, thirty, thirty-five, forty, forty-five, fifty, fifty-five, sixty, and older who were not receiving Social Security benefits or who did not have a registered online account. (The personal online registered accounts became available in May of 2012.)

In 2017, SSA posted on a blog that it would again stop mailing estimated benefit statements to most Americans. The SSA's new policy will be to mail statements only to people who are sixty or older who do not have an online account and who are not yet receiving Social Security benefits.

The statements are available in English and Spanish. For the latter, call 1-800-772-1213. Meanwhile, to keep up with your anticipated Social Security benefit, I recommend that you create an online Social Security account for yourself. Here's where to do that: https://www.ssa.gov/myaccount/.

When it comes to your Social Security benefits, however, the numbers aren't all you should consider. Here are some questions you need to ask yourself before you decide when you will start to take Social Security. Answer the questions as honestly and thoroughly as possible. If you can't answer the health questions, maybe you need to visit your doctor or talk to your elders about your family's medical history.

What is your family longevity history? If you come from a family that lives well into old age, postponing your benefits might make more sense than if your family members tend to die at a young age. Remember that delaying benefits results in higher monthly payments.

How is your health?

Even if your family longevity is poor, medical technology is changing rapidly, and people are surviving illnesses and conditions that were terminal just a decade ago. Preventive health measures, better nutrition, and the realization of the dangers of smoking or of a sedentary lifestyle have also increased the probability that you will have a long life, if you act on what we now know. If you are still working at full retirement age, consider delaying your benefits.

What are your cash flow needs? If your cash flow remains fine at full retirement age, it's likely because you are still working, so you might consider postponing your benefit until you are seventy. A major crisis facing today's seniors is health care expenses. Receiving a higher benefit later might make your retirement funding easier and provide additional resources to pay for health care or long-term care later.

Does your attitude about the future of the Social Security system impact your decision? This is a more important question than it might seem at first read. I know it actually impacts the behavior of some of my clients. Some take the position that they don't believe the system will be in place when they are truly elderly, so they want to get as much money out of the system as quickly as possible now.

Although I understand this reasoning—and certainly, I can't speak to the long-term viability of the system as we know it—I also know politicians like to be reelected, and allowing Social Security to fail would be political suicide, at least right now.

That said, there are no guarantees.

However, I would caution people not to allow their opinion of the system or their fear of the unknown to dictate their decision once they have answered all the other questions they need to ask themselves.

This is especially true if a larger, deferred Social Security benefit allows you to better meet your retirement cash flow needs. Your decision on when to take Social Security needs careful consideration. Interestingly, in the past, you could take Social Security early, and if you decided to defer the benefit at a later date, you just returned the money and delayed the benefit again. Of course, in practice, that almost never happened.

Nonetheless, the rules recently changed, and now you have a limited period of time immediately after making your decision to take an early benefit. Once that time passes, you must continue to take the reduced benefit for the rest of your life. Your decision becomes final. That is why it makes sense to spend some time now so you can make the decision that is best for you.

· · · · ·

Ashley: I am just so glad that I finally have a job that pays into Social Security. It's not in my field, but at least I'm earning something toward my eventual retirement.

Michael: I signed up for a personal registered Social Security account. My benefit at full retirement age will probably be higher than I think if I continue to earn more money throughout my career.

Lisa: I had no idea that I would lose so much of my Social Security benefit if I took it early and then continued to work some more. I might need to rethink my plans.

James: I have to decide whether to start taking benefits now or when I'm seventy. As long as I'm working, I'm tempted to defer payments as long as I can to receive the higher benefit later.

Peggy Doviak

. . . . .

WEEK 30 ACTIVITY

This week, I would like you to find a copy of your last Social Security benefits statement. If you aren't receiving them in paper form, you can register at www.ssa.gov to see the statement online. Once you find it, look not only at your benefits page but also at the page that lists the quarters that are counting toward your benefit. The IRS bases your benefit off your highest-earning forty quarters of pay. If you are young or have had a period of time in which you were underemployed, you might be able to replace the lower-earning quarters with higher-earning quarters. That could raise your overall benefit.

Before you decide on a retirement date, look at the difference in taking the benefits at different times, and remember that if you choose to take the benefit earlier than full retirement age, you can't also earn a large income. Your analysis will probably reveal whether you can take early retirement.

Finally, some people choose to receive income in a way that minimizes Social Security withholding through contract work or decisions made if you are a business owner. If you choose to do that, remember that those decisions will impact your benefit when you retire.

Sometimes the money that is saved today isn't worth the money that you will lose in the future.

. . . . .

Ask Peggy

Question: Peggy, what is the single most important takeaway from this chapter?

Peggy: The decision on when you should take Social Security benefits depends on many circumstances; however, each year you delay benefits, the amount grows by approximately 8 percent.

210

Notes

Use the following lines to jot down some notes about what you did this week. When you look back on it later, it will remind you of all the progress you've made.

_____

_____

_____

_____

_____

_____

_____

_____

_____

_____

_____

_____

_____

_____

_____

_____

_____

_____

_____

_____

_____

_____

_____

_____

_____

_____

_____

Chapter 31

Retirement: Medicare Pitfalls

The Man Who Wanted To Save a Dime but Spent a Dollar

A former businessman was a few years older than his wife. He had retired at age sixty-five, but his wife had a few years more to work. He knew he could take his Medicare benefit and pay the Part B premium, but it was cheaper for him to stay on his wife's insurance, so he did. Once she was ready to retire, he planned to go onto Medicare, knowing that as long as he had continuous insurance coverage, his premiums would be reasonable.

Then unexpectedly, his wife lost her job in a corporate downsizing. Almost immediately, she found another job and put him on her insurance again; however, he had been without any insurance for about a month. When he eventually applied for Medicare, he was horrified at the monthly premium cost—all because of the penalty for his not having had continuous medical-insurance coverage.

I know the details of all your Medicare benefits can be tedious, but I have seen two major errors that too many people make when it comes to Medicare benefits, and I want to discuss them in this chapter.

The foundation of *Medicare Part A* is a benefit you receive at the age of sixty-five, and at that time, you do not need to pay any additional money for it. Part A basically covers hospitalization.

Medicare Part B requires a reasonable premium when you turn sixty-five, and it basically covers physician costs.

Medicare Part D also has a premium that kicks in when you are sixty-five; it provides prescription drug coverage.

Medicare C, much less common, is a hybrid plan that doesn't so much provide benefits as it offers a private insurance option, and it also carries a premium.

On top of the Medicare benefits, many people purchase a Medicare supplement insurance policy to increase the level of benefits and/or decrease the out-of-pocket expenses that come with using your Medicare coverage.

Although this might seem pretty straightforward, a few traps lurk that you might not foresee. The first major error I have seen people make involves how they handle insurance if they work past the age of sixty-five.

Although Medicare is an automatic benefit at sixty-five, the Medicare system does not require you to purchase Parts B and D if you have coverage from your employer and you are still working. You might also have a working spouse and have coverage through that person's benefit package. Because no one wants to pay an unnecessary bill, people in this situation often choose to defer the B and D coverage offered by Medicare. The problem is what if something changes—your insured spouse loses a job or a company buys your spouse's company and changes the benefits package? Suddenly that outside coverage does not exist, and you will now face a major financial penalty when you do enroll in Parts B and D.

Always be careful to maintain continual coverage until you claim Medicare after age sixty-five.

You might consider even carrying double coverage for a few months if you are afraid you might end up with a gap—

and follow the strategies outlined below. Although people caught in this trap of a gap in coverage are extremely angry, and rightly so, don't blame the system. The whole concept of insurance only works if more money is paid in premiums than is paid in benefits.

If people were allowed to defer paying into Medicare until they were older than sixty-five or decided they needed the benefit, they would likely pay the premium about the time their medical bills began to increase because of their age or ailments. That would sink the Medicare system.

How do you avoid making such a mistake? You make sure you know the deadlines for Medicare enrollment. If there's even a chance you'll lose your outside insurance before the next Medicare enrollment period, pay the premiums to both insurance companies for the remainder of that year.

Yes, you will pay a little extra, but you will save thousands of dollars by not having to pay the Medicare uninsured penalty. Should something happen unexpectedly, you can maintain your insurance from the Consolidated Omnibus Budget Reconciliation Act, or COBRA, available from your employer after you separate from service until you are eligible to enroll in Medicare.

The legal definition of COBRA is complicated, but basically, it refers to the responsibility of most employers to make health insurance available to you and your dependents for a period of time after you are no longer employed by them. Of course, you have to pay for the insurance. And, yes, COBRA is expensive, but again, money well spent.

The second mistake I see people make concerns Medicare supplemental insurance policies. You've seen the ads describing different policies that are sold by a letter name. Don't confuse them with Medicare Part A, B, or D; both types of insurance classify themselves through letters of the alphabet.

Different Medicare supplemental policies, designated by different letters, cover different benefits, and you need to choose the one that meets your need. However, here's the catch—all Medicare supplement insurance plans sold with the same letter name have *exactly the same benefit*, regardless of who is selling the policy.

Therefore, you should choose a reputable company, but you should also shop these policies by price. No single carrier offers something different than any other carrier as long as you buy an equivalent policy. This allows you to choose a policy for price but also from the company you most trust.

Another error I see people make concerns their understanding of the benefits provided by Medicare supplemental policies. Medicare supplemental policies do *exactly* what they say—they *supplement* Medicare. They don't typically offer a benefit that Medicare refuses to cover, at least at the time of this writing. As a result, don't assume that you have a completely additional set of benefits in your Medicare supplement insurance policy when it comes to your health care coverage. You don't.

Most important, you need to know that none of these policies offers chronic, long-term-care solutions. To meet that need, you have to purchase a long-term-care policy or make other arrangements. It might not be perfect, but Medicare remains a great benefit that helps millions of senior citizens cover their health care costs efficiently.

$$\cdots$$

 Ashley: I like the idea that senior citizens can get assistance with their health care.

 Michael: My parents have talked about traditional Medicare benefits helping with long-term-care costs. I need to let them know that's not something Medicare does. We'll need to look into additional insurance for that.

Lisa: Medicare supplemental policies are so confusing. I tried to help my mother enroll in one, but I didn't know that all plans with the same letter name had the same benefits. That would have made it so much easier to pick one.

James: I'm planning to be on my employer's insurance and Medicare simultaneously for a short period of time. I would rather pay a little more in premiums than have a gap in coverage. Still, I need to keep a watchful eye on the timing as my retirement nears.

· · · · ·

WEEK 31 ACTIVITY

This week, you'll take some action or file information away for future use. If you are nearing retirement, take steps to ensure you have no gap in benefits if you are older than sixty-five. This is worth a conversation with your company's human resources department and some checking with the Medicare office. You might need to maintain double coverage for a short time to ensure you don't have a gap.

Study your Medicare supplement insurance choices carefully to be sure the plan you select has the benefits you need. Remember each plan with the same letter name should have the same benefits package, regardless of the carrier.

Medicare provides long-term-care coverage only for short, specific periods of time. Chronic long-term-care needs are not met by Medicare. You will need to make other arrangements for that.

Some other needs common to seniors are not covered by basic Medicare coverages. And because insurance only works if more people don't need the benefit than do, items such as glasses and hearing aids might not be covered. If you don't have insurance coverage for those items, you might want to look at adding such coverage after you've checked your budget to ensure that you can afford it.

· · · · ·

Ask Peggy

Question: Peggy, what is the single most important takeaway from this chapter?

Peggy: Although you do not have to begin paying Medicare premiums at sixty-five if you are covered by your own insurance policy or your spouse's, be certain not to have a gap in coverage, or your Medicare premiums will become much more expensive when you go to use them.

· · · · ·

Notes

_____

_____

_____

_____

_____

_____

_____

Chapter 32

Retirement: Early IRA Payments

The Technology Whiz Who Got Greedy

A young man entered the technology field at exactly the right time. Tech stocks were booming, and his start-up company went public. Almost overnight, he was a multimillionaire, and even better, when the next tech bust came, his company didn't go under.

In fact, it held up quite well.

By the time he was fifty years old, he had an impressive individual retirement account balance. His financial adviser explained some of the funds the man had in his IRA could be withdrawn early through a technique called 72(t). However, if he began to take early payments, he would need to continue to take them until he turned fifty-nine-and-a-half.

Excitedly, the tech whiz made the commitment, and almost immediately afterward, disaster struck. The key component to the tech device made by his company was found to emit high levels of radiation if the gadget was damaged. Fears of cancer caused the company's stock to plummet in value. The tech whiz watched in horror each year as the value of his company and his IRA dwindled away.

How to withdraw money early from your IRA is a pitch peddled at seminars and at gatherings of people who don't want to wait until they are fifty-nine-and-a-half to access their IRA money without penalty. This can sound especially seductive if you are retiring at fifty-five—maybe because you want to or maybe not—and a financial adviser generously offers to help you roll over your 401(k) into an IRA so you can begin to take distributions immediately without suffering the 10 percent early withdrawal penalty.

The downside is that most people cannot afford to access their IRAs early, because it will negatively impact their retirement cash flow too much. As you will recall, an early-distribution penalty is typically involved.

There is a work-around for that situation, but before you get too excited about it, you need to understand all the pros and cons and make sure it's not only what you want but is also the prudent thing to do in your situation.

The ability to establish substantially equal periodic payments, or SEPP, is based on IRS code section 72(t). Setting up a SEPP can allow you to access funds in your IRA at any age without penalty, but the rules are specific and strict.

Once you begin to take early payments, you must maintain doing so for five years or until you are fifty-nine-and-a-half, whichever is longer. That means if you begin to take early payouts at fifty-eight, you must continue to take them until you are sixty-three. And if you start at the age of forty, you must take distributions for more than nineteen years! That's a long commitment—and it could make a big dent in what kind of funds you have available in retirement.

If you decide to take early withdrawals, you will be given three formulas to calculate the amount of the SEPP: a formula based on the IRS table for required minimum distributions (RMDs), a formula based on an amortization schedule similar to how mortgage payments are calculated, and a formula based on an annuitization schedule similar to how annuity payments are structured. Only the RMD method changes the amount of annual distribution, based on your account balance. If you select the amortization or annuitization methods, the dollar amount is fixed. Because the formulas can be complicated, be sure you understand the process you are considering, and remember that if you are only in your thirties or forties, you are agreeing to a potentially long-term withdrawal system. You can, however, change your distribution methodology to RMD.

The market declines that impact your investment portfolio will not impact how much you have to take out of your IRA unless you have chosen the RMD method. It's also possible that you could have a required distribution schedule that exceeds your account balance. The IRS will allow you to fix this with a one-time change to the RMD method of calculating. However, even then, you must take distributions until the account balance is depleted. In the wrong stock-market environment, the results could be disastrous.

Once the calculation method is established, you can't take additional money from the account. Should you have another emergency that requires funds, the IRA will no longer be an available source of funds. Yes, it's not a great planning strategy to have to pay a 10 percent penalty plus taxes just so you can use your IRA for an emergency. But sometimes life requires that we adjust our plans.

If you don't have enough money to pay an unexpected bill and you don't have an emergency fund, the IRA is a readily available source of funds and is relatively easy to access. I'm just asking you not to let the ease overshadow the long-term cost. Take the time to calculate all the related costs. The total cost might surprise you. It might also make another option such as obtaining a loan or getting the money in another way a better option.

If you break the rules governing 72(t), you are subject to an IRS penalty on all the payments, even the ones you took correctly. This subjects you to the 10 percent early distribution penalty, interest, and penalties. The tax consequences are severe, and it's easy to make a mistake in implementing a 72(t) distribution.

Before you even consider taking substantially equal periodic payments, ask yourself why you want to begin to take distributions so early. Talk to your accountant and financial planner before you sign the documents. If you have calculated your retirement savings need, it is highly unlikely that you used a retirement age in your fifties. You might derail your entire retirement plan by getting in a hurry to take distributions.

After you retire, a better way to take funds between the age of fifty-five and fifty-nine-and-a-half is to leave some money in your 401(k). That money is yours to take once you are retired from your company, and it does not impose the 10 percent penalty as your IRA would.

Either method involves paying taxes, so there is little motivation to create a SEPP distribution schedule. Sometimes, the salesperson who creates the pitch is the one who will benefit the most from these plans.

· · · · ·

 Ashley: I'd have to be a gazillionaire before I would even consider doing something like a SEPP. The market is too volatile.

 Michael: If I've saved enough to retire at a reasonable age, I'm going to consider my financial plan successful.

 Lisa: I remember how many dot-com millionaires took their IRAs early. All it took was one market meltdown to destroy their financial world.

James. One financial adviser tried to convince me to take a 72(t) distribution when I was in my early fifties. I'm so glad I said no. It shows the importance of choosing the right financial adviser.

. . . . .

WEEK 32 ACTIVITY

The way to avoid having to take a 72(t) distribution is by doing good financial planning in advance.

In general, I haven't found such a distribution to be a good decision for most people, but you might be the exception to that.

If you are considering a 72(t) distribution, you need to ask yourself a few questions:

Why do you need the money early?

Could you review your budget and find funds elsewhere?

If you're worried about the stock market and that is the reason for your early distribution, have you looked at other available investments in your IRA, even including a money market that is outside market risk unless your account is very large?

If you opt for a 72(t), do you fully understand the terms, your responsibilities, and the risk?

How will you meet your retirement need once you are full retirement age?

. . . . .

Ask Peggy

Question: Peggy, what is the single most important takeaway from this chapter?

Peggy: Substantially equal period payments allow you to access your IRA funds early without penalty, but it is a complicated strategy, and distributions must be taken until age fifty-nine-and-a-half or five years, whichever is longer.

Notes

Use the following lines to jot down some notes about what you did this week.

Chapter 33

Retirement: Required Minimum Distributions

*The Client Who Didn't Know
All Good Things Come to an End*

An older woman was part of her family's business, and when the company created a retirement plan, it rightfully included her, even though she was seventy-five years old. Because the business was small, the financial adviser suggested a SIMPLE IRA for the retirement plan, and soon everyone was funding one. Because it was a company plan, the adviser assumed he didn't need to advise the client to take distributions since she was a minority owner. Ten years later, when a financial planner looked at the plan, he asked whether the woman was taking the required minimum distributions. When she said no, the planner panicked. She owed ten years of mandatory RMDs that she had not taken, along with a 50 percent penalty!

Even great things come to an end. The IRS is willing to let us defer taxation on money that we save for retirement, but it won't let us escape taxes on that money forever.

At some point, we must begin to pay required minimum distributions or RMDs. Almost all retirement savings accounts follow this requirement, including all IRAs except

Roths. Should the owner of the account fail to take the annual distributions, the IRS will levy a penalty equal to 50 percent of the amount that should have been taken.

It's important to note that you have considerable time before you need to take an RMD. Even if you retire early, you are not required to take a distribution from your company's retirement plan until you are seventy-and-a-half.

Qualified retirement plans that include 401(k), 401(a), 403(b), and other plans are not based on individual retirement accounts, so IRA distribution rules don't apply.

If you are still working at the age of seventy-and-a-half and you aren't a business owner, you don't have to take a distribution from a qualified plan until you actually retire—even if that is when you turn 100. If you are the business owner, the IRS suspects that you might never retire, so you have to take distributions at seventy-and-a-half even if you are still working.

IRAs are different. You have to take a distribution from a taxable IRA when you're seventy-and-a-half whether or not you are working, whether you are an employee or the owner.

If your company's retirement plan is based on an IRA, say a SEP or a SIMPLE, you also begin to take distributions at seventy-and-a-half even if you are still working and contributions are being made on your behalf. If you're in that situation, you receive the contribution from your employer, and you take the distribution. So how do you know how much you need to take? First you find your account balance on December 31 at the end of the year in which you turn seventy-and-a-half. Then go to www.irs.gov and look up Publication 590.

There are three IRS tables that provide formulas for calculating your RMD, depending on the type of IRA, but it might be easier to have your financial planner calculate it for you. At the end of Publication 590, you'll find the Uniform Table, which will provide you with a divisor factor. Take your account balance and divide by the number that corresponds with your age. That dollar amount is the amount of distribution that you must take. The RMDs can be consolidated for IRA accounts and taken from one account, but if you also have qualified retirement plans, you must calculate the amount you should receive and take it from each plan.

If there is a large age difference between you and your spouse, you might need to use the Joint Life and Last Survivor table instead. That table allows you to take a smaller RMD so that there is more remaining for the surviving spouse. If it is your IRA, don't use the Single Life table, even if you are single. That table is for inherited IRAs. Inherited IRAs require RMDs as well.

Inherited IRAs are handled differently depending on whether it was your spouse's IRA or, say, your father's or grandfather's. If the money belonged to your spouse, you have more options than if you are a non-spouse beneficiary. Talk to your financial planner to be sure you take enough distribution each year from each account that requires it.

You have some flexibility on the date of your first distribution. When you take your first RMD, you could wait until April 1 of the year after you turn seventy-and-a-half, but then you would owe two RMDs that year. The first one must be requested by April 1, accounting for the distribution you deferred from the previous year. The second distribution, due by December 31, meets the requirement for the one that you always needed to take that year.

Depending on the size of the IRA, it's theoretically possible that RMDs could change your tax bracket, so talk to your CPA before you decide to wait until the very last possible minute.

Roth IRAs don't have RMDs unless they are inherited. Roth 401(k) plans do. Roth IRA distributions also don't have tax due if they have been open for five years and you're at least fifty-nine-and-a-half. They also don't have required minimum distributions until they are inherited, so you can allow that account to remain invested and, it is hoped, grow if you have no need for the funds. Conversely, Roth accounts in a qualified plan require RMDs at seventy-and-a-half if you're retired. However, you can always roll the Roth account to a Roth IRA and avoid the RMD.

It's very important to understand and take your required minimum distributions.

All good things come to an end, and if you don't take the distribution, the IRS levies a 50 percent penalty against the amount you were supposed to take. And as always, it is a good idea to check with your CERTIFIED FINANCIAL PLANNER^{TM} practitioner and tax professional to be sure that you are doing everything correctly.

· · · · ·

Ashley: I enjoyed the chapters on cash flow more than this, but I know it's important. I'm going to take a break and then read it over once more. I've come this far. I'm not letting one chapter derail me.

Michael: I have my spouse as my beneficiary to all my retirement accounts. It's good to know that she has options on her distributions. We'll talk to our financial planner about it.

Lisa: When I turn fifty-nine-and-a-half, our company's HR coordinator says my Roth IRA will be available for tax-free distributions. However, I don't plan to take any until I need funds after I'm retired.

James: I'm close to needing to take RMDs. I was surprised to see how small of a percentage the IRS made me take each year.

· · · · ·

WEEK 33 ACTIVITY

This week, I want you to check the RMD treatment of all your retirement money.

One of the easiest mistakes to make involves forgetting to take a distribution from a SEP or SIMPLE if you are still working for the company. Ideally, your CPA or financial planner should remind you, but you don't want to miss a deadline because they forgot. You should also talk to anyone who stands to inherit money from you. Make sure that they understand the rules as well.

It will make life better for both of you.

· · · · ·

Ask Peggy

Question: Peggy, what is the single most important takeaway from this chapter?

Peggy: If you fail to take the required minimum distributions from your retirement accounts accurately and on time, the penalty is 50 percent of the untaken distribution amount.

· · · · ·

Notes

_____

_____

_____

_____

· · · · ·

Ask Peggy

 Ashley: Peggy, is it okay for me just to use a rule of thumb for my retirement savings because I am so young?

Peggy: Yes, it is, Ashley. In your twenties, you don't know what your spending habits will be in the future. In fact, just starting to save for your retirement in your twenties is a great thing! I'm proud of you. I would encourage you to try to save as much as you can, taking your current spending as the rule of thumb to use. I would hate for you to assume 80 percent of your current spending because I'm almost sure that is too low.

 Michael: Peggy, I inherited an IRA. What's the best thing to do with the distributions I have to take each year?

Peggy: Michael, I would encourage you to do something intentional with that money and not just put it in your pocket and watch it disappear. You could use that money to offset income that you could defer into a retirement plan. Technically, RMDs can't be used to fund an IRA, but the distribution could be used to pay your living expenses, freeing up income to put into the IRA. You could also set it aside to pay for holiday gifts or a family vacation.

 Lisa: Peggy, you said earlier you think Social Security will be there as a benefit. Do you think I can count on it?

Peggy: Lisa, nothing is certain. But I would be surprised, especially since you are already in your fifties, if your Social Security benefit wasn't there for you. It is possible that this could change—the full retirement age could be raised, or more of our income could be taxed. But I do believe that politicians will shore it up instead of allowing it to fail—if only because they don't want their offices mobbed with tens of thousands of angry senior citizens. Remember older Americans vote in high numbers, and they have been paying into Social Security for decades!

James: Peggy, as I think about it, I realize my three children are a wide range of ages. How can I best help them with the amount of required minimum distribution they will need to take?

Peggy: James, when you have one IRA, the required minimum distribution is determined by the age of your oldest beneficiary. So if you have beneficiaries with large age differences, the younger ones will have to take distributions more quickly than they might want after they inherit your account. If the account is large enough for it to make sense, you might divide one IRA into three IRAs and have one beneficiary for each IRA. Just be careful not to create accounts that are subject to additional fees or less favorable treatment because they are too small.

Taxes

Chapter 34

Taxes: Income Tax

The CPA Who Thought He Was Going Broke

Let me state the obvious: Except for a very small minority of Americans genetically predisposed to creating or studying the tax code with the joy most of us save for our hobbies, Americans do not particularly like doing their taxes.

Most people appreciate what our taxes make possible in our country and our communities—public schools, libraries, and universities; our national transportation system and law-enforcement agencies; food, drug, and safety programs; clean water and sanitation systems; our military, justice, and diplomatic service; and our social net of housing, education, and health services, among other things.

But they rarely relish preparing and filing taxes.

Taxes overwhelm most people, even those who study them and have a scholar's familiarity with the tax code. My hope is after reading this book, you will find that if you combine what you learn in these pages with the organizational efforts you've been making over the past few weeks as part of your 52-week journey to prosperity, doing your taxes this year will be the easiest it has ever been.

But let's start with a cautionary tale. An accountant was trying to calculate how much income tax he owed for the year. He had earned some extra money on the side, and he wondered what impact that would have on his tax liability. To determine how much he would owe, he multiplied the total income he had earned for the year by 28 percent, his "nominal" tax bracket. He was horrified to discover that he had massively underpaid his income taxes. He owed a huge tax liability! Although he had helped many clients in the same situation, it took him a couple of hours to figure out where he had gone wrong.

Basically, income tax is the tax that you pay on money that you have earned. Money that you earn working a job will always be subject to income tax.

Passive income that you receive from, say, renting a room out in your home or from profits from a stock portfolio, however, might be subject to income tax or capital gains tax, depending on the situation.

You might never have to worry about capital gains tax, but most of us, in addition to income tax, will pay sales tax—a flat tax that is levied on goods and, occasionally, services we purchase.

The final two types of taxes—gift tax and estate tax—will usually come into play only a few times in your life, if at all. However, the one tax you're almost certain to face in your lifetime is income tax.

Income tax is calculated using a progressive or graduated system. This means people who earn less money pay a lower rate of tax. For 2018, there will be seven brackets. The lowest bracket starts at 10 percent and the highest tax bracket tops out at 37 percent. To pay the highest rate, you will have to have earned more than $500,000 if you are single and more than $600,000 if married.

You might be wondering why isn't the marriage bracket $1 million for a married couple? That is what in the tax code is casually called a "marriage penalty," in which a couple filing jointly pays more than if they filed separately. The tax code also has "marriage bonuses"—more of them actually than penalties—in which a couple pays less together than they would alone.

Marriage penalties and bonuses are a result of the U.S. tax code simultaneously trying to satisfy three conflicting goals: equal treatment of married couples, equal treatment of married and unmarried couples, and progressive taxation.

In 2018, some of this will change, at least for couples making less than $300,000, but one place you will still see the "marriage penalty" is in the tax brackets themselves.

So what is a tax bracket? Think about a tax bracket as a bucket, with the tax brackets like a row of buckets lined up from smallest to largest. You start with the smallest bucket, the 10 percent bucket. You fill it up with the first $9,525 of your $100,000 salary if you are single, $19,050 if you're married filing jointly.

If you earned more than that, you move to the second bracket, the 12 percent bucket. You will put in it your earnings from $9,526 to $38,700 if you're a single filer, $19,051 to $77,400 if you're married and filing jointly. That $29,174 (single) or $58,349 (married filing jointly) will be taxed at 12 percent. And so it goes as you move up the rest of the remaining five buckets. Even if the percentages for the brackets change or if brackets are added or eliminated, the process remains the same.

The last percentage rate of the last dollar you earn—i.e. for the bucket holding your last dollar—is called your "nominal bracket." That rate is the rate at which any additional money you earn is taxed at, until you fill that bucket.

Sometimes when people get a raise, they see that it has moved them into a new tax bracket, and they panic. Like our frantic accountant, they mistakenly multiply their earnings by their nominal amount, the highest rate or biggest bucket they filled, to see what they will owe at the end of the year. However, the number arrived at in that way will actually end up being too high.

Remember that you fill each tax bracket successively until you have accounted for all your income. And many other things impact your tax liability besides what you make.

Your filing status will impact practically every number in the tax code, and I want to quickly mention one of them, "married filing separately," because many people don't understand it.

Remember how we talked about filling the tax brackets earlier? Well, if you and your spouse filed your earned income separately, you would each find yourself in a lower tax bracket, because separately, you don't make as much money as when you add your two incomes together. Suddenly you're very clever, and you have outsmarted the IRS!

Not so fast. Yes, you could try that strategy; it's called "married filing separately." However, the IRS is way ahead of you—remember that our tax code was written by people who love numbers and percentages and understand how they work in concert. Basically, if you try this strategy, you will be punished by the IRS in every other deduction use in your filing. Married filing separately rarely saves as much in taxes as it loses in deductions and credits.

Remember that 37 percent bracket for if you are single and earning more than $500,000? If you use married filing separately, that threshold number drops to $300,000. And the pain doesn't end there. Every other tax break is sharply limited. In fact, it is stunningly rare that a couple ends up paying less in taxes by filing separately. The moral of the story: Be sure you truly understand what you are doing before you try to get too clever with the IRS.

As you determine your tax liability, you and your family will automatically receive an exemption that effectively lowers your income total before you even begin to calculate your liability. The amount of that exemption depends on the number of family members in your household. You also get another deduction—either a standard deduction or an itemized deduction for certain expenses such as the interest paid on your home mortgage payments.

The standard deduction is easy; it's just a number provided by the IRS. The itemized deduction is calculated by your personal circumstances, including the loan interest you pay on your home mortgage. You might also find you're eligible for a tax credit just by meeting certain circumstances. Credits do tend, however, to be more available for those with lower income.

Be careful how you prepare your taxes. Typically, you have to file a return even if you don't owe any additional tax on top of what has already been taken out of your paycheck and submitted to the U.S. Treasury. If you don't, you could receive a failure-to-file penalty. Tax fraud is illegal and can be a felony. Some of the most famous criminals in the United States were ultimately arrested for tax fraud.

Yes, taxes are a serious business.

You cannot discharge tax liability through bankruptcy. Benjamin Franklin's observance that "in this world nothing can be said to be certain, except death and taxes" has endured since 1789 for a reason. And that is why I suggest you consult a CPA when doing your taxes, especially if there is anything complicated in your return or situation.

Why not have your financial planner do your taxes? Many financial planners do provide tax-planning guidance and education but rarely provide tax preparation. That is another reason to be sure you understand the scope of services that financial planners offer so they don't fail to meet your expectations.

And if you owe taxes, don't complain—at least not too much. Be grateful that you earned the amount of money necessary to cause such a liability. Most Americans would love to be in your shoes. I like to tell clients to be careful not to let a tax tail wag an income dog. Taxes are never 100 percent; you always make money from working.

Meanwhile, our taxes will continue to provide us with the services and security we have come to appreciate and expect in a civilized and modern country. Take every legal deduction, exemption, and credit you can. But once you have taken all that is available to you to reduce your tax liability, be grateful that you are prosperous enough to need to pay.

· · · · ·

Ashley: I always hated paying taxes, but maybe that's because I forgot all they make possible. I've read about countries with no clean water or sewage systems. I have to say: I want to do my part as a citizen.

Michael: I didn't know that my nominal bracket was my highest tax bracket. I never knew what "nominal bracket" meant before.

Lisa: I appreciate where my taxes go, but I need to take care of myself. I need to use a CPA to help me pay as little on my taxes as is legal.

James: I did think about trying to use the married-filing-separately classification once, but when I saw all the drawbacks, I realized my wife and I wouldn't save any money by doing that.

· · · · ·

WEEK 34 ACTIVITY
Your exercise this week will take longer than a week, but you will be glad you have done it. Every time you have any

type of taxable event during the year, put the receipt or document or document or data in a file folder or scan it to your computer or stick it in a shoebox! Even though the "shoebox of receipts" is the perpetual tax joke, the real joke is on you when you don't know where your documents are.

Vow to file on time, making your taxes a priority between January and April.

If you avoid doing your taxes because you owe money, change your withholding amounts. A large refund means you overpaid your taxes, but a small refund or zero balance is just the result of good tax planning.

· · · · ·

Ask Peggy

Question: Peggy, what is the single most important takeaway from this chapter?

Peggy: You fill income tax brackets like buckets, and the last bucket to be filled, which will be the highest percentage, is called your *nominal* bracket.

· · · · ·

Notes
Use the following lines to jot down some notes.

_____

_____

_____

_____

Peggy Doviak

_____

_____

_____

_____

_____

_____

_____

_____

_____

_____

_____

_____

_____

_____

Chapter 35

Taxes: Deductions and Credits

The Couple Who Wanted To Buy a House

A young couple was preparing to purchase a new home when they decided to ask their financial planner for clarification about how it would impact their taxes. The planner explained that they could take the interest they paid for their house loan off their taxes. They were amazed. That would significantly lower their annual tax liability.

Another financial planner overheard the couple and inquired, "You do know that won't lower your taxes by the amount of the interest? It lowers your taxable income by that much." The planner then went on to explain to the couple the difference between a tax deduction and a tax credit.

So do you want to report less income to the IRS or do you want directly to reduce your taxes? If you answered, "Yes, both, please," you are not alone. We would all like that. However, it doesn't work that way. So you need to know what deductions and credits do and how they differ.

Deductions lower your income. Tax deductions are deductions that the IRS lets us take as a result of expenses we have. We have our choice of taking either the standard deduction or itemizing our deductions. In either case, the total value of our deductions is subtracted from our adjusted gross income (AGI), the last number on the first page of your 1040 form. AGI is the basis we use when we calculate how much tax we owe. With a deduction, you will show less income than was reported on your W-2 or 1099, and that leads to lower taxes.

Tax credits are dollar-for-dollar reductions in taxes owed. They directly lower our tax liability. As a result, a credit is often preferable to a deduction. However, the IRS is aware of this, and so tax credits are usually given in smaller dollar amounts, and they have more restrictions on who can receive them. Sometimes you might make too much to receive a tax credit.

To make sure that you don't overlook a deduction or credit available to you, review your tax situation with your financial planner or accountant. You might well be eligible for something you're not taking. In the meantime, here are some important personal deductions and credits for you to review. It is not a complete list, and if you have a business, there are even more options. Descriptions of all of them are available on the IRS website, www.irs.gov.

Common personal deductions that lower your taxable income include:

Work-related deductions for the self-employed such as the cost of mileage for running errands for work, a home office, and business travel. The recent Tax Cuts and Jobs Act eliminated miscellaneous deductions, which included unreimbursed business expenses.

Investment deductions are allowed for some IRA contributions and other investment losses. Certain investment costs such as margin interest are also deductible.

Education deductions for student loan interest can lower the cost of higher education for you, your spouse, children, or step-children, but you must be liable for the loan.

Health care deductions are available if your medical bills typically exceed 7.5 percent of your adjusted gross income. This means for some of us that 92.5 percent of your AGI can be eliminated if your medical bills are high enough. This is especially useful if retirement assets need to be tapped to pay for medical bills.

Itemized deductions can include home mortgage interest, charitable contributions, and property tax. However, the recent Tax Cuts and Jobs Act also put limits on property tax deductions and state and local tax deductibility. Be sure to check to see if the changes impacted you.

Alimony paid might seem as if it should be a deduction, but the new tax law made it taxable to the payer. Alimony received is now tax free to the recipient.

Some of the earlier deductions mentioned may also fall into the itemized deduction section, including margin interest and health care.

Common personal tax credits that can provide a reduction in your taxes owed include:

Family credits for earned income, child and dependent care, and the child tax credit. These credits make it easier for families to pay for family expenses. Under the Affordable Care Act, a health insurance *premium tax credit* can offset all or part of your health insurance premiums for a plan purchased through one of the marketplaces. The income phaseout for this credit might be higher than you think. It's worth checking to see if you qualify.

Income and savings credits for most people with investment accounts. Credits for foreign tax paid might apply to you, as international mutual funds often use this credit. It can keep the fund from being subject to double taxation.

Education credits for lifetime learning help finance education beyond a traditional college experience. There is also an education credit for the first four years of college, the American opportunity credit, or AOTC.

Homeowner's credits for mortgage interest make home ownership more affordable for low-income taxpayers. The credit for alternative residential energy equipment allows homeowners to make utility-saving upgrades to their house. Low-income housing credits help offset the cost of rent.

Alternative motor vehicle credits are designed to encourage plug-in conversions and the purchases of electric vehicles and fuel-cell vehicles.

Tax relief in any form is welcome. Knowing the deductions available can help you make a better choice between itemizing or simply taking the basic deduction. And remember that some of the deductions are available even if you don't itemize. Although tax software can be useful to help you avoid missing these deductions and credits, often you have to know what you are reading before the software makes sense. Take some time to learn more about deductions and credits or work with a good CPA until you're comfortable on your own.

Just remember that you can't expect your CPA to be able to offer good tax-management strategies without understanding your financial situation. Consider making a written list of questions or matters unique to your financial or tax situation that you send in to the CPA well in advance of the tax deadline.

· · · · ·

 Ashley: I was so excited to learn that I could lower my health insurance premiums with the health care credit.

 Michael: My student loans are killers—sometimes I think I'll be paying on them forever. Being able to deduct the interest off my taxes, however, did lead to my getting a refund this year.

Lisa: I'm looking into the alternative-energy home-improvement credit—I bet the improvements would lower my electric bill, and if they shaved some dollars off my tax bill, so much the better.

James: Being able to use my retirement money to pay for long-term care in a way that is almost tax free will make our money stretch farther.

· · · · ·

WEEK 35 ACTIVITY

In this week's exercise, I want you to review deductions and credits with your tax professional. At the very least, review the list of deductions and credits provided on the IRS website, www.irs.gov. Be sure you aren't overlooking something that could save you a lot of money.

· · · · ·

Ask Peggy

Question: Peggy, what is the single most important takeaway from this chapter?

Peggy: The Tax Cuts and Jobs Act raised the standard deduction amount but eliminated or lowered many itemized deductions.

· · · · ·

Notes

_____

_____

_____

_____

_____

_____

_____

_____

_____

_____

_____

_____

_____

_____

_____

_____

Chapter 36

Taxes: What Is Capital Gains Tax?

The Millionaire Who Feared Paying Taxes

In his desire to pay less in taxes, a wealthy man refused to invest in anything other than his company's retirement plan. He kept the rest of his money in a savings account at a local bank, even though he wanted a nice retirement and wasn't sure he was saving enough to make that happen. He didn't want to invest his money because he feared owing taxes on it if he ever sold anything for a profit. His nominal tax bracket was more than 30 percent, and he didn't want to lose a third of his money in such a situation.

Fortunately, he shared this concern with his CPA, who reminded him that his investment growth wouldn't be taxed at his income-tax bracket if he held the investment for longer than a year. Instead, it would be taxed at the capital gains rate of 15 percent. The man was amazed by the low rate and how much lower his taxes would be than he had thought.

Taxes are baffling, and many of my clients are confused by the difference between income tax and capital gains tax. Understanding the difference between the two might save you some stress and provide you some effective strategies for lowering your own tax liability. Basically, income tax generally is tax paid on income you earn, whereas capital gains tax is tax paid on the sale of items you use or hold as an investment, such as selling collectible artwork or company stock or a building. Technically, this is "passive" income, or income you receive simply by holding or owning something.

Capital gains (or losses) are divided between short term and long term. A short-term capital gain is taxed at your current income-tax rate and levied on investments you have held less than a year. Long-term capital gains, assessed on investments you have held for longer than a year, is a flat rate that depends on your income-tax bracket and the type of asset you are selling.

If you are in the 10 or 15 percent tax bracket, you do not pay any capital gains tax. If you are in a higher bracket but earn less than $400,000, you owe a flat 15 percent capital gains tax on most standard investments. Those investments include stocks, bonds (the bond itself, not the interest), funds, and other similar items. If you earn more than $400,000 annually, depending on your filing status, you might owe a 20 percent flat capital gains tax on those same investments.

Other less typical types of investments have different tax rates. Taxable gains from Section 1202 on qualified small business stock that doesn't trade on the stock market has a maximum 28 percent tax rate. That kind of stock is most commonly held by small-business owners.

Gains on a collectible, such as the sale of coins, antiques, or art, is also taxed at a maximum 28 percent rate. Most investment real estate gains are taxed at a maximum 25 percent rate. Why are these rates higher?

The main reason is how difficult it is to determine that the gain is based on the true value of the asset. If you sell an asset for less than it is worth, you might show a lower profit and therefore less gain. Items such as small-business stock, collectibles, and real estate have usually provided the owner with more use, value, and pleasure than a stock and bond portfolio, and they are difficult to value as well. As a result, selling the asset for less than fair market value is more common. Selling assets for less than they are worth is also a common technique to pass assets between generations. The IRS is aware of all of this and wants to ensure they receive a fair tax percentage for such transactions.

Whether the capital gain is short term or long term, it is calculated the same way. You take the amount for which you sold the antique clock minus the amount you paid for it (the basis). The difference, or gain, is your capital gain, and it is the money that will be taxed. If you have money in a retirement account, it is not taxed when it is sold. Instead, it is taxed as a distribution when you withdraw it, and it is taxed as ordinary income.

Clients frequently worry that if we change investments in their IRA, we will trigger a tax. We won't. We trigger an income tax liability only if we take money out of the account. Selling one investment to purchase a different investment never triggers tax when that investment is inside a retirement account. It will, however, trigger a tax liability when the investment is inside of a nonretirement account.

Capital gains tax applies to taxable accounts. Because your capital gains rate is based on your income-tax bracket, if you expect to have a year in which you have lower income, it might also be the year to sell assets—be they your uncle's baseball collection you inherited or that property you've been wanting to unload—so you can take advantage of the lower capital gains rate.

What happens if you don't have a gain but a loss? Well, first you have to do something called "netting gains and losses," in which you calculate net short-term gains and losses and long-term gains and losses. Show both short-term gain and long-term gains, and you may pay short- and long-term gain. If one is a gain and one is a loss, you take the short-term/long-term gain/loss characteristic of the larger.

Say, if you have $300 in long-term gain and a $400 loss, that nets to a $100 loss. If you have a $300 long-term gain and a $200 loss, that nets to a $100 long-term gain.

Assume that once you have netted the gains and losses, you have a loss. You can offset any other capital gain with this loss, and if the loss exceeds all the gain, you can take an additional $3,000 of capital loss as a deduction on your taxes. If you have lost $3,000 more than your gain, you can carry forward that loss to future years. Even if you die, the loss is passed down to your heirs. Eventually, someone will get to deduct your loss.

It might be tempting, but do not let your taxes rule all of your investment decisions. Remember, capital gains and losses must be realized in order to have a tax treatment. That means that nothing happens until you sell an asset. Keep Grandma's Picasso, enjoy it, and watch it grow in value over the course of your life, and you will pay no taxes on that gain until the day you sell the painting.

On the other hand, holding a fund that has lost money in a taxable portfolio does not trigger any tax benefit either; conversely, unrealized gains don't create tax liability.

There are worse things than paying capital gains tax. Think of it as confirmation that your investment strategy worked.

· · · · ·

 Ashley: I didn't know that capital gains tax was different from income taxes—and often so much lower!

 Michael: Netting gains and losses gives me some idea on what I should look for if I want to harvest some investing gains.

Lisa: I knew I could change investments in my 401(k) but not that IRA investments don't generate taxes when I sell them.

James: I've lived long enough to have seen family heirlooms grow in value. It's nice that I don't have to worry about paying taxes on what they are worth now, unless and until I sell them.

· · · · ·

WEEK 36 ACTIVITY

This week, I want you to inventory your investments. Remember that retirement assets are not subject to capital gains tax. Determine the tax rates of your nonretirement assets. Keep these rates in mind, along with the net gains and losses, when you want to make investment changes.

· · · · ·

Ask Peggy

Question: Peggy, what is the single most important takeaway from this chapter?

Peggy: Capital gains tax is levied on investments at different rates, depending on the kind of investment and the length of time it is held.

· · · · ·

Notes

_____

_____

Chapter 37

Taxes: Inheritances

The Aunt Who Made Great Decisions

Although she had never earned a large salary, an elderly schoolteacher had managed to invest a little money during most of her working career. She had invested in products she knew and had collected a selection of major brand-name stocks. She did this regularly for fifty years. She had had the occasional setback as her portfolio was not well diversified, but overall, her choices had been great, and she had massive gains in her holdings.

She hoped to leave the investment portfolio to her nieces and nephews, but she didn't want them to pay a lot of taxes on the gift. As a result, she wasn't sure whether she should give them the portfolio while she was alive or wait to make it part of her estate after she died.

After a loved one dies, people often come to me with questions, and one of the most common fears is that they will have to pay estate tax on the money they have just inherited. Certainly, inheritances are received that are subject to estate tax, but most of the people who come to my office have nothing to worry about. The federal estate tax is owed only if someone inherits more than $10 million. And even then, the estate pays the tax, not the recipient of the money or assets.

If an estate is more than $10 million, the estate tax can take a sizable bite out of it. If you have assets over this limit, you need to see an estate attorney immediately about setting up a trust which can provide a way to lower your estate-tax liability.

Please do not go out and buy a whole-life insurance policy in your name to pay the estate-tax bill that your heirs will face. It's unlikely that you will need to purchase life insurance to pay estate tax. If you do, it should be purchased only after you have lowered your liability as much as possible through estate planning. And if you and your financial planner decide you should buy some life insurance, it probably shouldn't be in your name.

Even before the federal estate tax exemption went from $5.49 million to $10 million, 99.8 percent of estates owed no estate-tax bill in any given year, according to the Joint Committee on Taxation. Only the wealthiest .2 percent of Americans owed any estate tax. With the exemption doubled, experts anticipate only 1,700 estates in 2018 will owe federal estate tax.

A much more common event for most people when they inherit money is determining other types of taxability, and that depends on the characteristics of the inheritance.

If an account was taxable to the original owner, it will also be taxable to the person who inherits it. However, the tax code has a nice feature called a "step up in basis." That means the assets in the deceased's account revalue as of the date of death of the original owner. That price then becomes the basis for the person who inherits the account and later sells the asset. The capital gain becomes the difference in value from the date of death to the date of sale—instead of the date the deceased bought the asset.

One odd wrinkle to this is the "alternate valuation date." This rule says the estate can be valued either as of the date of death or exactly six months later. If the latter is chosen, the entire estate must take that date. Most of the time, this is more trouble than it is worth; however, if part of the estate appreciates dramatically in the six months after the money is inherited, it might be worth considering. Keep in mind that this is income received in a taxable account and/or the sale of investments in the taxable account that are subject to tax, not simply receiving the taxable account, assuming the estate doesn't owe tax.

Inherited retirement accounts remain taxable to the beneficiary. If the inherited account was funded in pretax dollars and if it is distributed entirely to the beneficiary, then all the money is taxable at the inheritor's income-tax bracket. However, it does not need to be distributed all at once.

Typically, the account will roll into an inherited IRA that can continue to be treated like an IRA if it is inherited by a spouse, but that requires required minimum distributions, if it is inherited by anyone else. The tax treatment and distribution rules of inherited retirement accounts can be tricky, and you should consult with a CPA or CERTIFIED FINANCIAL PLANNER™ practitioner to make sure you are taking enough distributions.

If the inheritance involves an annuity and the annuity has been funded with pretax dollars, usually as a retirement account, distributions are taxable to the inheritor. Retirement annuities are typically called "qualified" annuities. If the annuity was funded in after-tax dollars as a "nonqualified annuity," the distributions are a combination of growth and basis, and the growth portion of distributions is taxed at your income-tax rate.

Taxes on inherited assets can be a little tricky, but most of the time, they are not as cumbersome as people fear they will be. Careful planning while you are alive can help you make the tax liability and entire process easier for your heirs. Conversations with them can help both of you feel less apprehensive about what the future might hold and what will be due when.

· · · · ·

 Ashley: I'm ready for another chapter that applies to me!

 Michael: When I inherited that stock from my grandfather, I got to set its basis on the day I inherited it. I still own it, but that saved me a lot of potential tax liability.

 Lisa: I have never understood the taxability of annuities. This makes it clearer.

 James: We're keeping assets with more gain and giving our children items today that don't have as much tax consequence—and we're being careful to keep under the gift limit of $15,000.

· · · · ·

WEEK 37 ACTIVITY

In this week's exercise, I want you to look at your assets and consider the tax consequences if they were to be inherited by someone.

Without putting your financial plan in jeopardy, you might consider minimizing the tax consequences for heirs as much as possible.

If you have a taxable, highly appreciated asset, it might make sense to leave it in your estate, allowing your beneficiaries to receive the benefit of that step-up in basis.

Ask Peggy

Question: Peggy, what is the single most important takeaway from this chapter?

Peggy: Estate tax is paid by the estate, not the recipient, and the limits are high enough that many people will never have any tax liability.

· · · · ·

Notes

Use the following lines to jot down some notes about what you did this week. When you look at the book later, it will remind you of your progress.

_____

_____

_____

_____

_____

_____

_____

_____

Peggy Doviak

_____

_____

_____

_____

_____

_____

_____

_____

_____

_____

_____

_____

_____

_____

_____

Chapter 38

Taxes: Selling your Home, Sweet Home

The Couple Who Were Afraid to Downsize

After they had raised three great kids in a large home with a huge, grassy backyard, two married empty nesters wanted to downsize. They were tired of washing dirty windows, mowing, and paying property taxes on rooms that were never used. However, they were also afraid to sell their home. They had bought the house right before the birth of their first child, and he was now in his thirties with children of his own.

Even with fluctuations in the real estate market, their home had appreciated in value, and they didn't want to have to buy a new house that was as expensive as what they would be selling.

They were also afraid of the tax consequences of the gain they would recognize, especially if they pocketed the cash and did not put it into more property right away. Two of the most common questions I am asked by clients concern whether or not taxes are due when you sell your home or if you need to immediately buy a new house to avoid paying tax on any gain from the sale.

The answers are yes and no. In the past, you could put off paying any tax on a gain from the sale of a home if you used the proceeds to buy another home. This was called "rolling over" the gain from one home to the next. The tax on the original sale wasn't eliminated, just deferred to some future date.

You no longer have the option to postpone gain on the sale of your personal residence, although you would be surprised how many still think you do. But for home sales after May 7, 1997, you must choose whether to exclude the gain on the sale of your personal residence or to report the gain as taxable income in the year it is sold. The good news is that these days, the profit on home sales usually ends up to be tax free.

Because our country values home ownership, the tax treatment of your home is favored in several ways—indeed, more than ever before—and its sale is one of them. In 2018, you might be able to exclude as much as $500,000 of gain on the sale of your primary residence if you are married filing jointly.

If you are single, the figure is $250,000 of gain, with the very same limitations. Remember that gain is defined as the profit you make on the sale, basically the money you pocket over what you originally paid for the house and home improvements. For many people, this exclusion makes their home sale income-tax free. Even if you still owe some additional tax, it provides an amazing tax advantage.

That said, a few specific requirements must be met before you can be sure whether you will owe taxes. To begin with, you must own the home. This is straightforward enough, because you can't sell it if you don't own it! Nevertheless, the IRS lists ownership as the main criteria.

A trickier issue is that it has to have been your main home. If you own two homes, you can only exclude the gain on the home used as your primary residence. The IRS is picky about this, and you will need to show documentation proving that the house in question was your primary residence.

How long you have lived in the home is also an issue. To qualify for the exclusion, you must have used the home during at least two of the last five years before you sold it. That becomes important if you purchase a new home and keep the previous home as rental property. You need to decide whether you want to sell the first house before you reach this time limit or you will have capital gains on the sale of the home.

Short-term absences or vacations do not typically impact your qualification, even if you allowed a short-term renter to use the property while you were gone, say, on sabbatical as a professor or on an out-of-town assignment or a stint away caring for a sick relative. Other exceptions involve disability, a home that is destroyed or condemned, or a government job as uniformed or intelligence personnel. Serving in the Peace Corps also creates an exception.

I find that the biggest risk might be one that is not listed in the tax information. I have seen people purchase a new home and place their old home on the market. Then the old home doesn't sell. They aren't renting it or using it for any moneymaking endeavor. It just won't sell. If you are in this situation and it is getting close to your two-year window, go immediately to a tax professional to look at what your options are going forward.

Last but not least, you cannot exclude the gain if you claimed a home-sale exclusion within the previous two years. There are some wrinkles to this rule if something has forced an unexpected move. Usually, these involve a work-related move, a health-related move, or other unforeseeable events that were out of your control.

Finally, the IRS does not create a tax penalty for the dividing of assets during a divorce. If a spouse is transferring property to another spouse, the transfer of the home does not create a tax liability for the spouse giving up the house. The home is not treated as though it has been sold because it technically hasn't been. The marital property was already owned by both spouses, so letting one spouse retain all of it does not create a taxable event in the eyes of the IRS.

To take the deduction, you should also know that you can't have acquired the home through a 1031 exchange, or a like-kind exchange, within the last five years. This is an unusual situation, and it would involve exchanging a previous home for your current property. It is probably not anything you need to worry about.

A more likely tax issue is that you might have had a home office that you deduct from your taxes. If you take the home-office deduction, you might have also depreciated your home. This depreciation has to be "recaptured" and subtracted from the basis of your property when you sell it. Then if you sell the home for a gain and if you qualify to exclude the gain, you still must report this recaptured depreciation as income, which will be taxed at your ordinary rate. If you use the IRS's optional "safe-harbor" method to deduct your home office, no depreciation is deducted, and thus there is no depreciation recapture.

The decision on whether to depreciate your home is complicated and will require some thought before you decide how to handle it. Thankfully, by now you know to run such things by your financial planner and accountant.

Many people own their homes, and excluding the issues involving the real estate crisis of 2008–2009, the amount of gain on the sale of your home might well be the most you receive on any one investment in your whole life. Knowing the tax rules for excluding this gain can be financially beneficial. Talk to your financial planner and CPA to be sure you handle everything accurately. Selling your home, sweet home is even sweeter when it doesn't result in capital gains.

Ashley: I don't know if we even want to buy a house. It's so much responsibility and so expensive. I'm content to rent.

 Michael: I can't imagine my property ever gaining half a million dollars in value. I bet we never have to pay taxes.

Lisa: Even though I used and claimed a home office for several years, the tax savings related to the cumulative deductions against self-employment income still have been greater than the tax I will pay when I sell my home.

James: I'm not sure we are going to downsize, but I need to tell my friend Tom that he doesn't have to purchase another home to avoid the tax. We had both heard that old tax rule somewhere. I'm going to make his day!

· · · · ·

WEEK 38 ACTIVITY

Lucky for you, there is no exercise this week for you unless you have a home office or acquired your home through a 1031 exchange. If you have a home office, make sure you keep a file in which you track the amount you have taken in depreciation. When you sell your home, you will need that number.

If you have taken a 1031 exchange, make sure you keep the basis of the original property and the purchase price of any subsequent exchanges.

These steps will make it easier for you when you sell your home. For everyone else, just remember this information and share it with friends. Likely, you will have no tax impact if you sell your home.

$\cdots$

Ask Peggy

Question: Peggy, what is the single most important takeaway from this chapter?

Peggy: If you sell your primary residence and you have less than $250,000 gain if you are single or $500,000 gain if you are married, you have no tax liability in most cases.

$\cdots$

Notes

Use the lines below to write about what you did this week. When you look back, it'll remind you of your progress.

_____

_____

_____

_____

_____

_____

_____

_____

Chapter 39

Taxes: The Gift Tax

The Mom Who Broke the Law

A working mom had been careful not to give a daughter expensive gifts to compensate for her job sometimes making it impossible to attend every one of her child's sporting events, recitals, or school programs. Her daughter was turning sixteen now, and she was a great kid, on the honor roll every semester, and willing to pitch in around the house with little eye-rolling. Mom was hoping to surprise her with a nice car as a birthday gift. Even though the car wasn't brand-new, it was in great shape, a popular model with low mileage, and it would make a nice gift worth more than $20,000. Mom bought the car, not knowing she had just created a tax situation she had not anticipated.

Every year, thousands if not tens of thousands of tax-paying Americans unknowingly break the tax code rules. The fact that the IRS doesn't prosecute all of them speaks to the fact that the IRS really does have a heart.

So what rule are these otherwise law-abiding taxpayers missing? You may be surprised to learn it's the reporting of a taxable gift on a child's sixteenth birthday.

Of course, it's not the birthday that's the problem—it's the gift the sixteen-year-olds all have in common. Every year, thousands of lucky sixteen-year-olds receive a new car for their birthday, whether they need it or not. The cars can easily cost more than $20,000 or even $30,000, and that is where the problems arise. Now, had they bought their child a used economy car for $15,000 or less, there would have been no problem. They'd be paying less car insurance, and wouldn't have broken the tax code by exceeding the annual gift exclusion limit.

Gift tax is often a mystery to people who are otherwise savvy about the tax code. First, the tax isn't owed by the recipient, or in the case of the birthday car, your child. Anyone can give you a gift of literally any amount, and you will never owe any tax on the receipt of the gift. You are never subject to gift tax for a gift you receive, only potentially for a gift you give.

To avoid breaking the rule, you need to follow a few simple guidelines. First, each year, the IRS gives you the value of a gift you can give someone without any gift tax implications. That amount is called the annual exclusion limit, and it changes annually. The value of the 2018 exclusion amount is $15,000. Gifts less than or equal to the annual exclusion amount do not require a gift-tax return. There is also no tax due.

In fact, you can give gifts valued as high as the exclusion amount to as many people as you want. They don't even have to be relatives. Your spouse can also give a gift valued as high as the exclusion amount to anyone. If the two of you opt to give more than $15,000 apiece to one person, and the gift does not exceed $30,000, that is called "gift splitting," and it's a little more complicated. You still each need to file a gift-tax return.

However, it may help to know that the annual exclusion amount covers the entire gift.

The larger problem arises if you alone give a gift valued higher than the exclusion limit by yourself or more than twice that amount with your spouse to anyone in a year. That size of gift not only requires filing a gift-tax return with the IRS, but it also begins to work against your lifetime gifting limit of $11.18 million as of 2018. I know, I know—stop laughing. Many people never approach that amount, but you should know that today, gift tax and estate tax are computed on the same amount of exemption.

Although $11.18 million is a large estate, it is easy to reach when property is owned on either coast. For many people, the issue is not whether they reached the level of taxation; it is the failure to file a gift-tax return. To make it more complicated, each spouse would need to file the return because gift- and estate-tax returns are never filed jointly. Technically, failure to file could result in a financial penalty. To help ensure that you never fall into this trap, here are some additional tips.

First, if you and your spouse are both U.S. citizens, you can give an unlimited amount to each other. It's assumed that U.S. spouses regularly give each other much more than the exclusion limit per year, and gift tax is never owed on these gifts. However, if one of you is not a U.S. citizen, there are gift limitations between the citizen spouse and the non-citizen spouse. In 2018, that limit would be $152,000.

Charitable donations are not limited to the exclusion limit. Although there are deduction limits for charitable donations, the numbers are significantly higher for most people than the annual exclusion amount. We'll talk more about that later.

If you give money directly to a medical or educational facility *on behalf* of another person, it has no gift-tax consequences. Say a grandfather wants to help his grandson pay for college. He writes his grandson the check, and the grandson uses the money to pay tuition. If his check amount exceeds the gift exclusion, the grandfather has made a reportable gift on a gift-tax return. However, had he written the check directly to the university, a potentially taxable gift would not have occurred. Gifts to cover medical costs should be handled in the same way. Write the check to the medical facility, not the patient.

Gifts must be complete to be eligible for the gift-tax exemption. That means in order for the gift to qualify for the annual exclusion, the gift much be given completely, with no strings attached. To be considered a gift, nothing can be contingent on the actions of others. Say you want to give a vacation property as a gift to a friend or relative, but you would like to retain the use of it for a week each year. This retention causes the gift to be incomplete. You have to report it on a gift-tax return.

If you are planning a complicated giving plan, you should consult other professionals to be sure you are following all the rules. For most of us, it is usually pretty simple, but rapidly, the situation can become complicated. No one wants to be breaking the tax code without knowing about it, especially when all you wanted was to do something nice for someone.

. . . . .

 Ashley: I'm sorry my folks broke the rules, but I loved that car. I'm still driving it.

 Michael: We have a couple at our church—she's American, and he's from Brazil. I wonder if they know these rules.

 Lisa: I help Mom out financially from time to time and never knew it could result in a gift tax. I will be careful how I proceed going forward.

James: When it comes to helping with college for the grandchildren, I'm writing the checks made out to the university.

WEEK 39 ACTIVITY

Most of the gifts we give don't trigger a gift-tax return, and many of us will never pay gift tax. However, failure to file a gift-tax return when you need to, will cause you issues with the IRS if it finds out what you did. If you have given a gift that approaches the annual gift exclusion limit, discuss your future plans with your financial planner or CPA.

· · · · ·

Ask Peggy

Question: Peggy, what is the single most important takeaway from this chapter?

Peggy: Gift tax is paid by the giftor, not the recipient, and if a gift to any one person exceeds the annual exclusion amount, then a gift tax return must be filed, even if no gift tax is owed.

· · · · ·

Notes

Use the lines below to jot down notes on your week.

_____

_____

_____

_____

Peggy Doviak

_____

_____

_____

_____

_____

_____

_____

_____

_____

_____

_____

_____

_____

_____

_____

Chapter 40

Taxes: Charitable Donations

The Merchant Who Loved Ringing the Bell

In a small town, local merchants can almost be celebrities, and the owner of a popular diner was no exception. Not only was he a great cook, but he also had the reputation for being kind and generous, donating extra food to a local shelter and sponsoring Little League teams. Patrons knew the holidays were approaching when the bell and kettle appeared outside his restaurant, and no one gave more than he did, putting a crisp ten-dollar bill in the kettle at the end of each business day. When he did his taxes, he took that cash donation as a deduction. He had no idea it wasn't allowed because he had no documentation of the gift.

Many people like to be generous, giving, and helpful. Even more people like tax deductions. Fortunately, our tax code is written in a way to enable both goals to be met, allowing us to lower our taxes when we make charitable donations.

Restrictions to this do-gooding exist, however. You can deduct donations only if you itemize your deductions on your tax return. That means if you take the flat standard deduction, then your charitable donations will not decrease your tax liability. If your tax status varies between standard and itemized deductions (unlikely but possible), make your larger donations in the years when you anticipate itemizing on your taxes.

If you have documentation of the gift, the IRS allows you typically to take a charitable deduction of an amount as much as 60 percent of your adjusted gross income, or AGI, with certain income limitations. You can find your AGI amount on your tax return. Some charities have deductions that are limited to 20 or 30 percent of your AGI. For most of us, this won't be an issue because our donation level will be lower than that.

Still, I have seen it become a problem for older people with lower AGIs. They are trying to downsize, and they have items of considerable value that they want to donate. It isn't that difficult to reach 60 percent of your AGI if you are on a limited income and donating many of the major purchases you made in your lifetime. Planning ahead can help in this scenario. Ideally, you would begin to liquidate the estate late in one year and complete it in the next. A second option is to give items to family members and allow them to donate and take the deduction. Be aware, however, not to trigger the gift tax unless you're prepared to pay it or at least file a gift-tax return.

A second issue you might face when you take deductions is the allowable limit of the dollar value of your donations when your adjusted gross income is high. Because these numbers change regularly, you should check the current year's phaseout for itemized deductions at www.irs.gov.

Before you give, verify that the organization you want to assist is a qualified charity. Many people are surprised to learn that the money they donated, although going to a good cause such as a local family in need, did not go to an organization recognized by the IRS as a charity.

The IRS summarizes charitable organizations as those that are religious, charitable, educational, scientific, or literary. Donations to organizations that work to prevent cruelty to children or animals are also deductible. Not included for deductible contributions are political, lobbying, personal, and most civic and foreign organizations.

Always check the status of an unfamiliar charity. The IRS provides a searchable database and keeps the data in Publication 78. Not every eligible charity is listed in this database, however. For instance, churches are not on the list because donations to churches are always deductible. However, the database is a good tool to use with other charities.

To claim a donation deduction on your taxes, you must keep your canceled check or a receipt from the charity in order to claim the deduction on your taxes. The IRS no longer approves any cash donations without receipts. This doesn't mean you shouldn't give something to the bell ringer during the holidays. It just means you are practicing charity without a tax motive!

Although the IRS allows you to donate as much as 60 percent of your adjusted gross income to many charities, check with the charity and with the IRS if you are planning a large donation. As stated earlier, some charitable donations are limited to 20 percent or 30 percent of your AGI, depending on the charities. The rules are complicated and too detailed to discuss here, but typically, the IRS favors groups that benefit many recipients. The smaller or more private the group is that receives the benefits, the more likely the donation is to be limited.

When donating items, the IRS will not allow you to take a deduction unless the item is in good condition or better. Be sure you can justify the value you're claiming through one of the IRS-approved methods, including but not limited to expected sale price. The valuation rules are impacted by what you are donating. Different kinds of donations (land, household goods, clothes, art, stock, etc.) might be valued differently. Make sure you know the amount of the deduction and any related tax rules before you make the donations.

The amount you can deduct is also impacted by how the charity will use the item. If the item is seen as an investment that will be sold by the charity, your deduction is less than if the item can be used by the charity. This is why it's better to give that Persian rug to a church and camping equipment to the Girl Scouts.

The amount of documentation you need when donating items increases with the value of the item. If you place the value of a donation between $250 and $500, you must have a letter from the charity acknowledging the donation's value and must follow IRS protocol. If the donation values more than $500, you must also obtain a written, good-faith estimate of value. If the donation is between $500 and $5,000, you must have additional written documentation including but not limited to how you acquired the property and what it was worth when you acquired it, along with verification of value. If the item is worth more than $5,000, you also must obtain a formal appraisal. Those amounts might change over time, so be sure to check before taking the deduction.

If you keep any interest in your donated item, you impact the amount you can deduct, because the IRS views this ownership as creating an *incomplete* gift. Say you donate a piece of property and retain the right to vacation there for a week each year—you can't deduct the full value of the property, because you still control some of its use. This rule can become sticky, especially when creating charitable trusts, so consult a CPA before you attempt a complicated gift.

My final caution concerns donations of your own time. Regardless of the value of your skills, you cannot deduct the value of your time. If you play a musical instrument for compensation and you also play that instrument for free at your place of worship, you cannot take a deduction for the amount you would normally have charged for the latter, because it is considered a gift of time. The value of your time is *never* a charitable deduction, regardless of what your skills are or what you get paid elsewhere for them!

Even though the rules governing donated items can be confusing, it is likely that you can earn more money by donating an item than by selling it in a garage sale. Often in a garage sale, items are sold for a dollar or two when they are worth much more. A fair value that is deductible can generate more value than selling the item for a dollar. And this is especially true when you remember that garage-sale proceeds are taxable—and you can't deduct the time it took to run the garage sale.

Gift possibilities are almost endless, and amazingly, the tax code carves out rules for each of them. Even though the rules look numerous and complicated (I actually skipped the most complicated ones), they are straightforward when you look at them from a distance. The IRS supports the idea of charity and good works; it just wants you to deduct a fair amount for the donation, and it wants to be sure that your donation is truly a donation. I've seen what people earn in garage sales, and I believe that donating is a reasonable alternative, assuming you itemize your taxes. Of course, cash is the easiest gift, but be sure to get and keep that receipt!

· · · · ·

Ashley: Because I don't itemize, deductible donations don't apply to me, but I still like to donate as much as I can.

Michael: I thought I could estimate cash donations on my taxes. I'll start doing automatic payments to provide a record or get receipts.

Lisa: Mom needs to downsize, and I've encouraged her to have a garage sale. I bet she'll make more money if she donates the items, and it would be easier for both of us. She gets tired easily these days. And she still has clothes with the tags on them!

James: I should donate more while I am in a higher tax bracket. I can maximize my deductions, do good, and help the family finances.

· · · · ·

WEEK 40 ACTIVITY

Your project for this week is to create a system to help you keep track of your donations.

1. Create a way to track checks and auto-debit donations.

2. Remember that you cannot deduct cash without a receipt as proof of the contribution.

3. When donating items, keep all required documentation. Take photos of the items to justify your valuation.

· · · · ·

Ask Peggy

Question: Peggy, what is this chapter's takeaway?

Peggy: The IRS requires proof of any charitable gift. Gifts of cash are not deductible unless you get a receipt.

· · · · ·

Notes

_____

_____

Chapter 41

Taxes: Keeping Records

The Disorganized Woman

An elderly woman had lived a good and responsible life. Once her husband died, however, she just couldn't keep up. Although she wasn't that old, just seventy, she took to paying the bills (a job her husband had handled) and then throwing them in a drawer, then a box, then a bigger box, until finally, she had a spare bedroom full of bill boxes. She saved everything, but that was the problem. She saved *everything*.

When her children finally arrived like the cavalry to help her downsize, they opened the bedroom door and gasped at the sight of so many piles of boxes. When they opened the boxes, they found receipts, tax returns, and other financial data going back ten years. They wanted to help their mom organize the material and keep the five years' worth of documents that the IRS would want them to save, but they didn't know where to begin or even exactly what to save.

Remember when people told us that the personal computer would eliminate paper from our lives? We would keep all our files on our computer, and we would have no paper. Maybe your office is working to go paperless. Maybe you pay all your bills online using your phone. But much more likely, you do a lot of your personal business online, but you also still print out and save a paper trail. In a time of hacking, computer viruses, and identity theft, people might actually be returning to paper. And that means that for many people, paper continues to come in by the ream, seemingly every day. And even if you are paperless, if you go to help your parents, grandparents, or aunt clean out an old office or downsize a home, it's likely that they aren't. You may find boxes of receipts, checks, and tax returns in the attic or spare bedroom dating back to the 1950s or 1960s!

This begs the question: How long do you need to keep all that stuff? Fortunately, the IRS provides guidelines on how long you need to keep records, and this information can also be found on their website. However, I want to summarize it here, along with some suggestions.

First, keep copies of all your filed tax returns. Yes, all of them. If you can't stand to keep the paper, scan them and keep them electronically. The IRS recommends that you never throw them away. Of course, if you are cleaning out the attic and the tax returns are dated from the 1950s, I'll let you use your own judgment.

The IRS has further recommendations if you knowingly file returns with errors. Although it seems somewhat unbelievable, they have document requirements for such occasions. For example, if you made money you did not report and it exceeds 25 percent of the gross income that you did report, you must keep your records for six years. The IRS can audit for unreported income that far into the past. Even if it doesn't rise to the level of fraud, I don't need to remind you that the IRS takes a very dim view of this kind of behavior, and the penalties and interest will be harsh if they discover it.

Further, if you file a fraudulent return, you must keep the tax return indefinitely. Again, I can't stress enough: There is no statute of limitation on fraud. If you are practicing creative tax filing, I would strongly urge you to stop. Fraud can be defined somewhat loosely, and one person's creativity can be another person's fraud. But I suggest that you be wary of seminars that tell you never to pay taxes again. Any tax ideas you hear that do not resonate with what you always thought about the American tax process need to be researched and documented. That is not to say that you can't take every legal, even creative tax deduction and credit. The tax code is full of loopholes. Just be careful that you only seek out educated, thoughtful voices for your tax advice.

If you just don't file the return, keep the records indefinitely. There could be a failure-to-file penalty even when you don't owe taxes. It is better to file your taxes annually no matter what. Three years is the statute of limitations for a traditional audit, so keep your records for three years. Of course, there is a fine line between unpaid taxes and fraud. Once you know that you owe taxes, it becomes a gray area as to whether or not you are committing fraud. Again, that is not a path to take.

A situation you are more likely to experience involves an amended return. If you file for a refund or credit after you filed your original tax return, keep the records for three years from the time you filed the amended return or two years from when you paid the tax, whichever is later.

Sometimes you might learn that you—or even your accountant—made a mistake in a previous year's return. As long as that return can still be amended, there is no reason not to file for the refund or credit. Less commonly, although I have seen it, something will happen to create a theft or loss after you have filed the return. Within certain limitations, theft or loss can be deducted from your taxes.

As an employee, you need to keep records longer than your employer can be audited. You need to keep employment records for at least four years so you can prove how much money you actually received. If the IRS had an issue with your employer, you have records that support your tax return.

Many of us have property that might involve capital gains tax when we sell it. Be sure to keep all documentation about such assets until you have sold or otherwise disposed of the property. Then the way you dispose of the property will impact how much longer you need to keep the records.

Keeping the IRS satisfied is not your only concern. Other businesses can have an interest in your records, and some of your documentation might need to be kept longer than the IRS requires. Your insurance company or financing companies might require the records be held longer, usually as long as you hold or insure the asset. Remember you need to keep documentation showing the basis on all assets you are holding so that when they are sold, the gain can be calculated.

Assuming you are making a good-faith effort to do your taxes, you should be able to get rid of documentation after six years, although you should keep your tax returns permanently. Remember also to check with your creditors, insurance agents, and others associated with your assets before you throw anything away.

As for that box marked "Taxes 1958," it can probably be shredded without reading it!

· · · · ·

Ashley: I always thought once I'd done my taxes and filed them, I was done. It never occurred to me that I needed to save them.

Michael: I need to tell my friend Chris that he should keep employment tax records for at least four years. He's a neat freak and is always trying to get rid of paper he doesn't need.

Lisa: My mother has tax returns that date back to the 1950s. What a relief to learn we can get rid of some of those documents!

James: I was so glad I kept the information on the price I paid for those stocks when I got out of graduate school. When I sold them, I used my purchase price to support how much tax I should pay.

· · · · ·

WEEK 41 ACTIVITY

This week's exercise involves several tasks. First, the IRS has statues dealing with purposely misfiled taxes, so don't cut corners or cheat on your taxes. When the IRS catches up with you (and it probably will), your life can change for the worse. If your return rises to the level of tax fraud, the IRS can send you to prison.

Keep basis information on anything you'll have to sell for capital gain. If you need some time to find all of it, invest the time now. Otherwise, when you sell the asset, the IRS will make you pay taxes on all the money. If you hate clutter, you can scan documents and save them electronically. Remember to back up the documents in ways other than just on your computer's hard drive. If you have any questions, consult your financial planner and especially your CPA.

· · · · ·

Ask Peggy
Question: Peggy, what is this chapter's takeaway?
Peggy: Keep all of your tax returns indefinitely and the records supporting them longer than any audit period that might exist—it will ensure you can provide what the IRS might want should it ever come calling.

Notes

Use the following lines to jot down some notes about what you did this week.

_____

_____

_____

_____

_____

_____

_____

_____

_____

_____

_____

_____

_____

. . . . .

Ask Peggy

 Ashley: I thought getting a large tax refund was good. Are you saying I shouldn't be happy about getting one?

Peggy: There's nothing wrong with being excited about a refund. Most people are ecstatic to get one. Just remember it is only a function of getting money back because you paid more than you owed. And the government doesn't pay you interest on it! Your tax planning has been most efficient if at the end of the year you don't owe any tax and you don't receive a refund. That means you paid in the correct amount of tax over the course of the year.

 Michael: I heard when you sell your house, you have to pay taxes on the gain unless you buy another house right away.

Peggy: Michael, many people think that. However, if the home you sold is your primary residence, and you have met all the criteria, you can exclude half a million dollars of gain if you're married and file a joint return with your spouse.

 Lisa: Didn't the IRS used to allow a small amount of cash as a charitable donation without a receipt?

Peggy: Yes, Lisa, it did. However, that loophole has closed. Now, you need a receipt for any charitable donation, regardless of its size, to take the deduction.

 James: Peggy, I guess I don't have to worry about estate tax as much as I thought—and I must say that is a relief!

Peggy: That's wonderful James. Right now, unless you are extremely wealthy, you probably won't face an estate tax issue. But remember that the tax laws can change as swiftly as a wind comes up in Oklahoma, and all the individual tax changes for the Tax Cuts and Jobs Act will be sunsetting in just a few years. It's important that you monitor it, so you can plan accordingly.

Estate Planning

Chapter 42

Estate Planning: We're All Going to Die

The Businessman Who Wanted To Do It Himself

No one likes to think about dying, but it is the one thing we know will happen to each and every one of us. As the old adage goes, none of us is getting out alive.

While we might recoil from the thought of our life being cut short, we soon realize that the inevitable brings responsibilities. Most of us would be horrified at the idea of leaving the people we love in a bad situation because of our untimely death. We want to be prepared as much as we can be for our death, and we want to ensure the ones we love will be okay even when we are gone. That's why estate planning is so important.

This might well be the topic you're most interested in, but before you try to implement any of what we cover here, please talk to a good estate-planning attorney. I am not an attorney, and I am not giving you legal advice. In fact, some of the documents I discuss might have a different name in your state or might not even be recognized where you live.

What I hope to do is provide some educational tools as a starting place, a way to help you become familiar with the terms and concepts of estate planning. Only an attorney, however, can tell you if these strategies will work for your personal situation.

Consider the story of the successful businessman who'd been a lifelong bachelor. The man cared about his nieces and nephews as though they were his own children, and he had created a will leaving all his worldly possessions to them. To save some money, he had used a kit that he had ordered online to write the will. He did, however, listen when his financial planner suggested that maybe it would be wise to let an estate attorney take a look at the will.

When the man met with his attorney, he was surprised to learn that his entire estate would have to be probated in court because *no will* actually offers probate protection.

I remember when I was quite young, and my grandparents had a giant book on their bookshelf about how to avoid probate. At that time in my life, I thought I wanted to be a lawyer, so I tried to read the book. I was ten at the most, and it was the most boring book I'd ever read. I think I made it to page five or six. I haven't read an entire book about probate since, but I have studied it, and I find most of my clients either don't know what probate is or they don't understand it.

Basically, you create a will so that you do not die *intestate*, the legal term for dying without a will. When you do not have a will, your estate goes into the court system—except for that which is otherwise already designated, such as a beneficiary on a life insurance policy. The court then decides how your assets should be divided among your family members. This is obviously not ideal. Most people's lives are too complicated to let state law determine who inherits what of their assets.

So if your desires are anything other than the state-mandated laws of descent and distribution, you must have a will or another type of estate plan. In today's world of second marriages and blended families, not having a will or other estate plan can be disastrous as far as assets passing in accord to the true wishes of the deceased, or decedent (the legal term).

Even assets distributable by a will, however, are still subject to probate. Probate is the legal proceeding designed to be sure that your estate is settled properly, that your bills are paid, and that parties with an interest in your estate have an opportunity to be heard.

Probate takes time and carries an expense. Most people prefer to avoid it. However, a will is not the solution to avoiding probate. Assets are only protected from probate if they are in a trust, are provided to you as a beneficiary of say an insurance policy or an IRA account, or pass to you through some form of survivorship titling. Such assets can pass directly to you without a legal proceeding.

Although wills in your own handwriting are recognized in many states, you shouldn't try to create your own will in that way, because even a handwritten one must meet certain requirements before a court will recognize it. Find a good estate-planning attorney to help you draft something that honors your wishes.

Boilerplate wills, such as the will kit the uncle found on the Internet, are only as good as the service that drafted them. You could run into issues about their being accepted in your state or standing up in court should someone want to contest your final wishes. Even wills and trusts drafted by good attorneys can have problems in the legal system if someone wants to cause trouble. That's why an estate-planning attorney is worth the money.

Your will is only part of your estate and end-of-life plan. You might also need powers of attorney and documents related to health care decisions, such as a living will, advance directive, or durable power of attorney for health care if your state allows for them. You might also need a trust. An estate attorney can help you make those decisions.

Being willing to look into the future and recognize the challenges that will surely lie ahead for you and your family can be empowering—a chance to create a legacy that will help your family prosper, perhaps for generations!

· · · · ·

 Ashley: I need a will. I'll talk to my friend who is an attorney to see if she can recommend an estate lawyer to help me.

 Michael: I know too many folks who try to use online legal services or templates. They are just disasters waiting to happen.

Lisa: It is so important to keep a will up to date. My friend Beth had forgotten her ex-husband was listed as her beneficiary. She only remembered when she was reviewing her documents before going into the hospital for a major operation. If she hadn't gotten sick, she might never have remembered!

James: My father had a handwritten will. It held up in court, but then again, nobody was contesting it. I realize now it could have gone very bad if someone had. That's why I had my lawyer do mine.

· · · · ·

WEEK 42 ACTIVITY

This week, I want you to seriously consider getting a will if you don't already have one. A will is just about the most basic estate-planning document you can have, and I can't emphasize its importance enough. If you don't have a will and something should happen to you, assets can be tied up in court, and they might not pass to the people you want to receive them.

· · · · ·

Ask Peggy

Question: Peggy, what is this chapter's takeaway?

Peggy: A will allows your belongings to be distributed according to your wishes, but it does not exempt them from the potential of probate. Remember, probate is the legal process through which a deceased person's estate is properly distributed to heirs and designated beneficiaries and any debt owed to creditors is paid off.

· · · · ·

Notes

Use the following lines to jot down some notes about what you did this week.

_____

_____

_____

_____

_____

_____

_____

_____

_____

_____

_____

_____

_____

_____

_____

_____

_____

_____

_____

_____

_____

Chapter 43

Estate Planning: Advance Directives and Living Wills

The Really Lucky Snowboarder

A young man was a bit of a daredevil. He and his friends loved to snowboard, and he was always the fastest one down the mountain. One day he hit an icy patch, skidded off the run, and slammed into a tree. He had been unconscious for days when, almost miraculously, he woke up.

He realized such a happy ending had not been guaranteed. If anything had gone more wrong, his parents would not have had the authority to do what he knew he would have wanted them to do in such a situation. He was twenty-five—old enough to have his wishes carried out. But without a living will in place, on a different day, in a more serious situation, he might have lingered in a coma for years instead of dying with dignity as he wanted.

Do you remember Terri Schiavo?

She was the young woman who collapsed in her home and suffered severe brain damage from a lack of oxygen. She could not live on her own, and the hospital was keeping her alive with the help of machines. Her husband wanted to allow her to die—in accordance with what he believed were his wife's own wishes—but her parents did not. The U.S. Congress and the President of the United States entered the fight to keep Mrs. Schiavo alive. Ultimately, her feeding tube was removed, and she died—but only after several removals and reinstatements.

To this day, my heart breaks for all parties involved; everyone was simply trying to do what they thought was right in a complicated, emotional moment. You might not be able to say how you think her case should have gone, but I suspect most of us would not want our final illnesses playing out contentiously on the public stage. If Terri Schiavo had implemented an advance directive or a living will, most likely her situation would have unfolded privately, a family matter not a national controversy.

Advance directives and living wills are documents recognized by many states that allow us to express our intentions as to medical treatment if we are unable to make decisions for ourselves because we are incompetent or in a state of permanent unconsciousness. Because the rules vary from state to state, it's important that you create the documents that your state recognizes and that you update them if you have reason to move to another state.

Advance directives and living wills cover whether you want to receive hydration and nutrition using IV bags and feeding tubes and whether you want to be on a ventilator, and they can also cover additional circumstances.

Advance directives and living wills vary between states, so you need to consult with an estate-planning attorney to determine which device is recognized in your estate, if at all, and complete the document in the state where you live.

Many people and organizations misunderstand advance directives and living wills. Once, I read in a church bulletin that the church was opposed to living wills. I talked to the pastor after services, and I explained to him that the bulletin announcement was misleading.

Advance directives and living wills simply provide you with a document so your end-of-life wishes can be known. They can ensure that you receive the services you want as much as they can allow you to opt out of others. When they are properly informed, most people aren't opposed to the documents that comprise advance directives and living wills, even if they have a moral or ethical belief in what services should be provided in life-and-death situations. Instead, they oppose specific responses someone has made in an advance directive.

The pastor wasn't impressed with the information I shared that day, but I was still correct, and I want to encourage you not to let your beliefs prevent you from completing one. If you want to be kept on life support, that is a totally valid decision and is yours to make. However, it's the making of the decision that is so important here.

If you don't put your end-of-life wishes in writing in an advance directive or living will, how is anyone to know for sure what they are?

Your family members might claim to know what you want, but wouldn't it be nice to leave them something behind that will let them know for sure? Such times are difficult enough for any family without the stress of second-guessing someone's wishes in such a serious matter.

I like to think of advance directives and living wills as acts of kindness. No one wants the burden of needing to decide whether or not a beloved family member lives or dies. The advance directive or living will takes the decision out of your family's hands and puts it back into yours. Shouldn't we all be willing to be responsible for our own care?

The necessary documents can be downloaded from the Internet, but I recommend having a talk with your attorney about it—you want to be certain the documents will be recognized in your state. Be certain that you understand the document too as legal language can be confusing.

If the document needs to be updated to meet your state's requirements, an attorney can help you do that and keep the document updated as the years go by. It will cost a little money, but it could save heartbreak for your family, and it should keep your end-of-life decisions out of the news.

· · · · ·

 Ashley: I've heard of the Terry Schiavo case. I don't want that ever to happen to me.

 Michael: My wife and I both have advance directives, but I should make sure they are up to date.

 Lisa: I don't want my nieces and nephews to worry about making such serious decisions on my behalf.

 James: I've seen what happens when people don't have advance directives. If anything happened to my wife or me when we were traveling, I don't want there to be any questions as to what our wishes are.

· · · · ·

WEEK 43 ACTIVITY

This week, you need seriously to consider completing an advance directive. If you already have one in place, be sure it is up to date and recognized by your state (laws can change). Though you might find one online that seems to be reputable, don't risk it. As with your powers of attorney, these documents need to hold up when you need them, especially if the matter were to go to court.

Meanwhile, I want to you to finish reading all the related chapters here, because you might need several documents, and they are generally less expensive when purchased as a package. After that, it's time to visit an attorney.

. . . . .

Ask Peggy
Question: Peggy, what is this chapter's takeaway?
Peggy: Advance directives, often called living wills, can be completed in a way to allow your end of life wishes to be followed, but maybe more importantly the documents should save the people you love from having to make impossible choices about your end-of-life care.

. . . . .

Notes
Use the lines below to make notes.

_____

_____

_____

_____

_____

_____

_____

_____

Chapter 44

Estate Planning: Powers of Attorney

The Friends Who Promised To Take Care of Each Other

A middle-aged man had owned his business since he was in his late twenties. Over the years, he had developed a very close friend in his chosen industry, and they often consulted with each other about business deals. Although technically they were rivals, they didn't think of each other in that way, and they implicitly trusted each other.

As middle-aged people are prone to do, they began to talk to each other about growing old, which led to exchanges about their health and then to their estate plans. Although they wanted their spouses to make their health care decisions in case they couldn't, they knew neither of their wives had any interest in their respective business. Their solution was to create powers of attorney that would "spring" into effect for each other in the case of trouble. Each vowed to treat the other's business as his own until the actual owner was healthy and could make the financial decisions again.

What would happen if you became unable to make decisions for yourself or your business? What if you were unable to talk reasonably with a physician or write a check?

How would you know that someone you trusted was making medical decisions in your best interest, or how could you make sure someone was paying the utility bills for your home or your mortgage/rent in your absence? If you're a business owner, who would keep the business running until you could return?

Medical directives, or living wills, cannot dictate medical instructions for every scenario. Instead, they focus mainly on end-of-life decisions. As a result, you need to have documents in place that address the possibility of your incapacity, even if it is only to cover a short-term situation in which you cannot act on your own behalf. People tend to think about such things when going into the hospital for major procedures such as heart surgery, but we all know that people are incapacitated every day from elective surgery, hospital mistakes, and simple procedures no one expected to go wrong.

To cover such contingencies, you should consider having a power of attorney for health care, or what is sometimes called a medical proxy, as well as a power of attorney allowing for another person to manage your assets. Different people could hold your power of attorney for health care and for finance, or the same person could handle both jobs.

Powers of attorney can "spring" into effect upon your incapacity, allowing you full control of whatever they will oversee until then. They can be set up to handle a single event, such as someone acting as your power of attorney in a business transaction, which is typically known as a limited power of attorney. They can also be more general, giving that appointed person the ability to handle all your affairs with regard to your money or business or your health.

Appointing someone to have your power of attorney gives that person a great deal of control over your life. A springing power of attorney requires that you become incapacitated before the power of attorney takes effect. A doctor or panel of doctors makes the incapacity decision. Springing powers of attorney are more common when someone wants to make all of his or her own decisions and only wants someone else involved if it becomes absolutely necessary.

Again, the same person does not have to hold all your powers of attorney. Remember that an appointed agent, or attorney-in-fact, will hold great power. Horror stories of misused power are common enough that people approach this topic with fear. However, not having a power of attorney, even a springing one, can also end disastrously.

I know adult children who were unable to pay their mother's bills, because she didn't have any of their names on her bank account, and she couldn't pay her bills because she was unconscious in a hospital bed. The children were left scrambling, trying to find money. They weren't financially liable for her bills, but they didn't want to ruin her credit score and knew she would be devastated if she woke up and found that her bills hadn't been paid. Their plan was just to have their mother reimburse them if she regained consciousness or take the money from the estate eventually if she did not.

This is a situation in which a springing power of attorney would have worked well, allowing the mother to manage her own finances until an unexpected medical event.

No one enjoys thinking about situations in which we can't make our own financial or health decisions, but it happens every single day in this country. Better to be prepared than caught unprepared. Even routine surgery can leave a patient unable to function for awhile. Imagine how less stressful those visits to the hospital would be if you had your ducks all in a row as far as someone who could step in should anything go wrong or you required a few extra weeks to recover before resuming work and daily obligations.

An estate-planning attorney can help you decide whether you need a power of attorney for health care and finance and then can draft it for you. At least think about it. People who love you want to be able to help you when you need it, but you'll feel even better if you've already helped yourself.

· · · · ·

 Ashley: I should talk to an attorney about this—health emergencies happen to the young too.

Michael: I didn't know how important a power of attorney was until my friend Bob's knee was blown out in a pickup basketball game. He was on so many painkillers, he couldn't do anything—much less handle money.

Lisa: It was a difficult conversation asking Mom to give me power of attorney, but when it was all done, she admitted she was relieved to have a backup in case of an emergency. I think it brought us closer.

James: My wife runs the family finances already, thank goodness. She is both my finance and health care power of attorney, and I'm hers. I guess she knows I'll figure it all out.

· · · · ·

WEEK 44 ACTIVITY

If you don't already have a power of attorney for health care and finances, schedule an appointment with an attorney to get one. (To cut down on your expenses, you might finish the estate-planning section of this book first. You might need to discuss several things with the attorney, and it's best to be prepared and do it all at once.) Talk to the people close to you before you see the attorney, and explain to them what you want to do. Never appoint someone as your agent (or attorney-in-fact) without his or her knowledge and consent. Most people choose to have the same person as their agent (or attorney-in-fact) for all things, but you don't have to do that. Make the decision that works best for your situation. If you have a son who is a businessman and a daughter who is a doctor, it would be logical to make the latter your health proxy and to put your son in charge of your money matters.

. . . . .

Ask Peggy

Question: Peggy, what would you say is this particular chapter's takeaway?

Peggy: Powers of attorney allow people to handle your financial affairs or make health care decisions for you and can be written to take effect only on your incapacity.

. . . . .

Notes

_____

_____

_____

_____

_____

_____

_____

_____

_____

_____

_____

_____

_____

_____

_____

_____

_____

_____

_____

_____

Chapter 45

Estate Planning: Trusts

The Couple Who Found Unexpected Love

No one expected either of them to marry again—including themselves. He was a widower, and she had been divorced for years. They were in their sixties, and it seemed like a dream that they had found each other, much less that they might again be married. Both had money, and so practical matters needed attending to if they were going to tie the knot. As much as they loved each other, they also loved their grown children.

Both of them wanted to ensure that if one of them died, the remaining spouse would have no financial worries. However, after they were both gone, they wanted their respective children to have any remaining estate that they had brought into the marriage. They wondered if a trust might be just the answer.

I'm sure you've seen the cautions about how we are not supposed to practice law or give legal advice if we are not attorneys. You don't have to dig very far into the world of trusts before you understand why this is wise advice. Yes, cheap alternatives are advertised on TV and in the back of your favorite magazine, but trust me: The repercussions for not getting a personalized trust are much too severe to go that route. This chapter on trusts is brief, because trusts are so complicated that you truly need to seek additional professional advice before wading into one. Only an estate planning attorney can tell you if you need a trust and how to go about structuring it.

Basically, a trust is a relationship between a trustee and a beneficiary. Items held in trust are not subject to probate, and as a result, the items held in trust can be kept private or in confidence. Many people appreciate this feature.

It's important to remember that trusts are not just complicated wills. Trusts allow for much more flexibility and control than wills, and they give the trustmaker (or settlor) the ability to divide assets in a way that would be difficult to do in a will.

Trusts can allow different parts of a single investment to be held for the benefit of different persons or entities. You might create a trust that allows the income of a portfolio to go to a charity, whereas the portfolio itself ultimately goes to your children. A trust can also be used to help you take care of a second spouse while he or she is alive, while preserving assets for children from a previous marriage. The ability to divide assets is a unique feature, and it can be valuable while also serving many purposes.

Trusts can be used to protect children, the disabled, or a beneficiary who tends to spend too much money. Trusts can also be used in a gifting strategy, in which a charity receives income or the remainder (body) of a trust, and other beneficiaries receive either income or the balance. This is a useful tool to keep an asset in the family while allowing for a charitable donation of the income generated by the asset. Finally, trusts can defer or lower estate-tax liability. However, I should stress that even if you are not wealthy, you might still want or need a trust.

Trusts are either revocable (known as a "revocable living trust") or irrevocable.

Just as they sound, revocable trusts can be changed by the creator of the trust at any time while the creator is alive. Irrevocable trusts, once made, cannot be altered by the creator of the trust. As you might expect, irrevocable trusts are quite complex, but they can be useful in many situations. A properly structured irrevocable trust can hold assets in a way that can take them out of an estate, which has the potential of lowering the tax liability of the estate.

Some trusts are created as irrevocable life insurance trusts (ILITs). In these, the trust purchases life insurance that is used to pay estate tax liability when all other estate-planning strategies have been exhausted. Be sure you understand the structure of your trust if you choose to create one.

Once you have a trust, choosing the beneficiary or beneficiaries of your trust can be more complicated than you might think.

It can be tricky to list your trust as the beneficiary of an IRA, because some trusts are not treated with the same rules as individuals who inherit IRAs. If they're not drafted properly, trusts can be required to distribute IRA assets within five years rather than the lifetime distribution available through a required minimum distribution (RMD). If you now have your IRA beneficiary as your trust, you must talk to a knowledgeable estate-planning attorney to be sure you have not shortened the distribution period of the IRA to five years. That could be a very expensive mistake.

Trusts can be an important component to an effective estate plan. Talk to your estate-planning attorney, along with your financial planner and CPA. Make the effort to introduce these three professionals so they know each other and can work together on your behalf. You might find that you have the ability to structure your estate to your or your family's benefit in ways you never imagined.

. . . . .

 Ashley: It would seem that I need to start by getting a will rather than worrying about a trust.

 Michael: I always thought a revocable trust was used to avoid estate tax. I did not know that someone actually had to have an irrevocable trust to accomplish that.

 Lisa: I find that I appreciate the privacy I have with my assets in a trust.

James: When we were creating our trust, some of our friends suggested we just use a trust kit. I'm glad we used an estate attorney instead. I wasn't aware of everything charitable trusts can do.

. . . . .

WEEK 45 ACTIVITY

The professionals you choose to work with are so important. You might need a trust, and you might not. Before you decide, talk to an estate-planning attorney for an explanation of the advantages and disadvantages of a trust for you as it pertains to your own unique situation.

Trusts can be expensive, but you might have a situation that makes the need to have a trust a good option. However, take some time with this week's exercise so that when the time comes, you can make the right decision.

. . . . .

Ask Peggy
Question: Peggy, what is this chapter's takeaway?
Peggy: Trusts are complex, but properly structured they

can keep assets out of probate, aid in paying estate tax, and allow assets to be divided between the item, itself, and the income it generates.

. . . . .

Notes
Use the following lines to jot down some notes.

_____

_____

_____

_____

_____

_____

_____

_____

_____

_____

_____

_____

_____

_____

_____

_____

_____

_____

_____

_____

_____

_____

_____

_____

_____

Chapter 46

Estate Planning: Document Organization

The Children Who Couldn't Find Anything

The children were worried. Their father had always been extremely private about all financial matters. He had told them more than once that his finances were none of their business, and that they would find out soon enough how much money he had after he was dead.

But now, Dad was dying. And although his mind remained sharp, he still refused to share financial details with anyone. Their mom was very much alive but showing signs of fairly severe dementia. When they tried to ask her, she just smiled, laughed, and nodded her head. Dad had kept her on a need-to-know basis when it came to money matters too. Sadly, their father died, and the children were left to deal with their grief *and* finding their parents' assets. No one knew where anything was.

When we die, our families will miss us.

They might miss the stories we told or the rhubarb pie we baked for Sunday dinner or the way we laughed at their jokes. What we don't want is for them to miss the assets and insurance policies we have carefully saved just for them.

And by miss, I mean literally *miss* them, overlook them, and never find them.

This week's task will not only help you to live a more prosperous life, but it will also help your family and loved ones live less anxious and more prosperous lives. You will make this possible by telling them where everything they may need is before you can no longer do so.

Basically, my older clients fall into categories. The first category has a great relationship with the family, and in many cases, I know the children. Even if I have never met them, I know they have my contact information. I also know that they know where their parents' documents are located.

The second category of client doesn't have a great relationship with the family and might be afraid that the children are going to try to spend all the money or exploit them in other ways. Sometimes, their fear is valid, and sometimes, it develops over time. The third type of client, who is by far the most common, has never given any of this a thought. This chapter is written for them!

Everyone—be they eighteen or eighty—needs a list of financial documents that someone else can find. I'm sure you'll agree that seniors need such a list, but you might protest the idea of an eighteen-year-old needing a list of financial documents. I beg to differ. First, the habit of maintaining a proper financial cache is easier the earlier you start. Second, eighteen-year-olds are legally adults, and they have car loans and student loans and rental agreements and checking and savings accounts and medical insurance and these days, even possibly a credit card based on their own assets. They are old enough to marry; they might have children; or they can serve in the military and be sent to places where they might well die.

Let me say it again: Everyone needs to organize his or her financial documents into a list and then share that information with someone else. That trusted person can be a spouse, child, or friend. Sadly, I am including spouse because I have seen one spouse die and leave the other with no idea where anything is. Death is disruptive, and it often leaves surviving family members with impaired judgment.

As easy as it might seem to make a list, let me assure you, it's a tremendously important piece of your estate plan. So make it easy for your survivors to find your will, your trust, your investment accounts, and your insurance policies.

Some parents don't favor the idea of their children knowing what they might someday inherit, fearing with good reason that it might give them a false sense of security or even dull their motivation for earning their own money or making their own way in life.

The good news is that you don't have to provide the investment account balances to your children before you die. However, I should let you know that nothing makes my job as your financial planner easier than when I meet with you and your children and hear all family members are now informed and working together as a team.

I encourage my clients to make a master list of every asset, where it is located, the name of the professional to contact about it, and the contact information.

Take some time as you make this list. You might remember that you have an old savings account, a safe no one knows about, or a safety-deposit box at not one but two banks. Someone needs to know where all this is and, for the latter two, where you keep your keys or combination. With so much now done online, you also need to be sure the little book in which you keep your account names, user names, and passcodes is also included in the folder in which you keep this list—or a duplicate.

If you are a private person, you don't need to provide the list, but you should tell someone where it is. Some of my clients leave a note with me as to where the list can be found. Most clients have also provided me with insurance policies, brokerage statements, pensions, wills, trusts, and other financial documents. If you are working with a comprehensive financial planner, that person should prove to be of great value to your family in this situation.

Nothing is more stressful than the time right after someone has died. However, when a financial crisis follows a death, the pain is particularly difficult. If you had the assets set aside to take care of your family through the worst of times but they can't find the documentation or tools they need to access it, that pain will only be worse.

You've worked hard your entire life to create a financial legacy to leave your family. Make sure they can find it.

· · · · ·

Ashley: I have all my financial documents in my desk drawer at home. Jake knows exactly where everything is.

Michael: Wow, I never thought about this before! Almost everything I do is online, and yet I am 100 percent sure my wife doesn't know my user name or password for any of our financial accounts.

Lisa: It doesn't do me a lot of good to share information with Mom, because I'll probably outlive her. I need to give a list to one of my good friends. I love my nieces and nephews, but I'm not sure I want them to have full access just yet.

James: Between my attorney, my CPA, and my financial planner, everything is organized, and my wife is in the loop. She also knows I keep the key to our safety-deposit box hidden in a drawer in the dresser, but I bet nobody else does. I'd better tell my son.

· · · · ·

WEEK 46 ACTIVITY

This is such an important exercise this week, yet it is relatively easy to do. It just takes some time. I want you to make a master list of your accounts, including their location and any user names or passwords. List deeds, mineral rights, patents, safety-deposit boxes—literally anything with financial value. Let someone know where the list is located. Make sure the person who you believe knows about the list truly knows about them. It's worth a quick conversation.

If you are counting on someone your age to remember it, remember that person might be dealing with memory issues as well.

· · · · ·

Ask Peggy

Question: Peggy, what is this chapter's takeaway?

Peggy: As part of your estate plan, make a list of your assets, including passwords for critical websites and online accounts, locations of lockboxes and keys, insurance policies, investment accounts, and anything else your heirs might have difficulty locating—then, tell someone where the list is located.

· · · · ·

Notes

_____

_____

_____

Ask Peggy

Ashley: Peggy, I don't have a lot of money to pay an attorney. Do I need to create estate documents now?

Peggy: Ashley, one reason you create estate documents is to make it easier for the people you love to carry out your wishes if something happens to you. I am sure you wouldn't want to cause your parents and fiancé any more stress than necessary. I'm not trying to spend your money, but it's likely that you need at least a basic estate plan.

Michael: I never knew I could have a different power of attorney for finances and health care. How does it work?

Peggy: You could have one or two documents, but within the documents just clarify who you want to serve in each role. I would recommend you talk to the people you are considering for this just to give them a heads up.

Lisa: I remember the Schiavo case. It put everyone through so much pain. So, advanced directives can be used for accepting or rejecting medical protocols?

Peggy: Yes, advanced directives are only documents that express your wishes for your end-of-life care. Whether or not you want a feeding tube should not be a factor in whether or not you want an advanced directive.

James: Peggy, I didn't know I could use a trust to keep assets in the family while the income from those assets went to a charity.

Peggy: Yes, there are charitable trusts you can create that allow you to do that. Many people avoid making charitable donations of some assets, because they want to keep them for their children. Giving a gift of income can solve this problem.

More Planning

Chapter 47

Other Planning: Life Issues

The Parents Who Wanted To Help their Baby

A young couple considered themselves among the fortunate. They had both graduated from college without any student debt and found good jobs with retirement plans. The wife had given birth to a boy about eighteen months earlier, and now the couple wanted to start a fund for his college education. They laughed as they explained to friends that they weren't even sure he would go to college—or he might be a genius and get a full ride.

All they knew for sure was they wanted to give him what they had been given, and they figured a college education would, if nothing else, ensure he was a well-rounded, well-educated citizen. What they weren't sure about was whom to ask or what type of college savings plan to select.

College teaches us many things. We learn the skills necessary for a career, we learn what career speaks to us, we learn independence, we learn critical thinking, and ideally, we leave college better suited to contribute as Americans.

Even though a college education has come under criticism in some places recently, I believe college, ivy covered or not, remains necessary for financial success for most people, especially as our world becomes more complex.

Having at least an associate's degree raises earning potential and employment possibilities. Because of the value of a college degree, many people want to help the young people in their lives realize their full potential through higher education. However, I want to begin with a caution before we look at prudent ways to defray college expense.

The single best gift you can give your children is your own financial security. When it seems like everyone around us is buying their children nice cars and setting them up in well-decorated dorm rooms, I know you can feel as though you're letting your children down if you don't give them those things too. But children need security most. And although it might not feel like it, learning to make do and learning to work for what you want are two of the best skills you can pass on to your child.

That's why I don't feel bad when I say you have to have your own retirement plan in place before you try to save for your children's college. What that means is you must know how much money you will need to be secure in retirement, and you have to fund it sufficiently. You also need to have funding or insurance in place so that you are not left devastated by a disability, illness, or senior incapacity. Only then should you fund your children's college education.

If that seems selfish, remember that if you don't prepare for your retirement and future needs, taking care of you could fall to your children. And none of us wants that.

Even if you don't have any money to save, you can aid your children by helping them gain the skills to earn good grades in school, by explaining to them what good grades will mean down the road when it comes time to qualify for scholarships, and by looking ahead to all the options to afford and prepare for college. This begins in grade school, heats up in junior high, and becomes the main focus in high school. The family that waits to think about college until a child's senior year is a family doomed to be disappointed—a family that has already missed out on opportunities that could make college financially possible for their student.

I'm happy to say that you'll be surprised by how many free resources exist to help you. One great resource is IRS Publication 970, "Tax Benefits for Education." It provides more details on much of what we are talking about here.

As you get started with your plans, look into available grants and scholarships. Grants exist for many circumstances, including limited income. Scholarships are also issued for various accomplishments. Remember to look for ones that recognize exceptional talents, situations, ethnicities, or religious affiliations. There are scholarships for almost any imaginable demographic group. Typically, they are limited in number; there's no guarantee that your child will win one, but it pays to check it out. You might find that if your child becomes an accomplished Irish dancer or tuba player, it could be worth a nice little scholarship down the road!

Several tax credits provide free money to help pay tuition costs in the form of a dollar-for-dollar reduction in income-tax liability. The American opportunity tax credit and the lifetime learning credit both provide multiyear benefits if the student qualifies. The rules are specific, and you will need to review them in the IRS document. The American opportunity credit helps with the first four years of college, while the lifetime learning credit can be used to offset educational expenses over the course of your life.

Be careful about counting on either credit, however, until you do the math. The biggest limitation is the amount of income you can earn (annual gross income, or AGI). This can change annually, so be sure you review that number and all the other requirements.

Tuition and fees can be deductible on your income taxes for you, your spouse, and your dependents that you claim on your tax return. Again, there is a maximum AGI and additional rules, so check to see if you qualify. If you acquire a student loan to pay for your education, the interest on that loan is a deductible expense for a certain number of years.

Although other education savings vehicles exist, I would like to focus on two of them. The first is known as the Coverdell Education Savings Account. Although the amount that can be contributed each year is limited to $2,000, and there are AGI limits, it has a very interesting feature: The money can be used to pay for expenses acquired *before* the student goes to college.

The Coverdell could theoretically be funded for thirteen years, until the child reaches middle school or junior high, when expenses become higher. Then the entire amount, principal and growth, could be used to pay for band uniforms, sports equipment, or anything else that is an expense of a school-sponsored activity or a school-required purchase. The Coverdell does not have a tuition-only limitation. Any money remaining in the Coverdell could then be rolled into a 529 plan to pay for college.

The 529 educational plans have had a major change in 2018. The 529 plans used to be limited to post-secondary (think, usually, college) funding, but the new tax law allows the funds to be used to pay for private school tuition at the elementary and secondary level up to certain limits. The extracurricular expenses that can be paid out of a Coverdell cannot be paid using a 529.

One advantage of a 529 is the higher annual contribution levels each year.

Typically, that amount is limited to the amount of the gift-tax exclusion, so the giver does not have to file a gift tax return. Because 529 plans are created by the states, check the requirements of your state's plan, although most do not have an AGI limitation. This makes a 529 plan an easy vehicle to use to fund education.

Although you can make a contribution to another state's 529 plan, you cannot take a tax deduction on your state return for that plan. The only deductions are available for in-state plan contributions.

If you happen to live in a state without state income tax, there might be no deduction available, but it pays to check with the plan's rules.

I am going to share another bias with you here. In most cases, you will want to fund your own state's plan, and you rarely need a financial adviser to help you with it. Go online, enroll, and set up a way to fund it.

An adviser might try to convince you that your state's plan is inadequate and that you should use another state's plan that the adviser will help you choose. In such a case, you will pay advisory fees or commissions on top of any other costs of that state's plan.

That rarely is a wise move.

Although you will have to choose your investments, I tend to favor the age-weighted funds that become more conservative as children get older.

Yes, if there is a bad market when they are young and a good market as they approach college, they will earn less return. However, if the market takes the opposite path, they will not lose a lot of the portfolio right before they need it the most.

Of course, if you do not feel comfortable with doing this, hire a financial planner to help you decide how to proceed. And I'm sure there are times my strategy wouldn't work.

It's just a good overall rule of thumb.

Helping children learn, develop, and enter a fulfilling career is a great feeling. As long as your personal finances are in order, it is also a great achievement for you as a parent. Just remember that you don't want your own retirement savings to become ivy covered as you fund your children's education.

Ashley: College is so expensive. I can't imagine what it will cost twenty years from now. I think we'll start a family right after we're married, and because I want them to be able to pursue an education, we'll start setting aside for them what is prudent for us.

Michael: I wish I'd looked into financial options other than just taking out additional student loans. That has proved to be unnecessarily costly.

Lisa: I have many friends who have quit funding their 401(k) plans to put their children through college. I keep telling them that's a bad idea.

James: I think I'll look into a Coverdell plan rather than a 529 plan for my three-year-old granddaughter. It makes much more sense to fund something she could use in high school if need be.

· · · · ·

WEEK 47 ACTIVITY

This week's activity is more of a long-term task. First, return to the cash flow exercise from the first section of this book and look at the money that remains after you have paid your bills, funded your emergency fund, and contributed to your retirement plan.

The remaining cash flow could go to saving for college expenses for a child or a spouse or even you!

If you begin early enough in a child's life, the monthly amount you contribute could be low and still make a difference come college time. Many state plans have calculators on their websites that you can use to figure the potential impact of your contribution.

Then have a few honest conversations with your children about money while they are still in middle school or junior high. I'm sure you have already encouraged them to do their best in school—to master reading, writing, math, and science and to earn the best grades possible while they were still in grade school. Now that they have those good habits, it's time to build on them.

If your children have a particular interest or skill, they might look to refine this as they get ready to head to high school. It could give them additional college funding possibilities. Remind them of the continued importance of good grades—a young athlete with strong grades can broaden scholarship opportunities, even at out-of-state public and private universities. Well in advance of when you need it, look into any situational or ethnicity college funding available to your child—such funds are available for Native Americans students, among others.

Finally, have your children begin to take college entrance exams such as the ACT and SAT early in their academic careers. College admittance today has become a contact sport, and many applicants now take the exams multiple times. To be competitive, you need a great score.

But remember: Colleges also want well-rounded individuals who will contribute to the school's community, so make sure your children take time to volunteer, to work, to follow his or their passions, and to become the best version of themselves that they can be.

· · · · ·

Ask Peggy
Question: Peggy, what is this chapter's takeaway?
Peggy: College planning can take many forms, including your state's 529 plan and possibly a Coverdell Education Savings Account, but the best gift you can give your

child is your own financial stability, so please don't ignore your own retirement funding to pay for college tuition.

There are better ways to help your children.

. . . . .

Notes

_____

_____

_____

_____

_____

_____

_____

_____

_____

_____

_____

Chapter 48

Other Planning: Mortgages and Loans

The Serial Refinancer

His home was his biggest asset, a young entrepreneur had been told, and he took that advice seriously. He had purchased a home fifteen years ago, and he had refinanced it twice. Each time, he had stripped out the equity he had built and invested it into a business. He had begun with a fifteen-year mortgage, and if he'd done nothing, his home would be already paid off. But instead, it held almost no equity. Everything was fine until the entrepreneur made a bad business decision. The assets he had purchased with the equity were sold off for pennies on the dollar. He lost his business and, with it, his ability to make the mortgage payments. He didn't know what he would do.

Years ago, mortgages were boring.

They were typically issued for thirty years, and before you tried to buy a place, you saved 20 percent of the price, then you bought the house, you made your payment every month, with a little extra money if you could add it, and eventually, you owned your home—usually just before you were ready to retire. Before your bank would give you the mortgage, you had to prove to them that you could make the payments. Once you did this, the bank held the loan and celebrated your homeownership as much as you did.

Somewhere along the way as the investment world looked for more ways to make money, mortgages became commodities, investments to be bundled and sold. Lenders no longer demanded proof of your income.

Meanwhile, frightened by the dot-com disaster of 1997 to 2001, people sought investments that they perceived to be safer, and what could be safer than real estate?

Of course, such thinking worked until it didn't, and the great recession of December 2007 to June 2009 was when the floor fell out of the real estate market. That led to massive drops in real estate values and almost impossibly strict lending rules. And yet, people still want to buy houses. If you're one of them, here are a few things to consider when purchasing or refinancing a home.

Don't feel compelled to seek homeownership if it doesn't seem right for you, and don't ever buy more home than you can afford. And last but not least, please don't get pressured into buying more house than you want—or, ideally, than you need. Although it has the reputation of being the foundation of the "American dream," homeownership isn't the best planning strategy for everyone. You need to access your financial situation. And if buying a house doesn't fit into your financial plan, don't do it.

If you do want to own a home, purchase something that keeps your financial plan on track. You don't need to buy a house that costs as much as you are qualified to borrow, typically about 28 percent of your gross income.

I usually recommend that clients hold off buying a house until they save enough money to put down a sizable percentage of the price tag as a down payment. I realize that is an old-fashioned recommendation. However, I believe your life will be far less stressful if you put 20 percent down on that first home purchase—if only because it means the very first day you walk into your home, you will already be in the black with a nice bit of equity in the house.

Before you try to purchase a home, be sure to review your credit score and begin to work on it if it is low. If you need some strategies, review the chapter on ways to improve a credit score. Low credit scores can lead to higher interest rates or outright denial of the loan.

As with other financial products, loans have become complicated. Be sure you read all the fine print and understand what you've read. If something doesn't make sense or seems wrong, do research until you are sure you know what you are signing or ask your financial adviser. Tread carefully with those complicated mortgages. The best mortgages are straightforward and easy to understand. If you have to create an exotic arrangement to allow you to buy the house, you probably can't afford it!

When it comes to refinancing a house, you might very well lower your monthly payment, but you might also increase the total amount of interest you'll pay over the length of the loan. So even if you understand the paperwork, be careful if you are refinancing a home.

If you want to lower the interest rate, remember that in any loan, you pay more interest toward the beginning of the loan than you do at the end. Even though you might be paying a lower rate of interest, you will also be starting over as far as your time horizon. You might be improving your monthly cash flow, but you are also likely increasing the total amount you will pay for your loan. Of course, this isn't always the case, but it is the part of refinancing that no one seems to remember. And one last thing: Be sure to include all the additional closing costs in the equation before you decide whether refinancing is a good decision for you.

If you are trying to decide whether to take on a ten-, fifteen- or thirty-year loan, consider weighing the impact of mandatory higher payments against paying a higher interest rate. Although I love low interest rates as much as anyone, I also know that cash flow is king when it comes to economic stability. You need to know that whatever you decide to do, you will have to make that payment every month.

Get a mortgage without an early payoff penalty to allow you to make extra payments when you can. The more you can pay toward the principal, especially early in the life of your loan, the more years you might shave off your mortgage term. People are often surprised how an extra $100 a month quickly makes a dent in the principal owed.

Finally, pay attention to the interest-rate environment when you consider borrowing money. When you are the borrower, lower rates are better. If rates are comparatively low when you are reading this, it might make sense to consider borrowing money earlier rather than later. But, of course, you have to look at all your decisions within the context of your financial plan.

Your mortgage is probably the largest sum of money you will borrow in your life. It's a contract, and you should pay attention to the details so that you understand the agreement you are making with the bank.

For some people, purchasing a home is a great decision, but you need to decide what is best for you and your family, what will help you and your family prosper the most.

· · · · ·

 Ashley: I don't want to buy a house until we are sure where we will live. I know I don't want to work at the mall the rest of my life.

 Michael: I understand all of this, but sometimes it feels overwhelming to take on a debt for so long. I think we might want to look at refinancing from a thirty-year mortgage to a fifteen-year loan or maybe even try to pay it off early.

Lisa: I'm so glad I didn't refinance when I remodeled my kitchen. This way, I'll have my house paid off before I retire. Whenever I have a little extra money, I try to make an extra payment on the mortgage. It's amazing how even one extra payment a year will cut what I pay in interest as well as the length of the loan!

James: Thank goodness the house is paid for and has been for some time. It's nice to not have to deal with a mortgage payment anymore. And we're careful to stay on top of our property taxes and insurance payments.

· · · · ·

WEEK 48 ACTIVITY

If you are considering purchasing a house or refinancing an existing one, list all the positive and negative factors before doing so. Compare the total amount of interest you will pay with each of the options against any possible cash flow changes. Try to consider any life changes that might arise and whether or not they will impact your decision.

Reasons to buy: _____

_____

_____

Reasons not to buy: _____

_____

_____

Reasons to refinance: _____

_____

_____

Reasons not to refinance: _____

_____

_____

Monthly payment: _____

_____

_____

Total interest paid: _____

_____

_____

Anticipated life changes: _____

_____

_____

· · · · ·

Ask Peggy
Question: Peggy, what is this chapter's takeaway?
Peggy: Owning a home is fine, but be financially pre-
pared and don't buy more house than you can afford.

· · · · ·

Notes

_____

_____

Chapter 49

Other Planning: To Buy or Lease a Car

The Attorney Who Wanted To Keep Up With his Friends

A young attorney needed a car. He and his wife had some money saved, and he could easily have bought a decent used car and paid cash. However, he was getting a lot of pressure from his colleagues to buy something new and showy. They encouraged him to lease a car if he couldn't afford the purchase payments. He didn't feel it was in his best interest to lease a car, because he wanted something that he would actually own at the end of the process. But the pressure at the office to acquire more vehicle than he needed was intense.

The ads always look too good to be true—a sleek car zooming down city streets or banking around mountain curves. (Warning, this is a closed course and a professional driver. Don't try this, even if you buy our car.) Young men and women with perfect hair and stylish clothes smile at each other, his hand closing over hers on a close-up shot of the stick shift.

You, too, can have this experience at a lower price than you ever thought. Of course, in the fine print at the bottom of the screen, the end of the ad mentions that the monthly payment is a lease, not the purchase price. The car might be exactly what you want, and it might well fit into your financial plan. However, taking some time to weigh the advantages and disadvantages of buying or leasing a car is always wise. The following tables break down some of the more important considerations as you decide which option will work the best for your financial plan.

The first set of tables discusses buying a vehicle, and certainly that is a more traditional way of acquiring a car. I would, however, remind you that in most cases, a new car will depreciate about 11 percent the moment you drive it off the lot. Your best strategy might be to buy a used car that holds it value.

Buying Pros	Buying Cons
Once the car is paid off, it is yours to drive as long as you want	Without cash to pay for car outright, you will have to finance and pay interest
You have the ability to sell the car when you choose	Your credit score may impact the interest rate you pay
You can customize the car as you choose	Monthly purchase payment will nearly always be higher than monthly lease payment
If you damage the car, it is your decision whether to repair the damage	You have to sell the vehicle yourself or use it as a trade-in on the next vehicle
You have unlimited mileage; high mileage may impact trade-in value	Older vehicles may have higher repair costs

If you use your personal car for business, there are tax deductions that can come with it. Before you decide to lease a vehicle for business, however, be sure you will receive a tax benefit. It might tip the scale in the favor of ownership.

I favor purchasing a vehicle over leasing one, and for most people, I believe it is more cost effective. However, there are some advantages to leasing, especially from a business perspective. It's important that you understand what a lease can and cannot provide for you.

Leasing Pros	Leasing Cons
You are always driving a relatively new car	You never own a car
You don't need to save a down payment	You always have payments
Monthly lease payment will usually be lower than monthly buy payments	You are limited on the miles you drive without incurring a penalty
It may be easier to take as a business expense if vehicle is only a business vehicle	Minor damage can incur a major penalty
You will pay no sales tax	You can't customize the car
Your credit score will not be as much of a factor	You're committed to the vehicle for term of the lease; canceling early triggers a penalty

Whether you are purchasing or leasing a vehicle, read any and all paperwork carefully—don't let the salesman rush you or discourage you from doing this. Try to take the paperwork home so you can get out of the stressful environment of a car dealership. You might find that also puts you in the driver's seat when it comes to negotiating a better price for the car. As in every other aspect of financial planning, your personal situation will dictate whether you should buy or lease a car. The correct choice comes down to asking yourself the right questions.

Before you make a decision, ask yourself how long you want to drive the car. If you think it is a car you want to keep for a long period of time, then buying is probably the right decision. If you know you will turn it in after a year or two because you like to buy new cars or your work demands it, you might be better off leasing.

If you plan to use the vehicle in business, talk to your financial planner or tax professional before you make a final decision. They can help you determine whether you will receive the tax benefits you are anticipating.

Finally, before you buy or lease a car, be sure your cash flow is sufficient to make the payments—and pay the insurance. Some people are shocked when they see what the cost of buying a car tag and insuring a new vehicle has become.

Buying or leasing a car won't give you and your loved one beautiful hair or race-car driving skills. But that's okay. Slow, scenic drives are often the best!

. . . . .

 Ashley: I've learned I can't even go onto a showroom floor before I'm ready to take action. I love the smell of a new car!

 Michael: I thought I could get a tax break for business if I leased a car. I'd better ask my CPA if that's true.

 Lisa: I'm careful about everything else in my life. I like to drive a new car, but I've leased the last three. It works for me.

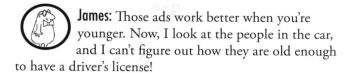

James: Those ads work better when you're younger. Now, I look at the people in the car, and I can't figure out how they are old enough to have a driver's license!

· · · · ·

WEEK 49 ACTIVITY

You might need to save this activity for the next time you are looking to purchase or lease a car. I have provided you with a similar copy of the comparison tables, except this time, I have given you room to write notes in each of the boxes. I have also structured the boxes to apply more directly to you as you consider your circumstances.

I want you to complete the boxes before you make your final lease/purchase decision. Although I tend to favor purchasing, the cash flow components of both alternatives are strong enough to make the activity worthwhile, even if you are considering purchasing the vehicle.

Buying Pro Questions	Buying Con Questions

Leasing Pro Questions	Leasing Con Questions

· · · · ·

Ask Peggy

Question: Peggy, what is this chapter's takeaway?

Peggy: Consider the advantages and disadvantages of buying or leasing a car, and remember that if you want an asset you can drive a long time without mileage or accessory limitations, buying might be the economical choice.

· · · · ·

Notes

_____

_____

_____

_____

Chapter 50

Other Planning: Identity Theft

The Grandmother Who Just Wanted To Help

When the phone rang late one night, a grandmother who lived alone was concerned. The phone never brought good news after midnight. On the other end of the call, she heard her grandson close to tears. He'd been arrested on what he called trumped-up charges while vacationing with friends in Mexico. If he didn't get money for an attorney that night, he'd face his accusers alone in court the next day.

The grandmother knew it was Spring Break and recalled her daughter saying something about the trip. She asked the sobbing teenager why he hadn't called his mother. He said he couldn't reach her. The grandmother got her purse, pulled out her credit card, and read the vital information into the phone.

After she hung up, she called her daughter, who answered the phone in a sleepy but alarmed voice. As Grandma started to explain what had happened, her daughter interrupted. Spring Break was next week. The young man who was supposedly in a Mexican jail was sleeping two doors down in his own bed.

Identity theft is a growing problem that most of us will find a need to address. Almost every day, it seems, a major financial institution or company or entity—be it a bank, credit monitoring service, retail conglomerate, online company, or the federal government—announces that it has suffered a breach. It might be a retail store's client credit card records or someone calling and pretending to be your grandson. Identity thieves constantly find new ways to try to steal personal information, and when they are successful, it can take years to clean up the mess.

Identity theft is a scary and complex topic; however, the breaches do tend to fall into categories. Each requires a slightly different defense plan.

Phone scams. Don't trust anyone who calls you and then asks for personal information over the phone. The caller might claim to be affiliated with a service you use, and your caller ID might even confirm that. Be wary. Get the problem the caller is claiming to report, and then call back using contact information you have in your records or find on the official website for the entity.

Know that the callers can be very persistent, acting as though you are in trouble or have made a mistake. A recent scam has involved someone claiming to be with the IRS, telling the victims that there is an error on their tax return and more tax is owed—the latest IRS fraud is someone claiming that an arrest warrant has been issued in your name.

Don't believe that. The IRS *never* calls to tell you that you are being audited or owe them money. Hang up right away.

If someone calls you, never give personal information over the phone, even if you think you know the person. And don't believe anyone who calls and claims to be a family member in trouble. Typically, this scam involves asking you to send money to get the person out of jail. The perpetrator counts on your not being very familiar with what your niece or grandchild might sound like when upset.

The con is that the person begs you not to call the parents and get the caller in trouble. Your job is to stay calm, ask where the caller is supposedly jailed, and end the call—then call other family members to locate the "jailed" grandchild or nephew. Don't be surprised if the missing child answers the phone when you call!

Internet and online scams. Do not open e-mails sent from people you do not know, but also be cautious about unusual or cryptic e-mails from people whose names you recognize. All too often, the latter means your friend's account has been hacked. And always, *always* resist the temptation to open an attachment you didn't know was coming, until you can confirm that it is legitimate.

Basically, keep your guard up. We're all aware that hacking occurs on high levels on a regular basis now, so you should assume that you are also at risk, even if you think you aren't. Be particularly suspicious of e-mails with misspelled words or obvious grammatical mistakes, whether you do business with the company or not. But also realize that identity thieves are constantly upping their game. Yes, there are still thieves who send e-mails that look as if they came from an illiterate Romanian prince, but more likely these days, the e-mail will appear to be an official request from an attorney or the government, possibly complete with forms attached.

That is why you should never respond to an unrequested, unsolicited, or unfamiliar e-mail, even if that e-mail request claims your account has been breached and you need to confirm your identity—at once!

The e-mail may look legitimate, but it is likely from a site that has been "ghosted," meaning an ill-intentioned outsider has hijacked the company's e-mail system. To avoid being caught up or fooled in such a situation, contact the company independently, explain what happened, and ask if there is anything you need to do.

Meanwhile, remember that it pays to change your passwords frequently—keep your user names and passwords in an easy to carry pocket-size notebook. When creating passwords, use letters, numbers, and special symbols.

To prevent your devices from being hacked, make sure your electronics have a virus protection program and keep it up to date.

You might think e-mails and other communications are safe while using your laptop in your hotel room or in a public Wi-Fi hot spot, but using public Wi-Fi is like screaming out your Social Security number in a crowded coffee shop. That means you shouldn't access bank information, investment information, or other sites that have your data readily available. If you have your own Wi-Fi service at home or on a portable device, keep a password on it to make it difficult for others to use.

Using social media is without a doubt a popular pastime, and most of us have at least one account, be it Facebook or Instagram or LinkedIn. Just be careful about what you post on social media. Approach it as if you were publishing it on the front page of a national newspaper.

And remember: Always avoid saying you are out of town or crowing about the two-week vacation you're about to take or even saying that you'll be going into the hospital for surgery. Thieves read social media posts to learn when your house will be empty, and you're just doing their work for them when you take a photo on the deck of a cruise ship labeled, "Bon voyage—see you in two weeks." With help like that, the thieves know they don't even have to rush!

Mail and printed material scams. It might seem a tad obsessive, but I suggest that you purchase a shredder and shred all documents that have personal information on them, even credit card applications or credit card checks conveniently sent by the card company. Buy a shredder that cuts in both directions, leaving the shredded paper in little squares.

Keep your printed checks in a safe place—even canceled checks that come with your monthly bank statement. I suggest you mail your bills at the post office rather than leave outgoing mail in your mailbox at home. Thieves drive through neighborhoods looking for raised flags. Then they steal the checks you are mailing and cash them or erase the ink and write them out to themselves. Go to the U.S. Post Office to send bills or set up an online payment system.

Make a little time each month to review credit card statements for bogus charges. Thieves often start with small charges first, hoping to confirm that the card is active but without tipping you off that they have access to it. Credit card companies used to allow you to disclaim most fraudulent charges, but they've recently added a shorter window in which you can report a problem. Be sure you understand your card's rules.

Other ways to avoid identity theft. Don't assume—and ask questions. First, ask any professionals who assist you how they protect your identity. Ask if they notify you if a data breach occurs—and how fast. Periodically check your credit report for abnormal activity. Try to stay up to date with the latest scams, and remember to keep software up to date.

To help you with all of this, you might consider hiring a monitoring service, but you need to be sure it is legitimate. Be sure you know what services you are purchasing and understand all the terms of any agreements before moving forward. I suggest you also do a quick search to learn what you can about the company and its parent company. This might be a good time to buy American.

My final tip is to encourage you to share all these ideas with others. Data thieves often feel emboldened by public complacency and a lack of law enforcement. The major hacks that are originating overseas are awful, but you can take many steps to protect yourself from the more petty and common ones.

Even though we tell ourselves that it is the young and naive or the old and trusting who are vulnerable to being scammed, in truth, it can be any one of us. It is a constant and ongoing fight with those who want to steal our identity. Yet with a little thought and attention, you can take many steps that are easy and effective and will make a difference when it comes to your personal security.

· · · · ·

 Ashley: I need to remember not to post photographs from my vacations until I'm home!

 Michael: I can't believe how many people use passwords without numbers or letters.

 Lisa: My mother told me that her friend received a phone call saying her grandson was in jail in Mexico. She doesn't have a grandson!

 James: I always review my credit card statements every month. Once in a while, I find a mistake, although so far I've never found fraud.

· · · · ·

WEEK 50 ACTIVITY

This week's activity is more general in nature. You might have discovered that you do something that puts you at risk. Maybe you put outgoing mail in your mailbox or post pictures of yourself while you are on vacation.

Make an effort to stop any and all of those behaviors that could put you, your family, or your home at risk—not to mention your finances. None of the changes is difficult or takes much time, but they are important to do.

· · · · ·

Ask Peggy

Question: Peggy, what is this chapter's takeaway?

Peggy: Never give identifying or credit card information to someone who calls you or sends you an e-mail; instead, contact the person or entity with contact information you already possess to make the payment.

· · · · ·

Notes

Jot down a few notes about what you did this week. When you look back at the book later, it will remind you of your progress.

_____

_____

_____

_____

_____

_____

_____

_____

_____

Peggy Doviak

_____

_____

_____

_____

_____

_____

_____

_____

_____

_____

_____

_____

_____

_____

Chapter 51

Other Planning: Being your Own Advocate

The Baby Boomer Activist

A baby boomer had come of age during the 1960s. Forever interested in politics, civil rights, and justice, she had campaigned, called, and picketed for decades. She had even been arrested a couple of times while protesting.

Fortunately, she had always been released quickly in such cases without charges, but her behavior drove her son crazy. He couldn't have cared less about politics until a piece of legislation arose that threatened his job. Suddenly he wanted to let the people in charge know that he had an opinion.

It's easy to believe one person can't make a difference. The status quo seems dominated by unlimited money and power. However, history says otherwise. That is the beauty of our form of government—one citizen can make a difference if you vote.

Your goal for this week is to begin to pay attention to laws, tax codes, and proposed legislation both locally, statewide, and nationally as it relates to you and your family's prosperity—from your quality of life to your neighborhood schools to your environment to your money.

We're not talking about a lot of time, just fifteen to thirty minutes a day listening, watching, or reading the news. Besides that, every American needs to take the time to understand the tax code. Most people who make mistakes on their tax returns do so out of ignorance. Not knowing the code can cost you deductions and credits to which you are legally entitled. It might even cause you to list a source of revenue in the wrong place, costing you money.

Not understanding taxes can also cause you to underpay your taxes. You might list revenue in the wrong place or handle a profit in the wrong way. The IRS has an excellent website, www.irs.gov, and it provides free online books and pamphlets that can be of assistance to you. Don't rely only on the marketing material provided by a company; that was created to represent that company in the best light.

Be aware of the laws that regulate the financial services industry. Make certain you understand every investment or risk management product before you agree to purchase it. Again, you will need to do your own research rather than just accept the material provided to you.

Remember that not everyone has your best interest at heart. And it doesn't help that many of the rules have fine distinctions and nuances that require careful study.

Fortunately, many organizations exist to help you. Within the industry, the Financial Planning Association, www.plannersearch.org, and the CERTIFIED FINANCIAL PLANNER™ Board of Standards' consumer site, www.letsmakeaplan.org, provide tips and updates.

Consumer protection groups and publications, such as AARP and *Consumer Reports*, also do their best to help the public understand key issues related to personal finance. Other specialized organizations, such as The Committee for the Fiduciary Standard, www.thefiduciarystandard.org, also provide excellent legislative updates. But when all is said and done, you have to become your own advocate. Once you know the issues, you need to write your elected officials when their legislation warrants it—and encourage others to do the same thing. Be a savvy financial consumer and a knowledgeable voter. It should go without saying that the latter is your right and your responsibility as an American.

Once you know the position of your elected officials, vote accordingly. Never even consider not voting in an election. Our vote is how we change or maintain the status quo. It's how we can affect legislative processes and outcomes. It's the most powerful tool we have as Americans.

It is easy to underestimate the importance of staying knowledgeable and informed as a citizen. It's easy to fall into the trap of believing our vote doesn't count. However, if we don't take a stand for our own best interest, it's unlikely that anyone else will. As the old saying goes, "If you're not at the table, you're probably on the menu."

· · · · ·

Ashley: I'm registered to vote but must confess I haven't done it often. I'm so busy. I'm going to look up the address to my polling place right now.

Michael: I didn't know that the IRS had consumer information. That would be a source I could trust. I need to check out its website.

Lisa: I need to do a better job of keeping up on current events. I had no idea they could impact the stock market or bond interest rates.

James: I like to check the political positions of my elected officials. It's like being a sports fan. It's confusing at first, but soon you know the names of all the players.

· · · · ·

WEEK 51 ACTIVITY

This week, I want you to take some steps to start staying informed about laws and legislation related to your finances. If you aren't registered to vote, go register. Then create a mix of news sources you trust, maybe the *Wall Street Journal* or Bloomberg for financial news, National Public Radio and the *Washington Post* or the *New York Times* for national news, combined with your local newspaper, television and radio stations, and online and cable options.

Yes, some of the information may be dry, but remind yourself that it is the ticket to making the most of your money and protecting both your prosperity and your country. We are all called to participate in this young experiment we know as the United States of America, and if you don't vote, our democracy suffers in the end.

· · · · ·

Ask Peggy
Question: Peggy, what is this chapter's takeaway?
Peggy: Stay up on laws and legislation that can impact your prosperity, and never miss an opportunity to vote.

· · · · ·

Notes

_____

_____

_____

Chapter 52

Other Planning: Whom Do You Trust?

My Mother Trusted a Broker

Well, it's Chapter 52, and that means this is our last story. It is actually my story—a cautionary tale about my mother, me, and a stockbroker!

In March 2000, shortly after my mother retired, a broker she was working with invested all of her 401(k) funds in dot-com single stocks and a technology fund. During their sessions, he expressed little interest in hearing about her goals or learning about her concerns or risk tolerance. When the market collapsed, my mother lost more than 40 percent of her holdings, because the broker had convinced her that she should not sell. Most of the companies her funds were invested in went bankrupt.

In 2002, I met a good friend of my husband who invested for a living, and I asked him how I could learn about the financial field. He mentioned several books and author names, and I sought them out. Reading them, however, quickly made me realize how many people do not understand investing and financial planning. Most people are as vulnerable as my mother was when she entered retirement.

I didn't want what that broker had done to my mother to happen to anyone else, so I changed careers from curriculum development and corporate training to finance. This book is the culmination of what I envisioned more than a decade ago—a book that would take the mystery out of personal finance.

I'm using this last chapter to provide recommendations that I hope will help you choose a financial professional. You will find some of the information echoed on other consumer-driven financial sites. However, I have added a few additional considerations that I believe you will find useful. There is no one more helpful than a good financial professional, and in my opinion, few professionals more dangerous than a poor or unethical one.

First, you need to know—and understand—the credentials of your financial professional. Although an alphabet soup of credentials exists, not all credentials are created equally. I believe if you want to work with someone to help you with the topics in this book, you should work with a CERTIFIED FINANCIAL PLANNER™ practitioner. The CERTIFIED FINANCIAL PLANNER™ Board of Standards has education requirements, ethics requirements, a disciplinary board, and a six-hour comprehensive exam with a pass-rate percentage in the sixties. It also requires thirty continuing education hours every two years. The Board also requires that an adviser have a bachelor's degree and three years of experience. It's a high standard to reach and maintain—and that's why you want your financial planner to have one.

There are other good designations; however, some designations do not require much academic rigor. Don't be impressed with a long list of letters after an adviser's name. Take the time to understand what they mean. If you need financial planning, the CFP® practitioner is the one to choose. Many consumer groups suggest finding someone with at least three years of experience. Of course, if everyone followed this advice, new planners would have difficulty entering the profession.

That said, experience does provide planners with knowledge they rarely have at the beginning of their careers. So if you are working with a less experienced planner, it might be best if the person is associated with an existing firm and mentored by more experienced planners. You also need to understand the background of your adviser. You can learn this by checking them out on websites associated with the regulating agencies. One such site is Financial Industry Regulatory Authority site "Broker Check," http://brokercheck.finra.org/Search/GenericSearch. There you'll find information on a broker, an adviser, or a firm.

Once you have completed the search, if an adviser has had disciplinary action in the past, you need to ask what happened, and you should get a reasonable explanation in writing. Someone glibly brushing off an issue scares me more than someone who admits to having made a mistake.

If you have concerns with an adviser's behavior, contact the adviser and supervisor. Written complaints must be kept in compliance files, and if the problem is a misunderstanding, this is the easiest way to resolve it. If that isn't effective, you can find consumer hotlines or phone numbers and e-mail addresses on regulatory agencies' websites. If you don't have Internet access, call your state's securities office for contact information on where to report a complaint.

Most people who work in finance are ethical, but you need to know what to do if something concerning happens. You also need to know how the adviser is compensated. Studies have shown that some people believe that they pay their adviser nothing. Other people admit that they have no idea how much the adviser is paid. Nothing is inherently wrong with any compensation structure, but you need to know who profits from your decisions—and how. You also need to know that the industry plays with this language to keep it vague. Fee-only advisers do not take commission; commission-only advisers take only commission; fee and commission, also known as fee-based advisers, take both types of compensation depending on the circumstances.

Some people charge flat fees; some charge by the hour; some charge based on assets under management; some get paid from companies for selling you products. Just remember this—*no one* works for free.

Be leery of people who aren't open about how they get paid. There is nothing wrong with asking advisers how much they will be compensated for their recommendations, and how much it will cost you. Tell them you would like them to explain and include your total fees—management fees, commissions, any expenses associated with the implementation, and any other costs. Again, I would recommend that you get this in writing.

Next, check the kinds of services the adviser provides and what type of client he or she cultivates. Think about this process as a job interview. You are interviewing people to see if you want them to work for you. For instance, do they provide financial planning services and portfolio management—do you need both of those things?

Sometimes, even CFP® certificants focus on portfolios. Will you have to transfer your assets to them? It might be a good idea to do this, but you need to understand their business model and why they are recommending that you do so.

Are you the largest or smallest client? Is there a minimum number of assets you must have to be a client or is there a minimum fee you will pay? What is involved in terminating the relationship? How easy will it be to transfer your portfolio away from the planner? Are the products proprietary, which could potentially impact your tax liability if you move the account? You want to be sure that the services provided match your needs and that you can afford the level of services you need. Advisers work in many different ways, and the cost for their services can vary greatly. Make sure you interview a few advisers and select the one that best meets your needs and budget.

To learn more, many consumer groups suggest asking the adviser to provide references. However, because of privacy issues, many of us cannot give out the names of our clients. Furthermore, some regulatory agencies do not allow the adviser to ask clients to provide references.

Nevertheless, there are still good ways of learning about the adviser. Internet sources, review sites, and social media can provide interesting insight.

And if the adviser frequently works with other professionals (I would want more than one) such as an attorney or a CPA, that person might be able to give you both insight into the caliber of peers the adviser associates with and a reference for the adviser. Clergy members, fellow civic club members, or the adviser's college instructors might also be able to provide insight. You can learn a lot about a person's character without talking directly to a client.

If the adviser is quick to show you awards, I suggest doing some checking. Real awards are great, and advisers should share that information with you. However, some awards are purely for selling the most products or even worse, the award is a piece of crystal that the adviser easily purchases. Being recognized by your peers or your industry is valuable—a sign of respect—and if legitimate, it should be part of your assessment. Just be sure you know what the adviser actually did to earn the award.

The next question, which can seem unimportant, is whether the adviser is a person you like. Financial people tend to be extroverts and very friendly, but the adviser should speak to you with respect. If you and your significant other go together, does the adviser talk to both of you? Does the adviser make you feel stupid or try to impress you too much? Were your questions welcomed? You should leave with a positive impression, but don't let a positive impression override the other criteria. Keep in mind that entire classes and marketing programs are devoted to how to appear caring to clients.

Ultimately, the *most important question* will be: Is the adviser willing to act as your fiduciary? Be careful here because the word *fiduciary* carries a legal connotation.

Besides putting your interests ahead of his or her own, a fiduciary adviser takes on a different role if you have a dispute. Generally, if you believe your financial professional has improperly handled your investments and you complain to regulators, you have to prove what the adviser did wrong. You have to explain how your risk tolerance was ignored, your personal situation wasn't taken into consideration, or some other issue wasn't considered.

However, when your adviser is a fiduciary, all you have to say in your complaint is that you believe your adviser has done something "wrong." It is then up to the adviser to show the regulators how he or she made appropriate decisions. In other words, the burden of proof for inappropriate behavior moves from you to the adviser.

This is a powerful legal distinction, and it explains why so many advisers want to dodge the responsibility. Of course, it's not hard to prove if the adviser has acted properly as a fiduciary and has documented the actions made.

Finally, not everyone is forced to act as a fiduciary. While legally registered investment advisory firms and their affiliated advisers hold a fiduciary standard, brokers do not. The existence of dually registered financial professionals who are both advisers and brokers might lead to the most confusion, because they can put the "adviser hat" on and take it off during the course of the engagement. It can be difficult for a consumer to know which standard such an adviser is following in any specific situation.

Many of us in the industry are working hard to make it a law that everyone who works with your money should hold a fiduciary responsibility, but it's a difficult fight. In fact, the rules around a mandatory fiduciary standard are being modified right now by the U.S. Department of Labor, the Security Exchange Commission, and CERTIFIED FINANCIAL PLANNERS™ Board of Standards. Again, be smart: Keep up with the legislation and rules. You can always demand to work with a fiduciary and can refuse advisers who don't hold to the standard. The voice of the public is the easiest way to change the law.

Recently, the DOL's Committee for the Fiduciary Standard, thefiduciarystandard.org, went so far as to create and adopt a fiduciary oath. Any financial professional you work with should be willing to sign this oath and share it with you. If the adviser won't sign the oath, don't work with that person. Once it is signed, be sure you keep it forever.

It's that important—your best interest is at stake.

The Fiduciary Oath

I will put my client's best interest first.

I will act with prudence; that is, with the skill, care, diligence, and good judgment of a professional.

I will not mislead clients and I will provide conspicuous, full, and fair disclosure of all important facts.

I will avoid conflicts of interest.

I will fully disclose and fairly manage, in my clients' favor any unavoidable conflicts.

I hope you feel better prepared now to choose someone to help you with your finances. Choosing the right person is an investment in time that pays both a good return and dividends.

As you move forward toward prosperity, your financial planner will be a partner and a resource, and you want the adviser to be someone confident enough to refer you to a specialist when the occasion warrants. That is not a weakness in your planner; it's a strength.

· · · · ·

 Ashley: I've always been intimidated by financial professionals. With the information I've learned, I'll be the one in control of the conversation now!

 Michael: I wonder if my fraternity brother Bob has any of these designations. He's always calling me trying to get me to invest money with him.

 Lisa: It's hard enough getting a financial adviser to take me seriously. When I go with my mother to a meeting, I feel as though her adviser is patting us both on the head.

 James: I'm glad we always worked with a CERTIFIED FINANCIAL PLANNER™ practitioner for almost as long as it has been a designation. I remember when our adviser got his certification!

· · · · ·

WEEK 52 ACTIVITY

I want you to consider my suggestions before you engage a financial professional. Even if you are already working with someone, you might want to review with him some of the points above.

Although I have covered the subjects I believe to be most important, you might have an issue that I haven't addressed. If I have skipped one of your concerns, please know that there are many consumer advocacy groups that can provide you with a list of questions to ask a financial professional before you work with one, including the CFP Board, www.letsmakeaplan.org; the Financial Planning Association consumer site, www.plannersearch.org; the National Association of Personal Finance Advisor's site, www.NAPFA.org; or the Garrett Planning Network's www.garrettplanningnetwork.com/about/how-to-choose-an-advisor.

. . . . .

Ask Peggy

Question: Peggy, what is this chapter's takeaway?

Peggy: Require a fiduciary level of care from anyone who works with your money, and don't work with them if they are unable or unwilling to promise it in writing.

. . . . .

Notes

_____

_____

_____

_____

_____

_____

_____

Ask Peggy

 Ashley: Knowing the IRS would never call me about an audit or to demand payment is such a relief. I've had phone messages from people claiming to be the IRS, and it is always so scary!

Peggy: Yes, it is, Ashley. The IRS will only notify you in writing if you are being audited. Just hang up on those calls and ignore those scary messages.

 Michael: The 529 plan usage changes in the new tax legislation mean I can only use it to pay tuition before college, not high school expenses?

Peggy: That's right, Michael. That's why the change has been seen as more favorable for private schools. Remember that if you qualify, the Coverdell ESA can be used for any approved school expenses, not just tuition.

 Lisa: Peggy, are you serious? A financial adviser doesn't have to always act in my best interest? Even when I've given them my life savings?

Peggy: I know, Lisa. It's galling. Investment adviser firms are fiduciaries, but firms who act as brokers don't have that legal liability. It's important to make anyone who handles your money act as your fiduciary—and get it in writing!

 James: I remember when average people stood up and got politically active in the 1960s. Many things changed. Can I contact any member of Congress?

Peggy: Yes, but unless you are a constituent, they probably won't speak to you. But do take time to know and talk to your own legislators and keep in contact with them, even if you have political disagreements.

The Bonus Chapter

The New Tax Cuts and Jobs Act

The Planner Looking for Accurate Information

Shortly after President Donald Trump signed the 2017 Tax Cuts and Jobs Act, a local financial planner was looking for accurate information about the new law. She knew it had major impacts for her clients' finances and planning, and she didn't mind doing the research.

However, what she found was that while the U.S. Congress had offered many ideas to reform the U.S. tax code, most of them were not in the final bill. The planner soon realized many of the articles about the bill were published before the bill was *signed*. As a result, some of them gave misleading information. She knew it wasn't "fake news," but rather the unexpected, last-minute changes typical in the law-making process. It was her job to make sure her clients knew what the *actual law* was and would mean for them.

· · · · ·

At the very end of 2017, Congress passed and the President signed an overhaul of our tax code. The Tax Cuts and Jobs Act makes changes to both corporate and individual tax law, but the majority of the *individual* deductions end after 2025. Of course, given the state of mind in Washington, D.C., the entire law could be revised by then too.

I am including this bonus chapter here for two reasons:

1. I believe in the old-fashioned idea of exceeding expectations or going that extra mile. The tax law changes came after this book was written, but both my publisher and I believe in the spirit of how a CERTIFIED FINANCIAL PLANNER™ pro approaches his or her work—basically that it was worth taking a little longer to add an extra chapter to make sure you, the reader got what you needed *now*.

2. I believe this bonus chapter is critical as you create a financial plan. Use it as an overview to the law, as I am covering only the most important changes at a summary level. Please also talk to your attorney, tax preparer, and financial planner to see what parts of the new law will impact you and your taxes. Lastly, unless otherwise noted, I assume a Married Filing Jointly marital status in the charts below.

Changes to Tax Brackets

The most basic change in the law is the tax rates, which are lowered for most filers, as you can see from the anticipated tax brackets for 2018 before the Act, compared to the new rates.

2018 Scheduled Rates Before the New TCIA

Marginal Rate	Single	Married Filing Jointly	Head of Household	Married Filing Separate
10%	$0-9,525	$0-19,050	$0-13,600	$0-9,525
15%	$9,525-38,700	$19,050-77,400	$13,600-51,850	$9,525-38,700
25%	$38,700-93,700	$77,400-156,150	$51,850-133,850	$38,700-78,075
28%	$93,700-195,450	$156,150-237,950	$133,850-216,700	$78,075-118,975
33%	$195,450-424,950	$237,950-424,950	$216,700-424,950	$118,975-212,475
35%	$424,950-426,700	$424,950-480,050	$424,950-453,350	$212,475-240,025
39.6%	Over $426,700	Over $480,050	Over $453,350	Over $240,025

New 2018 Rates Under the New TCIA

Marginal Rate	Single	Married Filing Jointly	Head of Household	Married Filing Separate
10%	$0-9,525	$0-19,050	$0-13,600	$0-9,525
12%	$9,525-38,700	$19,050-77,400	$13,600-51,800	$9,525-38,700
22%	$38,700-82,500	$77,400-165,000	$51,800-82,500	$38,700-82,500
24%	$82,500-157,500	$165,000-315,000	$82,500-157,500	$82,500-157,500
32%	$157,500-200,000	$315,000-400,000	$157,500-200,000	$157,500-200,000
35%	$200,000-500,000	$400,000-600,000	$200,000-500,000	$200,000-300,000
37%	Over $500,000	Over $600,000	Over $500,000	Over $300,000

Changes to Personal Exemptions

Prior to the new tax law, you had personal exemptions for you, your spouse, and your dependents—unless you earned more than $300,000 Married Filing Jointly (MFJ). In 2017, the amount was $4,050 apiece, which means that a married couple with two children would be able to lower their taxable income by $16,200. However, the Tax Cuts and Jobs Act eliminates personal exemptions, so the reduction is no longer available.

Changes to Standard Deductions

The standard deduction amount has increased by $5,500 for Single filers, now giving a $12,000 deduction amount. For Married Filing Jointly, the amount has increased by $11,000, to a standard deduction of $24,000.

Changes to Itemized Deductions

Because of the increases in the standard deduction, fewer people will have deduction limits high enough to itemize. If you still benefit by itemizing, it's important to understand how the new Act impacts what you can deduct.

1. The income limit for allowable itemized deductions has been suspended for higher-income individuals.

2. Mortgage interest (qualified residence interest) is still deductible up to indebtedness of $750,000, down from the previous level of $1 million. Home equity mortgage interest is no longer deductible. Mortgages acquired before December 15, 2017, retain the previous level.

3. State and local income taxes, state and local personal property taxes, and other state and local taxes are no longer deductible individually; however, taxpayers can claim an aggregate itemized deduction up to $10,000.

4. Personal casualty and theft loss deductions can only be claimed on events attributable to a federally-declared disaster area.

5. Gambling losses can only be deducted to the level of gambling winnings.

6. Previously, charitable contributions had a 50 percent limit, which has been increased to 60 percent.

7. Purchases for college athletic seating are no longer deductible.

8. Through the year 2019 and including 2017, the Adjusted Gross Income threshold for medical deductions is eliminated, causing medical expenses in excess of 7.5 percent of AGI to be deductible, outside of Alternative Minimum Tax liability, regardless of age.

9. Beginning in 2019, alimony is no longer deductible to the payor-spouse, it is included in taxable income. Alimony is not considered income to the payee-spouse. This should also remove alimony as funds that could be used to fund an individual retirement plan, or IRA, for the payee-spouse as it no longer meets the income test.

10. Moving expenses are no longer deductible except for members of the Armed Forces in specific circumstances.

11. Entertainment, meal, and transportation expenses are no longer deductible as business expenses, although meals purchased at the place of business or nearby, for convenience purposes, retain their 50 percent deductibility.

12. All deductions under the classification of Miscellaneous Itemized Deductions are no longer deductible, including but not limited to the home office deduction, hobby expenses, adviser fees, license fees, uniforms, dues, and work-related tools/supplies/education.

Changes to Alternative Minimum Tax

Fewer people will owe alternative minimum tax due to changes in both the exemption levels and the exemption phaseouts. For Married Filing Jointly filers, the exemption level increased from $84,500 to $109,400. Additionally, the exemption phaseout level increased from $160,900 to $1 million. These changes likely cause the Alternative Minimum Tax only to impact very high net worth individuals as long as the tax changes are in effect.

Changes to Retirement Plans

Although several changes to allowable retirement plan contributions were proposed as the Act was being finalized, in the end, amounts were not impacted. However, it's important to know that advisory fees are no longer deductible. Additionally, if investors make a Roth conversion from a traditional IRA, they can no longer recharacterize the conversion back to the traditional IRA. This means that if an investor has money in a traditional IRA, opts to pay the taxes that would be due and transfer funds into a Roth, he or she cannot later (but within the same year) recharacterize that amount back into the IRA.

Changes to Estate, Gift, Generation-Skipping Transfer Tax

Estate tax, gift tax, and generation-skipping transfer tax have always had exemption amounts that allowed people to give assets to others without paying taxes on the transfer. The Tax Cuts and Jobs Act doubled the amount of this exemption, allowing individuals to transfer $11.2 million and married couples to transfer $22.4 million before tax is due. Additionally, in 2018, an inflation adjustment allows $15,000 to be gifted, and the gift is excluded from filing a gift tax return.

Changes to Small Business Taxes, Deductions

Small businesses are impacted by the Tax Cuts and Jobs Act in several ways. The loss of the entertainment deduction for businesses along with the personal lost deductions of home office and office supplies, all discussed earlier, have a negative impact on the small business owner.

However, the Tax Cuts and Jobs Act does allow for a deduction of 20 percent of qualified business income from pass-through business entities like S corporations. Qualified Business Income is tricky and doesn't include reasonable compensation amounts. Instead, it's the income in excess of this, likely often reported on a K1. Some service businesses are excluded from having QBI income, so small business owners will want to research this carefully.

Closing Thoughts

The Tax Cuts and Jobs Act made many changes to the tax code, and even the IRS is concerned that the scope will make enforcement difficult. For some people, the Act will lead to less tax liability; however, for others, the results may not be as rosy. Losing the personal exemption deduction will be difficult for large families, and the loss of many itemized deductions makes it difficult for most people to benefit from itemizing. This increases the impact of the lost exemptions.

The lower tax brackets will be helpful, especially to higher net worth taxpayers, as will the change to AMT. In short, it's complicated. Talk to the tax, legal, and financial professionals in your life to help you maximize your tax savings, even though you can no longer deduct their fee—it remains the prudent thing to do.

Afterword

Congratulations—you finished the book! I hope you learned a few strategies along the way that can help you implement your financial plan.

Before I go, I would like to leave you with a few final thoughts. I know your life is busy, but do try to look at these topics periodically. A new job, a baby, a marriage, a divorce, or other life changes can impact your financial circumstances and change what you need from your financial plan.

We call the profession *financial planning*, because it is recursive, circling back on itself as life happens.

Don't be shy about asking the appropriate professionals to answer your questions and provide guidance. No single book can provide a do-it-yourself financial plan, because so many of the topics are quite complex. I've hit the high points here, the must-knows, but there is more to learn. And remember: You might have individual circumstances that impact what works for you and is in your best interest.

The information in this book changes with the tax code and legislation. Even as I was writing it, the laws changed, and I had to revise a chapter or two.

That's why it pays to have—and to talk with—your financial team. They are no good to you if you don't.

And don't think of this as good-bye. You can find me at www.PeggyDoviak.com, where I will be providing updates to chapters as they happen. And if a question arises, please feel free to post it on my website at "Ask Peggy." Who knows—you might inspire a chapter in my next book.

Be prosperous!

—**Peggy Doviak**

Acknowledgments

Nancy Berland, thirty years ago, I met you in the unlikely setting of a craft show. You were a glamorous published author, and I was a wanna-be writer. Twenty-eight years later, you breathed life into this project and brought it into being. Thank you!

Jeanne Devlin, editor of the award-winning Road-Runner Press, thank you for believing in a business book with fifty-two chapters! You are insanely talented, and I am so proud to be one of your authors.

More thanks than I can express goes to my husband, Richard Doviak, my tireless supporter and payer of bills when I opened a financial firm with no clients! Rich, your belief in me and insistence that I had to write this book kept me strong and inspired.

Robert Con Davis-Undiano, my professor, mentor, and friend, thank you for reminding me that it isn't enough to say you want to write a book. You actually have to write it.

Thank you to my amazing content editors: Sheryl Garrett, Carol Alexander, Ken Carlyle, Mike Cates, Kristi Isacksen, and Parker Lowe. Thanks to my dear friend and artist, Sue Frueh, who gave form to Ashley, Michael, Lisa, and James. Thank you also, Patty Reed, for helping me see the forest through the trees.

Special thanks and all my love to my aunt, Margaret Beggs. And finally, thank you to my precious mother, Martha Frazier. Without you and your confidence in me, none of this would have happened.

About the Author

Peggy Frazier Doviak is a CERTIFIED FINANCIAL PLANNER™ practitioner with a master's in finance and a doctorate in education. She hosts the syndicated radio program *Ask Peggy* and speaks frequently on personal finance. Visit her at www.PeggyDoviak.com.